by Andy Harris

HTML5 Game Development For Dummies®

Published by
John Wiley & Sons, Inc.
111 River Street
Hoboken, NJ 07030-5774
www.wiley.com

Copyright © 2013 by John Wiley & Sons, Inc., Hoboken, New Jersey

Published by John Wiley & Sons, Inc., Hoboken, New Jersey

Published simultaneously in Canada

For general information on our other products and services, please contact our Customer Care Department within the U.S. at 877-762-2974, outside the U.S. at 317-572-3993, or fax 317-572-4002.

For technical support, please visit www.wiley.com/techsupport.

Wiley also publishes its books in a variety of electronic formats and by print-on-demand. Not all content that is available in standard print versions of this book may appear or be packaged in all book formats. If you have purchased a version of this book that did not include media that is referenced by or accompanies a standard print version, you may request this media by visiting http://booksupport.wiley.com. For more information about Wiley products, visit us www.wiley.com.

Library of Congress Control Number: 2013932120

ISBN: 978-1-118-07476-3 (pbk); ISBN: 978-1-118-26144-6 (ebk); ISBN: 978-1-118-22261-4 (ebk); ISBN: 978-1-118-23652-9 (ebk)

Manufactured in the United States of America

10 9 8 7 6 5 4 3 2 1

About the Author

Andy Harris is the author of numerous books on gaming and web development. He taught himself computer programming by building games on the TRS-80 model I, and hasn't stopped playing yet.

Andy taught special education for several years while also working as a contract programmer. Eventually he found himself at Indiana University/Purdue University – Indianapolis teaching computer science full time. He currently serves in the computer science department as a senior lecturer, where he is responsible for the freshman computing program. He also teaches game and web development.

Andy is also a regular columnist for a major homeschooling magazine, where he writes about how to use and teach computing at home.

You can learn more about Andy or ask him a question at his website: http://www.aharrisbooks.net. Visit this site to see every example in this book, and to see what else Andy is doing these days.

Dedication

I dedicate this book first to Jesus Christ my personal savior.

Acknowledgments

First acknowledgment always goes to my amazing wife Heather. I couldn't write books without you, but then I couldn't do much of anything without you. I love you dearly. A big thanks to Elizabeth, Matthew, Jacob, and Benjamin. Now you know what I was doing in the office all that time.

Thank you also to my students, current and in the past. I've learned much more from you than you ever have from me. A special shout goes to the In-Grace high school group and CSCI N301 classes, for helping me test the projects in this book.

A huge thank you goes to Tyler Mitchell, for his contributions to the simpleGame Engine, especially the animation system. Thank you Tyler, for your incredible contributions. I'm looking forward to incorporating your other ideas into a future version of the program.

Thanks to Tom Dunlap for additional testing and support. Without Tom, the game engine might not have some of its key features.

Thanks to Katie Feltman, for years of friendship and support. I appreciate you understanding what I wanted to do with this book and helping to make it happen. Blessings to you in your new endeavors.

Mark Enochs once again plied his magic on this book. Thank you, Mark, for putting so much energy into this project. You're a good friend and a great partner in this process.

Thank you to my editors Linda Morris, Melba Hopper, and Mark Enochs, and thank you to my tech editor Russ Mullen. Thanks also to the many people at Wiley the author never meets, but who add to the book.

A huge thank you goes to the various open source and creative commons authors that contributed to this project. Look for specific individual attributions in the various projects. A special thank you goes to the folks at open game art, Kreiner's tilesets, and Ari's sprite lib. I made up for my own lack of art skills by utilizing the talents of these incredible artists, and I truly appreciate their generosity.

The biggest thanks goes to you for reading this book. If you've read any of my other books, thank you so much for your support. If this is your first book with me, welcome aboard! I can't wait to share the fun of game development in HTML5 with you.

Publisher's Acknowledgments

We're proud of this book; please send us your comments at http://dummies.custhelp.com. For other comments, please contact our Customer Care Department within the U.S. at 877-762-2974, outside the U.S. at 317-572-3993, or fax 317-572-4002.

Some of the people who helped bring this book to market include the following:

Acquisitions and Editorial

Project Editors: Mark Enochs, Linda Morris

Senior Acquisitions Editor: Katie Feltman

Copy Editor: Melba Hopper

Editorial Manager: Leah Michael

Editorial Assistant: Annie Sullivan

Sr. Editorial Assistant: Cherie Case

Cover Photo: © Anton Novikov / iStockphoto

Cartoons: Rich Tennant (www.the5thwave.com)

Composition Services

Project Coordinator: Patrick Redmond

Layout and Graphics: Carrie A. Cesavice, Joyce Haughey

Proofreader: Melissa D. Buddendeck

Indexer: BIM Indexing & Proofreading Services

Publishing and Editorial for Technology Dummies

    Richard Swadley, Vice President and Executive Group Publisher

    Andy Cummings, Vice President and Publisher

    Mary Bednarek, Executive Acquisitions Director

    Mary C. Corder, Editorial Director

Publishing for Consumer Dummies

    Kathy Nebenhaus, Vice President and Executive Publisher

Composition Services

    Debbie Stailey, Director of Composition Services

Table of Contents

Introduction

I've been working on this book for about 35 years. I've *always* liked inventing games. Even as a kid, I would try to think up new kinds of board games with paper and pencil. I must have come up with hundreds of terrible game ideas.

When I was a teenager (in the early '80s,) I got access to a computer. That changed everything. Sure, you could do cool things with it, but my favorite part was how I could make any game I could imagine. I learned how to program specifically so that I could write games.

Eventually, I grew up (at least chronologically) and turned my computing skills to "serious" pursuits like commercial programming and teaching. But I never forgot about games, and I still write games for fun. Whenever I get a new machine or programming language, I master it by creating games. Playing games is fun, but making them is incredible.

Game programming was simple in the early days because computers couldn't do much. As things have become more complicated and expectations higher, it's become harder and harder to get into game development. Today's technology is incredibly capable, but it can be overwhelming to a beginner. Programming is hard enough, and game programming is often even more difficult.

I want to concentrate on the main ideas of programming and game development without being overwhelmed by details, and it seems I'm not the only one. People still want to create games for themselves, and they're willing to learn how to write computer programs to do so. What they need is a way to learn real programming and make some fun games without being overwhelmed with arcane details, and without spending a ton of money on software and equipment.

If you want to learn programming through game development in HTML5, you need a tool to hide some of the more arcane details. I developed an open-source (and completely free) game development library designed specifically to make programming and game development easy to learn. Even if you've never programmed before, you should be building a game or two after your very first session, and by the time you're halfway through the book, you'll be building your own web-based arcade games.

About This Book

This is the book I wish I'd had 35 years ago. It's my sincere hope that this book changes your life by giving you the tools to build the great games that are perhaps germinating within you.

As you read this book, you'll develop a lot of skills:

- ✔ **HTML5:** This markup language is the foundation of the modern Internet. Although you won't uncover every detail of HTML, you will master enough to make a functional web page.

- ✔ **CSS:** This language allows you to change the way a web page looks. I've written books much longer than this one about HTML and CSS, but in this book, you'll learn enough CSS to make your pages and games look good.

- ✔ **Computer programming:** Most of the book focuses on the JavaScript programming language. You find all the main features of any programming language, including variables, loops, conditions, functions, and object-oriented programming. These are the ideas taught in most introductory computer science courses.

- ✔ **Game development:** Games are a specific type of programming, and in this book, you use the `simpleGame` library to build powerful and interesting 2D games. You discover how games work with space and time, how to build sprite objects, and how to handle things like sound effects, collision detection, and multi-state game elements.

- ✔ **Mobile development:** The games you write in this book will work on any modern browser, including the one that comes with your smartphone or tablet. The `simpleGame` library incorporates a number of mobile features, including the use of touch input, a virtual joystick mechanism, and tilt control access.

What You Will Need

One of the best things about HTML5 and JavaScript development is how easy it is to get started. Any modern computer will do. (I tested on Windows 7, Ubuntu Linux, and Mac OSX.) You probably already have everything you need on your computer. There is absolutely nothing else you'll need to buy. However, I do recommend that you download and install a few free programs. Chapter 1 goes into some details about the specific tools to install, but here are the tools you need to start with:

✔ **Your background:** I don't assume any programming or web development knowledge. If you already have these skills, you'll have a great time. If you're just getting started, you'll probably need to concentrate on the first few chapters before you're ready to do things toward the end of the book.

✔ **An HTML5-compliant browser:** My personal favorite browser is Google Chrome because it follows the standards you use in this book very well. It's available on every operating system, and it has very helpful debugging tools. The latest version of any major browser will probably be fine.

✔ **A good text editor:** You should really have a dedicated programmer's text editor. I like Komodo Edit because it does everything you need, provides some help for programmers, works well on multiple operating systems, and is free.

✔ **A graphics tool or two:** You'll probably want to do some artwork for your games. I recommend GIMP (a very powerful free raster graphics package) and Inkscape (an equally impressive vector graphics tool).

✔ **An audio editor:** I really like Audacity, a powerful and free audio recording and editing tool.

Links to all of these programs are available on my main website (www.aharrisbooks.net/h5g). Chapter 11 highlights these and several other great game programming resources.

How to Read This Book

People from many different backgrounds can use this book.

If you're brand new to computer programming, I suggest going through the whole book in order. The ideas in the book generally build on each other. HTML provides the basic framework for your games, so you can start there. If you're already comfortable with modern HTML and CSS, you can skip ahead to the JavaScript sections.

If you know how to build web pages but you're new to JavaScript, begin by looking into JavaScript to see how this language is similar to the language you already know.

If you're comfortable with programming and JavaScript, you can move straight to the chapters on the simpleGame engine and discover how to make your own games quickly and easily. If you're an advanced JavaScript programmer, you'll particularly like Chapter 12, which explains many of the technical details of the game engine.

If you're an experienced programmer, you can jump to the game starters in Chapter 13. Each one is a partially completed game in a different genre. Try your hand at building a whack-a-mole game, a role-playing game, or a tile-based world.

Of course, feel free to just start where you wish. If you find that you're not following an idea, you may need to go back to review something presented earlier in the book.

Each game and example in the book is on my website at `www.aharris books.net/h5g`.

To see examples from my other books, or to drop me a question, or just to see what I've been up to, you can also go to my main website at `www.aharrisbooks.net`.

How This Book Is Organized

I organized this book by renting time on a supercomputer and applying a multilinear Bayesian artificial intelligence algorithm. No, I didn't. I don't even know what that means. I really just sketched it out during a meeting when I was supposed to be paying attention. In any case, this book is organized around the main milestones you'll need when becoming a game programmer.

Part 1: Building the Foundation

HTML5 gaming lives on the web, so you need to know a little bit about how the web works. I show you the bare essentials of HTML and its companion language CSS. I also show you how JavaScript fits into the mix and introduce programming with JavaScript. Along the way, you find all the essential elements of computer programming, and you build several simple games.

Part 11: Basic Game Development

In this part, I introduce the `simpleGame` engine, which was designed from the ground up to give you a fun and reasonably easy start into game programming. You find out how to incorporate the engine into your own projects, how to build your own sprite objects, and how to create your first arcade game from scratch.

Part III: Diving Deeper

After you understand the basics, you'll no doubt be curious about the more advanced features. In this part of the book, you apply a basic physics model for more advanced motion. You build sprites that fall with gravity, skid around the screen, and orbit planets realistically. You discover how to make your games work on mobile devices like phones and tablets. You find out how build a virtual joystick interface and read the motion sensor built into many of these devices. Finally, you look over the formal documentation of the simpleGame library to understand more about how this library works and what it offers.

Part IV: The Part of Tens

The *For Dummies* series is famous for its "Part of Tens." Some of the best material in the entire book is here. When you're ready to understand how the simpleGame library does all the magic, you can look into ten key ideas behind the engine. You see some of the math and programming concepts used to build the engine. I also have a list of ten (or maybe more) resources for game developers. Check here for great tools, graphics libraries, sound resources, and more.

We Even Use the Internet Thingy!

Because this book is about developing games for the web, you won't be surprised that it has a web page. These are games, and you really shouldn't just look at them in a book. You really need to experience all these examples in a web browser. You can find every example in the book on my website at www. aharrisbooks.net/h5g. You can run all the programs in the book, and you can also view the code I used to make them (Ctrl+U on most browsers). This site is also helpful as you're collecting your tools. I added a link to every tool or library I recommend throughout the book.

Of course, there are other things on the site, too, like links to my other books, a forum for questions, and a place you can send me an e-mail if you run into any problems.

I'm looking forward to seeing you on my main website at www.aharris books.net.

Icons Used in This Book

Every once in a while, a concept is important enough to warrant special attention. This book uses a few margin icons to point out certain special information.

These are tidbits of additional information you ought to think about or at least keep in mind.

Occasionally, I feel the need to indulge my "self-important computer science instructor" nature, and I give some technical background on things. These ideas are interesting but not critical, so you can skip them if you want. However, you might want to memorize a couple of them before you go to your next computer science cocktail party. You'll be the hit of the party.

Tips are suggestions for making things easier.

Be sure to read anything marked with this icon. Failure to do so might result in a plague of frogs, puffs of black smoke, or your program not working like you expect.

Where to Go from Here

Thank you for buying this book. I truly hope you find it fun and useful. I had a great time writing it, and I think you'll enjoy using it. I'm looking forward to hearing from you and seeing what you can do with the skills you pick up here. Drop me a line at andy@aharrisbooks.net and let me know how it's going!

Also, be sure to visit the companion website for this book at www.dummies. com/go/html5gamedevfd, where you'll find files and images used throughout the book. For updates to this edition, check out www.dummies.com/go/html5gamedevfdupdates. For helpful tables and other information, check out the book's Cheat Sheet at www.dummies.com/cheatsheet/html5 gamedevelopment.

Part I
Building the Foundation

The 5th Wave   By Rich Tennant

"Games are an important part of my
website. They cause eye strain."

In this part . . .

*H*TML5 games are built on the web. Before you can push the limits of what the web can do, you need to have a basic command of fundamentals. This part provides a quick overview or refresher on basic web technologies, at least enough so you can start writing games.

Chapter 1 introduces the key components of HTML5 and CSS. If you've never used HTML before, you'll find the concepts pretty easy to understand. If you're an old hand at HTML, you may still want an overview of HTML5. Even in this very first chapter, you build an adventure game while learning how to create the HTML and CSS infrastructure you'll use for more advanced games.

Chapter 2 introduces the JavaScript programming language and explains how it's used to interact with web pages. You use JavaScript throughout the book, and the techniques described here will be used for scoreboards and user input. As you explore these topics, you build the classic Word Story game.

Chapter 3 introduces all the main ideas of computer programming including data conversion, loops and branches, functions and parameters, and arrays. These ideas form the foundation of all computer programming, and you'll see them in practically every game you write.

Chapter 4 combines all the ideas in the first part to build a complete number-guessing game. You find out how to put together a game development plan, how to work with random numbers, and how to assemble a game with a lot of moving parts.

Chapter 1

Playing on the Web

Two particular flavors of programming have always appealed to me: game development and web programming. These have historically been very different kinds of programming, with vastly different tools and techniques.

With the advent of HTML5 and its related technologies, these two formerly different forms of programming are finally one. In this book, I show you how to build basic video games entirely with free web technologies.

Soon enough you'll be building games with moving elements, animated characters, and realistic physics. You'll discover a number of interesting web technologies as the book progresses, but they all build on two basic and related technologies: HTML and CSS. Web-based games are web pages first, so you need to have a basic grasp of web development before you move on to the more elaborate game development.

HTML has been around for a long time. Although the latest version (HTML5) has a lot of new features, it's still very similar to older versions. HTML is a markup language, which means it's designed to help you determine the types of elements in a page. In this chapter, you find out how to build a web page in HTML5. I don't cover all the details, but enough so you can make any basic page.

HTML is about what things mean, but another language, Cascading Style Sheets (CSS), is about how things look. Typically, CSS and HTML are used together to build a page and style it. In this chapter, you also learn enough CSS to add basic style to your pages. You'll be able to add colors, change where things are positioned, and make basic changes to fonts.

Of course, this is a game development book, so you develop a game even in the very first chapter. You learn how to build a simple "choose your own adventure" game. It's a pretty fun way to practice your web development skills.

Web-based game development has a number of interesting aspects:

- ✔ **The technology is freely available.** If you have a reasonably modern computer, you already have everything you need to get started. You don't need to buy anything at all, although you probably will want to download a few free tools.

- ✔ **It can be easier.** Game programming is well known to be one of the more difficult forms of programming. This is especially true when you use one of the traditional programming languages, like C++. The languages used in this book are quite a bit more friendly for beginners.

- ✔ **You can reach a huge audience.** Anybody with a modern web browser can play your games instantly. They won't need to install plug-ins like Flash, and they won't need to download your game, as it appears immediately in the browser.

- ✔ **You can write mobile games.** Mobile gaming is very hot. The traditional approach to writing mobile games is to use native application development tools. The web approach I use is much simpler than the native tools and bypasses app stores for much easier distribution.

- ✔ **It's fun.** Game development is a hoot. You get to build your own world, set up a story for the player to interact with, and see what happens.

- ✔ **It's a great start to more "serious" programming.** Games are cool, but some people think they aren't really serious. Even if you're not aiming for a career in the gaming industry, the skills you learn in this book help you learn web development and programming. If you work through the exercises in the entire book, you'll learn advanced programming techniques such as object-oriented programming (OOP), local data storage, and animation loops.

Building the Framework

Game development with web technologies has been attempted for years, but the new technologies change everything. For this book, I'm using a number of technologies as a foundation:

- ✔ **HTML5:** HTML5 is the newest version of HTML (the primary language of the web). It offers many new capabilities. All of the other new technologies are built from the HTML5 foundation.

- ✔ **CSS3:** CSS (Cascading Style Sheets) is a language that applies formatting to the structure determined with HTML. The new version of CSS adds some new features that allow great gaming options. For the first time, you can easily scale and rotate web elements, as well as animate and add shadows.

- ✔ **JavaScript:** JavaScript is a full-blown programming language. If you want your game to really do anything interesting, you need to learn how to program. Don't worry. JavaScript is a reasonably easy language to use, and modern implementations have more than enough power.

- ✔ **Canvas:** In the past, it was very difficult for the user or programmer to draw dynamically on a web page. The new `canvas` tag adds this ability to web pages, making it much easier to build a game and add it to your page.

- ✔ **SimpleGame:** Although HTML5 and its related tools do make it possible to build games, there are a number of advanced techniques to learn. I show you everything you need to build games on your own, but to speed things up, I provide a game engine called `simpleGame` that simplifies this process. This tool allows you to create powerful Flash-style games after only a few chapters!

- ✔ **Multimedia tools:** Games are truly multimedia applications, so you'll need some media assets to work with. I introduce my favorite tools for building games, including free tools for developing sketches, graphic images, 3D models, and audio.

Setting Up Your Workshop

You won't need a lot to get started, but a number of tools are helpful. All are free and work on every major platform (Windows, Mac OS X, and Linux).

Web browsers

All the games created in this book require a modern version of HTML and related technologies. To run the programs, you need a modern browser. Here are the browsers I check the programs with:

- ✔ **Google Chrome 13+:** The Chrome browser by Google has become a favorite of HTML5 developers. It has very good support for HTML5 standards, and it has one of the speediest JavaScript engines around. It is available for all major desktop operating systems.

✔ **Mozilla Firefox 6+:** Firefox is one of the most popular browsers. It has very good support for HTML5 features. It has a strong add-on system that allows you to add extensions. The Firebug add-on turns Firefox into a high-powered programmer's tool.

✔ **Apple Safari:** The Safari browser is standard on all Apple products, although it's also available for other systems. Safari and Chrome use the same underlying engine (so they have similar behavior) but they are not identical. The iPad and iPhone devices have a form of Safari built in.

✔ **Opera:** The Opera browser is popular among some developers because it has very good support for standards. It offers versions for the Wii and some mobile devices.

✔ **Internet Explorer 10:** Microsoft has long frustrated web developers by choosing not to follow the standards completely. Internet Explorer 10 finally supports most of the tools you need for game development, but sadly, it's not available unless the user is running Windows 7 or greater. Fortunately, all of the other browsers are available on any version of Windows.

A programmer's editor

You'll need some type of text editor to work with all the various files. Most operating systems come with a default editor, but these often do not have enough power for a programmer's needs:

✔ **Notepad:** If you use Windows, you're familiar with the ubiquitous notepad program. It does the job, but it's very simplistic. When you start to get serious, you'll want features like line numbers, support for multiple files, and syntax highlighting. Notepad doesn't have any of these features, but it's fine if you're just getting started.

✔ **TextEdit:** If you're using a Mac, you know TextEdit. It is much more powerful than its Windows counterpart, but it still has some problems. Be sure to save all text in plain text format (TEXT – Save as Text) or your programs won't work correctly.

✔ **Gedit:** If you're a Linux user, you're probably using something like gedit. It's probably the best of the default text editors, but it still doesn't have every feature you might want.

✔ **Word:** Don't use it. Word processing is different than text editing. All the fancy stuff that Word does for you (fonts, spacing, paragraph formatting, and so on) are ignored in programming and will just cause problems.

So if none of these programs are ideal, what should you use? I think a programmer's editor should have the following features:

- ✔ **Syntax highlighting:** Some editors can recognize what kind of code you're writing and add color hints so you can see what's going on. For example, all comments might be blue. This is incredibly helpful when you're programming.

- ✔ **Line numbers:** Sounds like a simple thing, but it's often really important to know what line a certain error is on, and many basic editors do not have this feature.

- ✔ **Multi-file support:** Often a program like a game consists of more than one file. It's nice to have some sort of tab system that allows you to edit multiple files at once.

- ✔ **Code completion:** A number of editors help you write code by guessing as you type. This works surprisingly well and can really help you remember syntax.

- ✔ **Remote file management:** Sometimes you have files out on a web server somewhere. A number of editors allow you to work on remote files as if they were on your machine.

My current favorite editor is Komodo Edit. It does all of these things, works the same on all major operating systems, and is totally free. If you don't already have a favorite text editor, I recommend trying this one. Check my website www.aharrisbooks.net for a link to the current version (7 as of this writing).

Graphics tools

Most games involve some form of graphics. You may be able to find everything you need, but usually you'll need to modify or create your own graphics images. The most popular graphic editor on the planet is Adobe Photoshop. It's very capable, but it can be expensive. I prefer Gimp, which does everything you need, and is free. Look at Chapter 11 for help and resources on using Gimp to create game graphics.

Modern browsers (finally) support another type of graphics called *vector graphics.* This style of graphics can be easier for building game characters than programs like Gimp or Photoshop. My favorite vector editor is Inkscape, which is also described in Chapter 11. I used both Inkscape and Gimp to generate the graphics shown in this chapter and throughout the book.

Users often expect 3D graphics, but 3D games are much more difficult to build. If you're interested in making your game *look* like a 3D game, you can use a 3D modeling tool like Blender to build your graphics and then produce 2D images for the game. Blender is also discussed in Chapter 11.

Links to all these tools are available on my website at www.aharrisbooks.net.

Audio tools

Modern games also require audio. You'll definitely want to include sound effects. You'll need a tool that can record and manipulate sounds. Audacity is a wonderful free tool that helps you with this process. Like all other tools, I've provided a link to this program on my website at www.aharrisbooks.net. You can learn more about editing sound for your games in Chapter 11.

Building Your First Game

Enough background. Let's make a game!

The first game will be a simple take on the old "Choose your own adventure" genre. This game uses nothing but HTML and CSS and can get as simple or complicated as you want. This game highlights the adventures of an aspiring game programmer. I create it in a cartoon style (mainly because I've got no artistic talent). Figure 1-1 shows the first screen in the game.

Figure 1-1:
The first page of my epic adventure game.

On each page, you are given a situation. Most situations involve making a choice, which takes you to a new situation.

The overall plan for the game is shown in Figure 1-2.

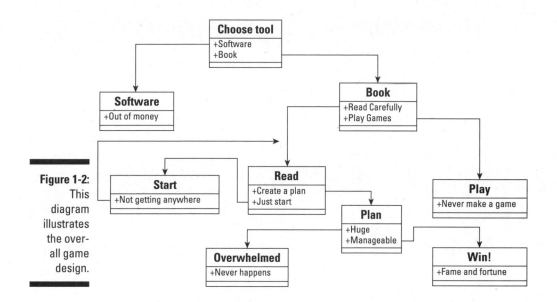

Figure 1-2:
This
diagram
illustrates
the over-
all game
design.

Adventure games have a particular pattern (which computer scientists would call a *finite state machine,* but everyone knows gamers have more fun than computer scientists). Each situation could be considered a *node*, and in each node, the player has to make some sort of decision. The decision determines which node the player travels to next.

Of course, the question is how to generate the various nodes. There are many solutions, but one of the easiest is to simply build a web page for each node. That's exactly how I do it in this chapter.

Building a Basic Page

Here's the great thing. You can learn how to build web pages at the same time you learn how to build a node for an adventure game. If you already know how to make pages, you should still follow along because I use a new fancy-dancy form of web development in this book. Old versions of HTML were pretty limited, but the latest version (HTML5) is a fully capable game programming platform.

The basic web page is nothing but a text file. Figure 1-3 shows one example.

Figure 1-3:
A basic web
page.

To make this page, all you need to do is open a text editor (see "A programmer's editor" earlier in this chapter for my suggestions on which editor to use). Then type the following code:

```
<!DOCTYPE HTML>
<html lang="en-US">
<head>    <meta charset="UTF-8">
    <title>Adventures of Goo Goo</title>
</head>
<body>
    <h1>Adventures of Goo Goo</h1>
    <p>
        You are Goo Goo, an intrepid adventurer.
        Your goal is to become a game developer.
        Best of luck to you as you begin.
    </p>

</body>
</html>
```

Although this isn't the fanciest page on the Internet, it provides a pretty good foundation for everything I do in this book. Before you look at the details, note the following:

- ✓ **It's written in plain text.** Even with fancy editors, web pages are really nothing more than plain old text.

- ✓ **There are some funky <> things in there.** The angle braces indicate *tags*. A tag is like instructions to the browser. The various tags indicate how the browser should treat the various parts of the document.

- ✓ **Most tags are containers.** Most of the tags seem to happen in pairs, for example, <head> and </head> or <p> and </p>. That's because tags usually contain other things (like text and other tags, for example).

- ✓ **This page is written in HTML5.** If you know something about web development, you may have seen different forms of HTML (HTML4 or XHTML, most likely). This book uses HTML5, which is a bit more capable than the earlier versions. Fortunately, it's also actually easier to use.

- ✓ **The code is indented.** Although web browsers don't really care how code is formatted, programmers do care about such things. Typically, I indent every time I begin a new structure, so I won't forget to end every container. If you look carefully at the code, it's pretty easy to see through the indentation that everything has a beginning and an end.

- ✓ **The code doesn't look exactly like the page.** What the user sees in the web browser isn't exactly what was written in the text editor. This is deliberate. Unlike a word-processing program, web pages are designed as code that is interpreted by the browser.

Even before you understand all the details of the code, you can probably guess a lot about what's going on. HTML is pretty easy to follow most of the time. The key to understanding HTML is to know what the various tags mean. Here are the tags used in this page:

- ✓ **<!DOCTYPE>:** This special tag is used to indicate what kind of document is being built. The exclamation point indicates it is a special tag meant to send a message to the browser. <!DOCTYPE HTML> means the page will be built in HTML5.

- ✓ **<html lang = "en">:** The html tag is a container for the entire document. Web pages begin with <html> and end with </html>. In HTML5, the html tag specifies the language. I build my websites in English, so lang = "en" indicates that.

- ✓ **<head>:** The head of a document is a lot like the engine compartment of a car. A lot of important stuff happens here, but it's not where the users usually go. For now, the head is relatively empty, but as you write more complex games, much of your programming code will go here.

- ✔ **`<meta charset = "utf-8">`:** The meta tag provides information about the document. There are many different types of meta tags, but the most commonly used in HTML5 sets the character set. The utf-8 character set is the one usually used with English.

- ✔ **`<title>`:** Each web page has a title. The title traditionally appears in the browser's header bar (but this is not always the case). The title is also shown when a user searches for a page with a search engine. It's important that the title describes the page.

- ✔ **`<body>`:** If the head is the engine compartment, the body is where the driver and passengers go. All the content the user typically sees is described in the body section of the page.

- ✔ **`<h1>`:** This tag indicates a level-one headline. An h1 tag is the most important headline on your page (so typically you'll only have one). Subsections of your page may have level two headlines (signified by `<h2>`). Headlines go all the way to level six (`<h6>`), but it's unusual to go much deeper than level three. (Even in a book this size, I rarely use level three.)

- ✔ **`<p>`:** The p tag marks a paragraph. Paragraphs are the most important units in writing, and they are the foundation of web pages as well. Most of the text in your pages is contained inside a paragraph. You can have as many paragraphs as you want.

It's tempting to think that using HTML is just like working in a word processor, but that's not completely true. Most modern word processors use a technique called WYSIWYG (What You See Is What You Get). In the print world, this makes sense because the end result of a word-processed document is a print document, and printers can be controlled very precisely. The web doesn't work that way. You web page may be viewed on a huge projector, on a big desktop monitor, on a smaller notebook, on an iPad, on a smart phone, and on a tiny feature phone screen. Each of these devices determines exactly how the page looks.

In HTML, we don't exactly control how things look. Instead, HTML code describes what things *mean*. It's a crucial difference. You'll still get to suggest how things look with a technology called CSS, and these suggestions will usually be followed. Web coding is about trading precise control for amazing flexibility. All in all, it's a good trade.

I'm covering HTML pretty quickly here, and it's actually a bit more complex than I'm making it out to be. If you want a more complete introduction to HTML and CSS (and a bunch of other technologies) please check out one of my other books, *HTML, XHTML, & CSS All-In-One For Dummies*, published by John Wiley & Sons. It's chock-full of information.

Dressing up the page

I've created the first page of my game, but it isn't very exciting. It would be nice to dress it up. There are many ways to do this. The first way is to provide an image. Take a look at Figure 1-4.

Figure 1-4:
Now the
page has a
picture.

Adding a picture really spices up the page. It's not the world's greatest game yet, but at least it's a bit more interesting than it was. Here's the new code. (Note that I bolded the part that was added.)

```
<!DOCTYPE HTML>
<html lang="en-US">
<head>
    <meta charset="UTF-8">
    <title>Adventures of Goo Goo</title>
</head>
<body>
    <h1>Adventures of Goo Goo</h1>
    <p>
        <img src = "GooGoo1.png"
             alt = "Goo Goo makes a game!" />
    </p>

    <p>
```

```
        You are Goo Goo, an intrepid adventurer.
        Your goal is to become a game developer.
        Best of luck to you as you begin.
    </p>

</body>
</html>
```

The key to adding images is a tag called (cleverly enough) <img>. The img tag allows you to add images to your page. Here's what you need to do to add an image to a page:

1. **Obtain a picture.**

   This seems obvious, I suppose, but it's true. In order to display a picture, you need to have one. You can use an image editor to create or modify a picture or grab a picture you already have.

2. **Put the picture in the right format.**

   On the web, only a few image formats are universal. Most web images are in .png, .jpg, or .gif format. The best format for a simple line drawing like my image is .png. You may need to use your image editor to modify the image type if it's not already in the right format.

3. **Put the image file in the right place.**

   Typically, you'll move the image file to the same directory as the web page itself. (I'm not a fan of a separate images directory unless there are a large number of images in a document. Things get complex enough without adding another layer.)

4. **Create a container for the image.**

   An image is considered an *inline* element. That means it is meant to be placed inside some sort of container. The most common container is a paragraph, so I place the image in its own paragraph. (You can combine an image with text in the same paragraph, but the formatting becomes trickier, so I'm just making a paragraph with a single image in it.)

5. **Add the <img> tag to the document.**

   The <img> tag tells the browser how to retrieve and display the image. It needs a little more information to do its job, so it has a couple of special elements called *attributes*.

6. **Use the src attribute to indicate where the image is.**

   The src attribute is used to tell the browser where it will find the image file. If the image file is in the same directory as the HTML page, all you need to do is list the name of the image file. (Note that capitalization matters — the filename on the page must be exactly like the one in the operating system.) The filename must be enclosed within double quotes.

7. **Use the** `alt` **attribute to describe the image.**

    It's possible the image will not display. If there is a problem download-ing the image, or the user has a visual disability, the `alt` tag is used to describe the image. The `alt` tag is also used by search engines to determine the contents of an image. Like all attributes, it is enclosed in double quotes.

8. **End with a slash.**

    Because the `<img>` tag won't contain any text content, it isn't consid-ered a container, and it doesn't have a closing tag. Indicate the end of the tag with a slash character.

Providing a link

Right now, your game has a single page. That's not much of a game, but you're gonna fix that. One of the biggest features of HTML is how it allows you to link pages. This linking mechanism is a perfect way to make an adven-ture game because you can build a page for each node, and link all the nodes together to make the game. For the first link, modify the page you're working on so it leads to the first decision. Figure 1-5 shows the newest version of the first page of your adventure. Note the link in the bottom left of the screen.

Figure 1-5: The page now has a link to the first decision.

This page is starting to look pretty good. It has a heading, an image, some text, and a link. The link looks something like ordinary text, except it is blue and underlined. If you click on it, presumably your browser will go to a new page.

The code for the new version of the page (`addLink.html`) builds on the previous examples. As usual, I've bolded the new part.

```
<!DOCTYPE HTML>
<html lang="en-US">
<head>
    <meta charset="UTF-8">
    <title>Adventures of Goo Goo</title>
</head>
<body>
    <h1>Adventures of Goo Goo</h1>
    <p>
        <img src = "GooGoo1.png"
            alt = "Goo Goo makes a game!" />
    </p>

    <p>
        You are Goo Goo, an intrepid adventurer.
        Your goal is to become a game developer.
        Best of luck to you as you begin.
    </p>

    <p>
        <a href = "chooseTool.html">Begin your adventure</a>
    </p>

</body>
</html>
```

The only new section is a paragraph containing a link. Here's how you add a link:

1. **Create a paragraph or other container.**

   A link is an inline tag (like the `img` tag). It cannot stand on its own, but needs to be inside a container. The paragraph is a great container, so just build a paragraph with the `<p></p>` set.

2. **Use the `<a>` tag to create an anchor.**

   The links in a web page are called *anchors* and are generated by the `<a>` tag.

3. **Add the `href` attribute.**

   The `href` attribute stands for *hypertext reference* and it indicates the file the browser navigates to when the user clicks the button.

4. **Include the name of the new file.**

   You need a filename so the browser knows where to go when the link is clicked. You haven't built the file yet, but that's okay. From the diagram listed in Figure 1-2, you know that the first decision point will be "choose tool," so call the next page `"chooseTool.html"`.

5. **Add the text of the link.**

   The next text ("Begin your adventure") appears on the web page as a link. Any text that is placed between the `<a>` and `</a>` tags is a clickable link.

6. **End the anchor with `</a>`.**

   The `</a>` tag ends the anchor and subsequent text looks like ordinary text.

Of course, you should look at the code in your browser to see how it looks.

If you are looking at my example online, it indeed goes to another page, but if you're writing your own version, you'll get an error when you click on the link. That's exactly what you should expect because the page you're linking to doesn't exist yet. Just stay with me and it will all make sense soon.

Beautifying the page

The first page of your adventure works pretty well, but it sure is ugly. HTML does not produce beautiful pages, but there's another tool that can help a lot. CSS (Cascading Style Sheets) is a technology that allows you to add visual appeal to a page described in HTML. Figure 1-6 illustrates the page with a little CSS dress-up.

CSS code is a special language that allows you to modify the visual appearance of a page. CSS and HTML work together to give you a great deal of control of your page's appearance. There is a lot you can do with CSS, but this example adds the following features:

- ✓ **The background of the page is yellow.** You can change the background color of most elements, including the page itself. (I know you can't see yellow in this black-and-white book, but you really should be playing along on the website.)

- ✓ **The headline is centered.** You can also modify the alignment of text. I think headlines look better centered.

- ✓ **Paragraphs are centered.** I want to center each paragraph.

- ✓ **The anchor is black instead of the default blue.** The default blue color of a link didn't seem to fit with my color scheme, so I changed the anchor to black.

Figure 1-6:
With CSS,
the page
looks nicer.

All of these changes are possible through CSS. Take a look at this version of the code, and you can see how I've added the style instructions:

```html
<!DOCTYPE HTML>
<html lang="en-US">
<head>
    <meta charset="UTF-8">
    <title>Adventures of Goo Goo</title>
    <style type="text/css">
        body {
            background-color: yellow;
        }
        p {
            text-align: center;
        }
        h1 {
            text-align: center;
        }
        a {
            color: black;
        }
    </style>
</head>
<body>
    <h1>Adventures of Goo Goo</h1>
    <p>
        <img src = "GooGoo1.png"
             alt = "Goo Goo makes a game!" />
    </p>

    <p>
```

```
        You are Goo Goo, an intrepid adventurer.
        Your goal is to become a game developer.
        Best of luck to you as you begin.
    </p>

    <p>
        <a href = "chooseTool.html">Begin your adventure</
        a>
    </p>

</body>
</html>
```

As usual, I've bolded the interesting part. I didn't actually change anything in the body of the page. Instead, I added a new element to the head, called a *style*.

The `<style></style>` tag is special because all code inside the style is interpreted as CSS rather than HTML code. CSS works by defining certain elements and then describing various attributes of these elements. Each type of tag in the page can have its own style rules defined. For example, look at this portion of the CSS style:

```
body {
    background-color: yellow;
}
```

A number of interesting things are happening in this passage:

- **Part of the page is specified for modification.** Any part of the page that has a tag can be modified through CSS (although it doesn't make sense to modify things the user cannot see, such as the head). This particular style segment applies to the body. Any styles applied to the body influence the entire page.

- **A list of rules will be enclosed in braces ({}).** After you indicate the part of the page you want to change, you can start listing rules. The braces indicate the beginning and end of the rule sets. It's traditional (though not absolutely necessary) to indent all the content in braces.

- **Each rule is an attribute/value pair.** CSS defines a bunch of properties or characteristics of a page element. Most of the properties can be applied to any element. Assign a value to a property to determine how the element changes.

- **Change the `background-color` property.** The property names are usually pretty easy to understand. They are technically a single word, so you'll sometimes see a dash, as in `background-property`.

- **Add a colon (:).** After you describe the property you want to change, add a colon to indicate you're about to provide a value.

✔ **Set the background color.** You can then indicate a color. There are many ways to do this, but for a simple color like yellow, you can simply type the color name.

✔ **End the rule with a semicolon (;).** Each rule ends with a semicolon. This is a common rule in programming languages.

✔ **Repeat with more properties if you wish.** I applied only one rule to the body, but you can add as many rules as you wish.

There are many style rules, but I needed only a few for this example. Here are the rules I used in this page:

✔ background-color: This indicates the background color of the element. You can either indicate the color with a color name or use hex values like #FF00CC (if you know how to use them).

✔ text-align: The text-align attribute indicates how text lines up inside the element. You can set text alignment to left, center, right, or justify.

✔ color: The color attribute describes the foreground color of an element. As with background-color, you can often simply type a color name.

 I'm showing you a small tip of the CSS iceberg here. There is much more to know about how to modify elements. If this is all new to you, I recommend my much larger book *HTML, XHTML & CSS All-In-One For Dummies*, published by John Wiley & Sons. I've also added a more complete bonus chapter on CSS on the website for this book if you need a more complete introduction.

Making a style reusable

This game will consist of many pages, and all should use the same style, so I'm going to pull out a really amazing CSS trick. You can devise a single style and reuse it among many pages. Take a look at the code for externCSS.html:

```
<!DOCTYPE HTML>
<html lang="en-US">
<head>
    <meta charset="UTF-8">
    <title>Adventures of Goo Goo</title>
    <link rel = "stylesheet"
          type = "text/css"
          href = "gooGoo.css" />

</head>
```

```
<body>
    <h1>Adventures of Goo Goo</h1>
    <p>
        <img src = "GooGoo1.png"
            alt = "Goo Goo makes a game!" />
    </p>

    <p>
        You are Goo Goo, an intrepid adventurer.
        Your goal is to become a game developer.
        Best of luck to you as you begin.
    </p>

    <p>
        <a href = "chooseTool.html">Begin your adventure</
            a>
    </p>

</body>
</html>
```

The neat thing about this program is what's missing: The style code is not there. Instead, you find this mysterious-looking code:

```
<link rel = "stylesheet"
    type = "text/css"
    href = "gooGoo.css" />
```

This little code snippet indicates that the CSS code is in another file. Essentially, it tells the browser, "Go find a file called gooGoo.css, and you'll see the CSS code you need there."

Of course I've created such a file. Look it over, and you'll find it eerily familiar:

```
body {
    background-color: yellow;
}
p {
    text-align: center;
    font-size: 200%;
}
h1 {
    text-align: center;
}
a {
    color: black;
}
```

Of course you've seen this before. It's exactly the same code I used to have inside the style tags. Now, however, it's in its own file.

This doesn't seem like a big deal, but it's really useful when you start building systems (like this adventure game) with multiple pages that use the same style. I put the same link code in every page, and then I can change the style of every page in the system by changing a single file. Genius!

Building the next node

That's enough work for the first page. The good news is that the groundwork is entirely laid. The next page is easy to build. Figure 1-7 shows how it looks.

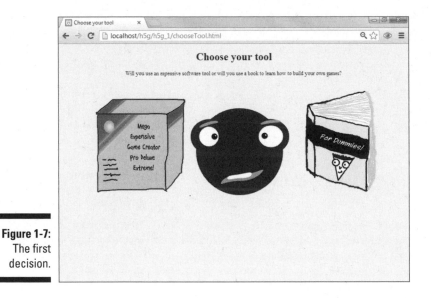

Figure 1-7:
The first
decision.

This second page is much like the first, except there are a few differences:

- **The headline defines the node.** Use a heading to encapsulate the current situation.

- **A small text segment describes the new problem.** Most nodes are really decision points, so use a small text segment to illustrate the situation the adventurer currently faces.

- **This page has three images.** I've created a picture to illustrate each of the two options that the user currently faces.

- **Two of the pictures are also links.** If the user clicks either of these images (the book or the software), she is taken to the corresponding page of the game.

Look over the code for `chooseTool.html`, and you'll see most of it is really familiar:

```html
<!DOCTYPE HTML>
<html lang="en-US">
<head>
    <meta charset="UTF-8">
    <title>Choose your tool</title>
    <link rel = "stylesheet"
          type = "text/css"
          href = "gooGoo.css" />
</head>
<body>
<h1>Choose your tool</h1>
<p>
 Will you use an expensive software tool or will you use a book to learn how to
                build your own games?
</p>

<p>
  <a href = "software.html">
    <img src = "MEGPE.png"
         alt = "Expensive Game Software" />
  </a>

    <img src = "GooGooConfused.png"
         alt = "confused Goo Goo"/>

  <a href = "book.html">
    <img src = "Dummies.png"
         alt = "Dummies book" />
  </a>
</p>

</body>
</html>
```

Building this type of node (with a choice) is pretty easy.

1. **Begin with a standard HTML5 page.**

   Use the same framework as the first page. All the standard HTML stuff goes in there, like a `head`, `body`, `h1`, and a paragraph or two.

2. **Add a link to the external style sheet.**

   Here's where building the external style sheet pays off. Now you can simply link to the existing sheet without having to rewrite everything. Better yet, if you decide to change something, one sheet rules them all.

3. **Describe the problem.**

   Use a standard paragraph to describe the problem.

4. Make an image for each choice.

I just drew a (bad) image for each of the options. Use the standard `img` tag to display the images. Remember that images belong in a paragraph. Because these images are typically displayed side by side, I put them in the same paragraph.

5. Two images are links.

The `<a>` tag turns text into a link, but if you surround an image with an anchor, the image becomes a link. Use the original diagram to determine what page should be displayed when the user clicks on the image.

Adding a sound effect

If the user chooses the expensive software, she is taken to a page that looks like Figure 1-8.

Figure 1-8:
This page has a funny sound effect.

Most of the page is built like the other pages in this project, but it does have a new feature. Note there is a little bar under the image with a Play button. This indicates an audio sample that can be played. If the user clicks the Play button, he hears Goo Goo's anguished cries of pain and frustration. (Seriously, you've got to go to the website. A book just can't do this corny sound effect justice.)

You might wonder why the user has to click the Play button. Couldn't I make the sound play automatically when the user gets to the page? Yes, I could, but it's generally considered bad form to have a web page automatically play a sound without the user's permission. It's not a big deal in a game, though, and this particular application is somewhere between a game and a web page. Look ahead to Chapter 6 for information on how to add sound effects to your games.

Sound has long been one of the biggest headaches for web-based gaming. Web browsers could never agree on a good way to handle sound, which is one reason Flash became the de facto standard for web-based gaming.

However, HTML5 provides native audio support, so there's finally a good way to get sound effects working in any modern browser. Look at the code for `software.html`, and you'll see how it works:

```
<!DOCTYPE HTML>
<html lang="en-US">
<head>
    <meta charset="UTF-8">
    <title>Software</title>
    <link rel = "stylesheet"
          type = "text/css"
          href = "gooGoo.css" />
</head>
<body>
    <h1>Software</h1>

    <p>
        <img src = "mad.png"
             alt = "mad" /> <br />

        <audio controls = "controls">
            <source src = "mad.ogg"
                    type = "audio/ogg" />
            <source src = "mad.mp3"
                    type = "audio/mp3" />
            <a href = "mad.mp3">play sound</a>
        </audio>
    </p>

    <p>
        You chose the software, but now you have no money,
        and you can't figure out how to use it anyway.
    </p>


    <h2>You Lose!</h2>
```

```
    <p>
        <a href = "begin.html">Try again?</a>
    </p>
</body>
</html>
```

The new tag is called `audio`. It is designed to make it easy to incorporate audio clips into your web pages. Here's how to add audio to an HTML5 web page:

1. **Obtain your audio clip.**

    The cleanest approach is to build your own audio samples. I love Audacity, a free recording tool available for every major operating system. A link to Audacity (as well as an add-on library you'll need for recording MP3 files) is available on the website for this book. See this book's Introduction for more on the website and Chapter 11 for a bit more about Audacity.

2. **Store MP3 and Ogg versions of your sound.**

    Although every modern browser supports the audio tag, they don't all agree on the format. Some prefer MP3, and some prefer Ogg. Store both formats for the best results. (You can use the export command in Audacity to easily export files to Ogg and MP3 format.)

3. **Create the `<audio>` tag.**

    The `<audio>` tag is a relatively new HTML5 tag. You can either place it on its own or inside a paragraph or other container. I placed mine in a paragraph because I thought it looked better. I also used a special tag called `<br />` to force a line break so the audio controls show up on their own line.

4. **Designate whether controls will be displayed.**

    Because you're going to be polite and not automatically play the sound effect, you should let the user control the audio directly. The `controls = controls` attribute (defined by the department of redundancy department) does the trick.

5. **Add a `source` element for each format.**

    For maximum effectiveness, I ship both an Ogg and an MP3 version of each sound effect. The source element inside the `audio` element allows me to define as many audio source files as I want. The browser goes through the list of sources until it finds one that works.

6. **For each source, indicate the audio type.**

   The audio types are self-explanatory: audio/ogg or audio/mp3.

7. **Include a fallback anchor.**

   If the user has a really old browser, you can provide a link (with an ordinary anchor tag) that plays the sound in an external window. It's not very satisfying, but at least it works.

Add another page for a victory

Because this chapter is getting long, I simply add one more page that displays when the user makes the right choice. The final page looks like Figure 1-9.

Figure 1-9:
Choosing the right answer has incredible rewards.

Though you can't tell from the screen shot, this page features another silly sound effect. You really have to look at this project on the website.

There is really nothing new about this final page. It uses the same techniques as the other pages.

Here's the code for the `book.html` page:

```
<!DOCTYPE HTML>
<html lang="en-US">
<head>
    <meta charset="UTF-8">
    <title>Read a book</title>
    <link rel="stylesheet"
          type="text/css"
          href="gooGoo.css" />
</head>
<body>
    <h1>Read a book</h1>
    <p>
        <img src = "gooGooHappy.png"
             alt = "Happy Goo Goo" />
    </p>

    <p>
        You chose to read the book. <br />
        You learn all there is to know about building
        web-based games in HTML5. You win! <br />

        <audio controls = "controls">
            <source src = "whooHoo.mp3"
                    type = "audio/mp3" />
            <source src = "whooHoo.ogg"
                    type = "audio/ogg" />
            <a href = "whooHoo.mp3">WooHoo</a>
        </audio>
    </p>

    <p>
        <a href = "begin.html">Start over?</a>
    </p>

</body>
</html>
```

This simple page has all the same features as the other pages.

Making it your own

Of course, this adventure game is pretty short. It needs several more nodes. However, you know everything you need to make your own. Try designing your own game. Then use HTML5 to create each node, use CSS to design the pages, and add links to connect the nodes.

Chapter 2

Talking to the User

• •

• •

*A*lthough HTML and CSS are pretty cool as they are, games are really about interactivity. You can get a small amount of interactivity through hyperlinks, but for the really fun stuff, you need to write computer code.

Most people think that computer programming is a challenging skill, but it's actually not that hard to learn. You already have everything you need to get started: a text editor and a basic web page.

Modern web browsers all have built-in support for a programming language called *JavaScript*. JavaScript is a reasonably easy language to learn, and it provides more than enough power for some really fun games. Here are a few key features of JavaScript:

- ✔ **It's a scripting language.** This class of programming language tends to be a bit easier for beginners than more formal languages such as C++ and Java. Scripting languages are more focused on ease of programming than squeezing every ounce of performance from the computer. However, they still have plenty of power to make cool games.

- ✔ **It's tightly integrated with HTML and CSS.** HTML and CSS are used to provide the visual parts of the program (like the actors in a play) and the JavaScript code is the script that tells the actors what to do.

✔ **It's a powerful and modern language.** Some programmers act as if JavaScript is not a serious language. That is not a fair characterization. Modern versions of JavaScript are capable of some very sophisticated behavior, as you see throughout this book.

✔ **It uses object-oriented programming.** Object-oriented programming (OOP) is a specific style of programming that allows you to describe objects (like parts of the web page, or the robot zombie opossum in your game). Building a game consists of building the various objects and putting them together to make them work.

✔ **It is based on events.** As your code is running, various events trigger actions. For example, you want certain things to happen when your code loads in the browser, when the user clicks on a button, or when your hero collides with the dreaded pickle of doom.

JavaScript is a completely different language than Java, despite the similar names. Sometimes Java programmers like to act all superior, but don't believe it. Java and JavaScript are both terrific languages, but they're designed for different jobs, like a tennis racket and a baseball bat.

Traditionally, JavaScript is used to interact with specially designated parts of the page called a *form*. Forms provide basic interface elements to allow the user to enter data.

Making an Interactive Form

The basic style of interaction with the user involves creating a form and interacting with it. A form is simply a part of the page that accepts user input. The input can be from text boxes or more advanced elements like drop-down lists, radio buttons, and so on.

You can use ordinary HTML to create these elements, but if you want to read the user input, you'll need a programming language. That's where JavaScript comes in.

Figure 2-1 illustrates the game you write later in this chapter.

After the user enters some words, she clicks the Tell the Story button, and the results are shown at the bottom of the page, as in Figure 2-2.

This type of game is a Word-Story-style game, and it's a great first interactive program to write. You learn everything you need in this chapter to create your own word game.

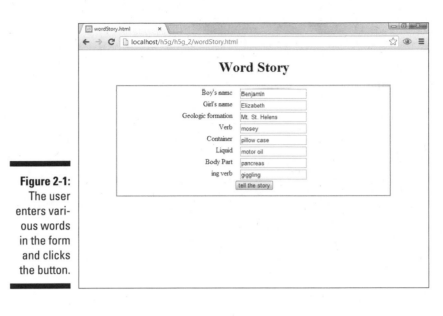

Figure 2-1:
The user
enters vari-
ous words
in the form
and clicks
the button.

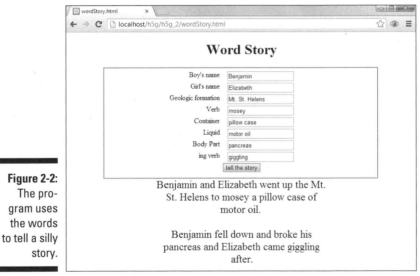

Figure 2-2:
The pro-
gram uses
the words
to tell a silly
story.

Adding JavaScript to Your Page

JavaScript is a programming language embedded within the web browser. It
works very closely with HTML. In fact, HTML forms the user interface of most
JavaScript programs. Where HTML provides the structure of a web page and
CSS provides the visual interface, JavaScript adds action. Here's an extremely
simple example:

```
<!DOCTYPE HTML>
<html lang = "en">
<head>
  <title>alert.html</title>
  <meta charset = "UTF-8" />
</head>

<body>
  <h1>Add quick JavaScript to a page</h1>
  <p>
    <button type = "button"
            onclick = "alert('I said not to click me!')">
      don't click me
    </button>
  </p>

</body>
</html>
```

This looks a lot like an HTML page because that's mainly what it is. Here's what's interesting about the page:

- ✔ **It has a button.** The `<button>` tag creates a button on the page. This button isn't in a form (although often they are). Note that HTML buttons don't do anything when you click them. You're about to change that. There is more than one kind of button, so use the `type = "button"` attribute to indicate that it's a normal button.

- ✔ **The button has an** `onclick` **attribute.** `onclick` is an *event attribute*. It's a special attribute of form elements that allows you to specify what should happen when an event occurs. The `onclick` attribute signifies what should happen when the user clicks on a button.

- ✔ **The value of the** `onclick` **attribute is JavaScript code.** You can use the `onclick` attribute to attach a single line of JavaScript code to your button click. In this case, that line is `alert('Hi there!')`.

- ✔ **The** `alert()` **command pops up a message box.** The alert command is used to send a message to the user without changing the structure of the page. Alert is easy to use, but it's annoying for the user. See the later section, "Modifying the page itself," for details on a more elegant way to talk to the user.

- ✔ **Any text inside the alert's parentheses is displayed to the user.** In this case, the message box will contain the greeting "Hi there!"

- ✔ **Note that I used single quotes.** JavaScript and HTML both allow single and double quotes. Because this JavaScript code was embedded in an HTML statement, I used a combination of single and double quotes to keep the browser from being confused about which quote was which.

When you load `alert.html` into your browser, it will look like Figure 2-3.

The great thing about buttons is that users are guaranteed to click them. If you want to be absolutely certain the button gets clicked, tell the user not to click it. It works every time. When the user inevitably clicks the button, she will see what is shown in Figure 2-4.

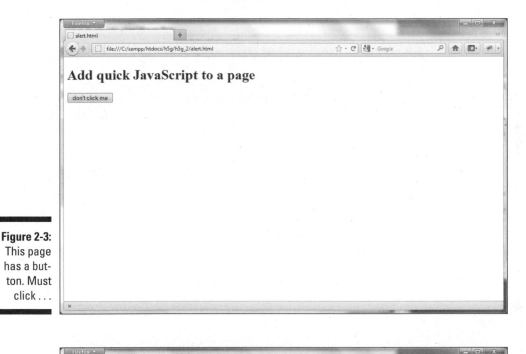

Figure 2-3:
This page has a button. Must click . . .

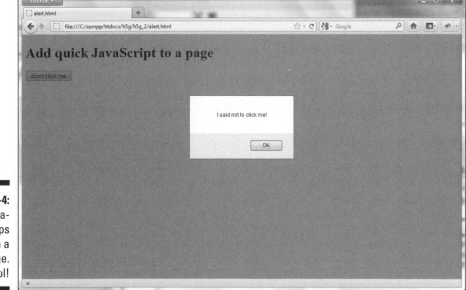

Figure 2-4:
A little dialog box pops up with a message. Cool!

The dialog box is called an *alert*. It's a simple tool, but it's an easy (if somewhat annoying) way to send the user a message.

The actual appearance of the alert dialog box differs based on your browser and operating system, but something pops up.

Creating the custom greeting

Buttons are nice, but it would be nice to allow the user to input some sort of data and then do something with the output. HTML allows you to create *forms*, which are special parts of the page designed for user input. Figure 2-5 shows one of the simplest possible forms:

Please type your name [   ]   submit

Figure 2-5:
The user
can enter a
name and
click the
button.

Although the input.html form shown in Figure 2-5 won't win any beauty contests, it has all the main features of a form. There's a label that describes what the user should do, an input area for the user to type in, and a button to do something when the user clicks on it. (Don't get your hopes up too much. The button in this version doesn't do anything, but I change that in the next example.) The code for input.html is short and sweet:

```
<!DOCTYPE HTML>
<html lang="en-US">
<head>
    <meta charset="UTF-8">
    <title>input.html</title>
</head>
<body>
    <form>
        <fieldset>
            <label for="txtName">Please type your name
        </label>
            <input type="text"
                    id = "txtName"/>
            <button type = "button">
                submit
            </button>
        </fieldset>
    </form>
</body>
</html>
```

Nothing horribly fancy here, but there are some new elements:

- ✔ **A `form` element:** It probably won't surprise you that a form is created with the `<form>` tag. Every once in a while, HTML makes sense. Any elements that are meant to allow for user input are expected to be placed in a form.

- ✔ **A `fieldset` element:** The form is just a logical container. It explains that the elements inside the form are used for input, but you still need some type of other container to hold the elements. The special `<fieldset>` tag is designed for exactly this purpose, so I put a `fieldset` pair inside the form.

- ✔ **Labels:** Labels are special HTML elements that are meant to describe a form element. They aren't absolutely necessary (earlier versions of HTML did not have them), but they can be useful. Labels have a special `for` attribute that helps connect the label to a specific input element.

- ✔ **An input:** There are a number of elements used for user input. Most are variations of the `<input>` tag. A text box (as used in this example) is `input` elements with the `type` attribute set to `text`. Note that I also assigned an `id` attribute to the `input` element. The `id` is used to connect a label to an input, and it is used later when JavaScript code wants to retrieve data from the `input` element.

- ✔ **A button:** Most of the time, forms just sit there, waiting for user input. All the real action happens when the user clicks on a button. For that reason, most forms have at least one button. The button has a `type` attribute, which must be set to `button`.

It may seem redundant to tell a button that its type is button, but it's a critical step. There are a number of different types of buttons. If you don't specify which type of button you're creating, HTML assumes you want a Submit button. This type of button is used in a totally different type of programming (on the web server) and submits a blank request to the web server, which causes your page to refresh rather than taking any other action. For the type of programming you'll do in this book, ensure you've set all buttons to type button.

Making the magic happen

If you've been following along, at this point you can type your name in the box of input.html, and you can click the button, but nothing happens. That's because you have to tell the browser what you want it to do. The onclick trick allows you to do simple things, but if you want to do something more interesting, you'll need to connect the button to a block of code called a *function*. Figure 2-6 shows greet.html, which adds this functionality to input.html.

The HTML is almost completely unchanged. The only difference is in the button code. The button now looks like this:

```
<button type = "button"
        onclick = "greet()">
    submit
</button>
```

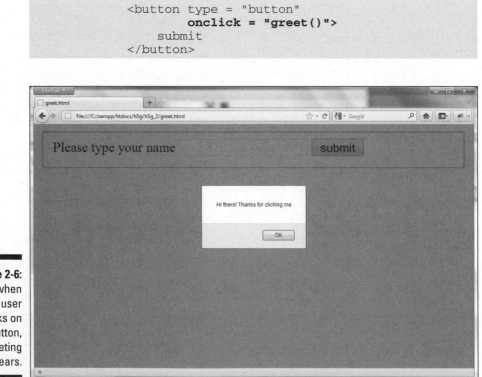

Figure 2-6:
Now when the user clicks on the button, a greeting appears.

The new feature is an `onclick` attribute. You can attach one line of JavaScript code to an `onclick` attribute. In this example, I tell JavaScript to run a function called `greet()`. That function doesn't exist yet, but that's the next step.

Most of the time when you want to add JavaScript code to a web page, you'll put it in the header, inside a `<script></script>` pair. Here's the JavaScript section in whole:

```
<script type = "text/javascript">
    function greet(){
        alert("Hi there!  Thanks for clicking me");
    } // end greet
</script>
```

These few lines hide a lot of sophisticated goings-on. Here's what you're doing in this code:

1. **Designate the beginning of a script segment.**

   The `script` tag is normally placed in the HTML header area. It indicates to the browser that the enclosed code will be in a programming language.

2. **Indicate the code will be written in JavaScript.**

   The `type = "text/javascript"` piece indicates that the following code is written in the JavaScript language. There are a few other language options, but they are rarely used.

3. **Create a function.**

   Most of the time, you'll store code in containers called *functions*. A function is a container for a block of code. At the simplest level, a function allows you to call several lines of code with only one name. Right now, I'm making a function called `greet()`. Remember, the `onclick` property of the button calls `greet()`. So, when the user clicks the button, any code in the `greet()` function will happen. Cool, huh?

4. **Dress up your function.**

   Functions are a very important part of programming. You need to know a few rules to make them work well for you. After the function name, you need a pair of parentheses. (They are empty for now, but later on you'll add content here.) A function always begins and ends with squiggly braces (`{}`). It's traditional to indent all of the code inside the function. (By "traditional," I mean that all programming teachers and bosses absolutely require it. Trust me. You need to get in the habit of doing it.)

5. **Use appropriate punctuation.**

   In English, it is important to end each sentence with appropriate punctuation (a period, question mark, or exclamation point). JavaScript has similar rules. In general, every line that does not have a squiggly brace needs a semicolon (;) to indicate the end of the line. Make sure it's a semicolon, and not a colon (:). It makes a huge difference.

6. **Greet the user.**

   This function is simple. It creates a basic greeting for the user. It ignores the user's name for now, but that will be in the next example. For now, appreciate that you can put any code you want inside a function and connect that function to a button. It's a pretty powerful tool.

7. **Comment the ending.**

   The two slashes after the close brace are a *comment* indicator. A comment is a note for programmers embedded in the code. Comments are ignored by the computer, but they're very useful for programmers. There are a number of places to put comments, but one of the more useful is at the end of a function. As your code gets more complicated, you'll have a *lot* of closing braces, and they can get hard to keep track of. Add a comment to each closing brace so it's clear what you're trying to close. It's a great habit to learn now as you're getting started.

A program where everyone knows your name

The `greet.html` page asks the user's name, but it doesn't do anything interesting with it. That requires a new concept, called a *variable*. A variable is simply a name for a chunk of computer memory. Variables can hold all kinds of information: words, numbers, even parts of the web page. A big part of programming is knowing how to create and use variables. Here's another version of the greeting program that uses variables to give a personal response. First I show you everything, and then I explain the details:

```
<!DOCTYPE HTML>
<html lang="en-US">
<head>
    <meta charset="UTF-8">
    <title>greetName.html</title>
    <script type = "text/javascript">
    function greet(){
      var txtName = document.getElementById("txtName");
      var userName = txtName.value;
      alert("Hi, " + userName + "!");
    } // end greet
    </script>
</head>
<body>
    <form>
```

```
        <fieldset>
            <label for="txtName">Please type your name</
            label>
            <input type="text"
                    id = "txtName"/>
            <button type = "button"
                    onclick = "greet()">
                submit
            </button>
        </fieldset>
    </form>
</body>
</html>
```

This program does something more interesting when you click the button, as you can see from Figure 2-7.

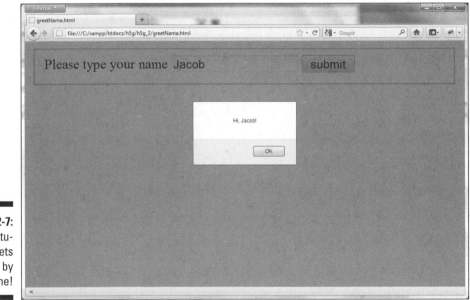

Figure 2-7:
Now it actually greets me by name!

Essentially, the program does these things:

1. **Get access to the text box.**

    The web page and the JavaScript code are different (if related) entities. Before I can get access to the *contents* of the input field, I need to give JavaScript access to the input field. I make a variable to refer to the text element.

2. **Retrieve the name.**

   The user's name is stored in the `value` property of the input field. I'll make another variable to refer to the name.

3. **Output the greeting.**

   Now I have everything I need, so I make a new greeting. This greeting combines some actual text with the user's name. I use the standard `alert` mechanism to create an easy greeting.

Implementation is not difficult once you know what you're trying to accomplish, but you do have to learn some new skills. Here's how the actual function works:

1. **Create a variable for the input element.**

   The `var` statement creates a new variable. A variable is simply a place in the computer memory. Whenever you create a variable, you must give it a name. I call my variable `txtName` because it's the text field containing the user's name. (See the upcoming sidebar for tips on naming things.)

   ```
   var txtName = document.getElementById("txtName");
   ```

2. **Attach the input element to the variable.**

   Before you can work with a part of the page, you need to tell Java Script what you're working with. Essentially, you create a variable to represent any important elements of the form. The command `document.getElementById()` expects the `id` of an element in the current page and returns a reference to that element. The first line of the function asks for the page element called `txtName` and creates a JavaScript variable also called `txtName`. When this line of code is finished, a variable called `txtName` refers to the HTML element of the same name.

   ```
   var txtName = document.getElementById("txtName");
   ```

3. **Create another variable for the user's name.**

   The `txtName` variable refers to the input field, not the actual name. If you want the user's name, there's another easy but important step. Make another variable called `userName`. This variable contains the actual name.

   ```
   var userName = txtName.value;
   ```

4. **Extract the user name from the text field.**

   Text fields have a `value` attribute. If you have a variable referring to a text field, you can read or change the value of that text field. Take the `value` property and assign it to the `userName` variable.

   ```
   var userName = txtName.value;
   ```

Naming things

One of the most important jobs a programmer has is naming things. Programmers invent stuff all the time, and the names you choose for these things can have a big impact on how easy your code is to use and maintain. A few conventions have emerged over time. Follow these, and you should be good in pretty much any language.

✔ **Make names meaningful.** It's much easier to determine what *userName* means than *X*. Whenever possible, create a name that describes what the thing does. In the best-written programs, the variable names are chosen so clearly a reader can understand the program without comments.

✔ **Use the name to convey the type of information.** When you're naming a variable, describe the kind of data the variable will contain. If you're naming a function, describe what the function does (usually function names look like verb phrases). If you're naming a file, describe what sort of content the file has.

✔ **Be careful with punctuation.** Spaces and punctuation have special meaning in most languages, so use them carefully when naming things. Generally, you should avoid all spaces and punctuation symbols. Often the underscore character is allowed, but you should not use any other punctuation in the name of a function, a variable, a file, or an object.

✔ **Use camel-case.** It's common to use all lowercase and to use uppercase to indicate word boundaries (as in *userName*). Note that you'll see other capitalization traditions in your travels. Object names are often capitalized, and constants are usually all uppercase. I point out these exceptions as you come across them.

✔ **Make the size reasonable.** You want the name to be long enough to be clear, but not so long that it's difficult to type.

5. **Greet the user.**

   Use a standard `alert` statement to greet the user.

   ```
   alert("Hi, " + userName + "!");
   ```

6. **Include the value of** `userName`**.**

   The alert statement can contain plain text: `alert("hi")`. It can also contain the value of a variable: `alert(userName)`. Note that if you don't include quotes, the alert statement prints the *value* of the variable, not the variable name itself. If you want to get fancy, you can combine actual text and variables, like I do in this program. Use the plus sign to combine variables and standard text.

   ```
   alert("Hi, " + userName + "!");
   ```

Modifying the page itself

It's great to have a program that greets the user by name, but the dialog box is a little annoying. It would be even better if the program could modify the web page directly. As an example, Figure 2-8 looks a lot like the other pages, but after the user clicks the button, the greeting is embedded directly into the page!

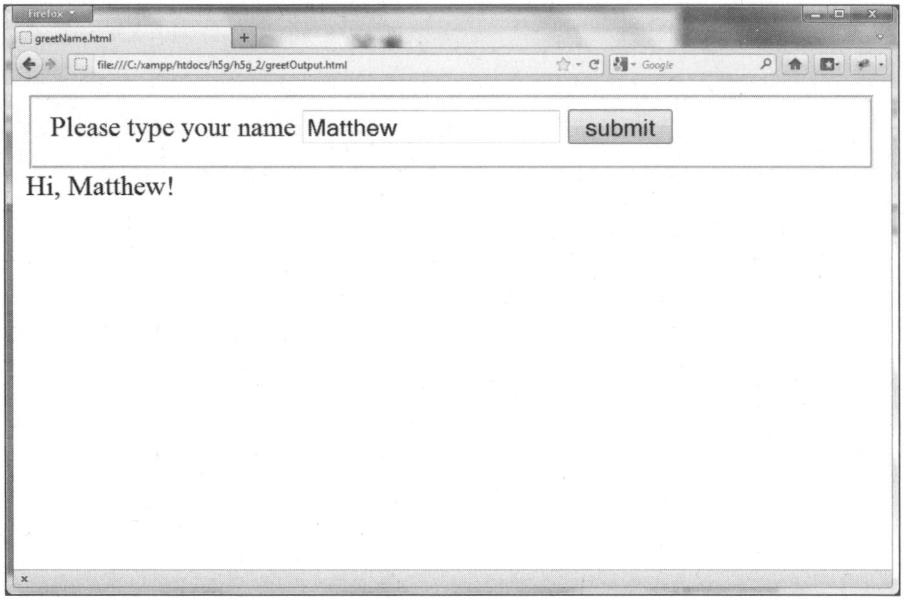

Figure 2-8:
This program embeds the greeting into the page.

The new version of the program is called greetOutput.html, and here it is in its entirety. (The new code elements are highlighted.)

```
<!DOCTYPE HTML>
<html lang="en-US">
<head>
    <meta charset="UTF-8">
    <title>greetName.html</title>
    <script type = "text/javascript">
        function greet(){
            var txtName = document.getElementById("txtName");
            var userName = txtName.value;
            var output = document.getElementById("output");
            output.innerHTML = "Hi, " + userName + "!";
        } // end greet
    </script>
```

```
</head>
<body>
    <form>
        <fieldset>
            <label for="txtName">Please type your name</
        label>
            <input type="text"
                   id = "txtName"/>
            <button type = "button"
                    onclick = "greet()">
                submit
            </button>
        </fieldset>
    </form>
    <div id = "output">empty</div>
</body>
</html>
```

The code isn't shockingly different, but there are some new elements:

1. **Create an HTML element for output.**

   Add an HTML element to the page that will contain your output. I'm using a standard `div` element. Be sure to give the element an ID so you can refer to it in code. You'll generally make this element empty, but I like to put something in there (like the word `empty`) so I can tell where the `div` is. After your program is working, you can take out any place-holder text.

2. **Create a variable for the output element.**

   Use the `document.getElementById` trick to create a variable representing the output area. You can use this method to create a variable for any HTML element, not just form inputs.

3. **Modify the output's contents.**

   All HTML elements that have beginning and ending tags have an `innerHTML` property. If you change the value of the property, you change what's displayed inside the element. You can place any legal HTML code here, but I simply want to create the greeting.

Adding style to your forms

The greeting page is now pretty functional, but it doesn't look very good. At the moment, all the form elements are bunched up together. It would be nice to have them lined up neatly. CSS can fix that. Figure 2-9 shows the page with a custom style attached.

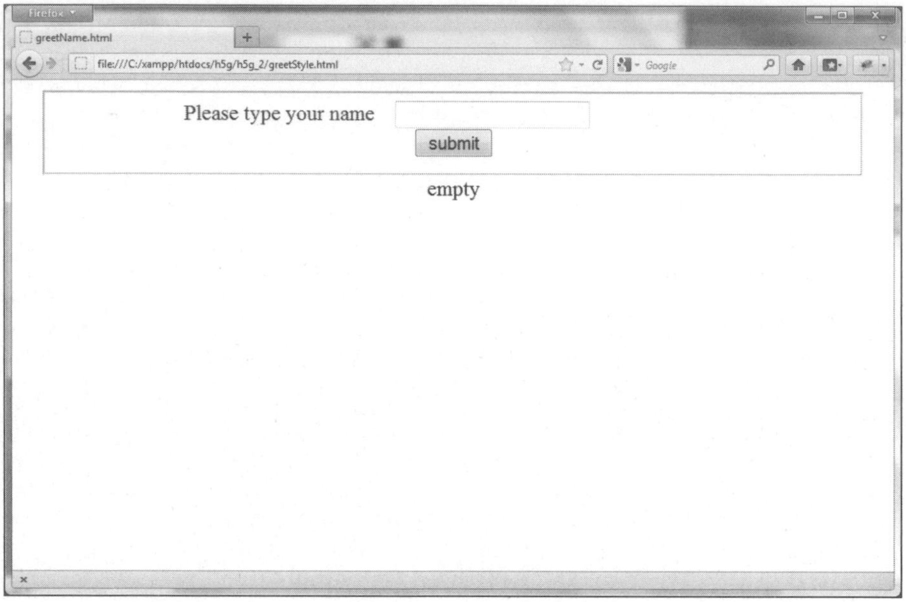

Figure 2-9:
Now every-
thing is lined
up neatly.

That's fine, but it can get a little messy. Sometimes you might want to put all the CSS code in a separate file and call it in when you need it. This offers a couple of advantages. First, the CSS code stays out of the way until you need it. Perhaps more importantly, after you've stored a set of CSS rules in a separate file, you can reuse them across multiple HTML pages. So if your game uses the same style across 100 pages, you only have to write the style rules once. Changing the style in the external sheet changes all the pages that use that style. It's pretty easy to build an external style sheet:

1. **Create a new empty file.**

   Use a plain text editor (usually the same one you use to build HTML pages). Be sure to save the file with a CSS extension. Save your CSS file in the same directory as your HTML files. I saved my file as `form.css` so I can reuse it any time I want to display a form.

2. **Type the CSS rules in the new file.**

   You don't need to use the `<style></style>` pair in an external style sheet. It's already understood that you're defining CSS. Otherwise, write your CSS code exactly like you would inside the `style` pair.

3. **Add a `link` tag to the HTML header.**

   In the HTML's header area, you can add a `link` tag to indicate a linkage to an external style sheet. Set the `type` to `text/css`, the `rel` to `stylesheet`, and the `href` to the name of the style sheet you just created.

Do it with style

Of course, you need to apply some style rules to make the page look nice. Typically, you should line up the labels and their corresponding input elements. A number of handy style rules make pages lay out better. Look over these new style rules:

✔ text-align: The text-align rule changes the alignment of text inside an element. It only works on block-level elements. Use text-align to align your text to the left, right, center, or to justify it. You do not use text-align to center elements, just to center text within an element. (See the margin rule described later in this list for element alignment.)

✔ width: Use this rule to determine the width of an element. You must define a width whenever you use float. The width can be specified in pixels (px), percentages (%), or by character width (em).

✔ margin: The margin determines the space between the outside of the element and the text. You can define separate margins for all sides (margin-left, margin-top, and so on) or you can define all the margins at once with the margin rule. If you set left and right margins of a block-level element to auto, you center that element.

✔ float: The float rule removes the element from the normal placement rules and places it using a new rule set. If you float to the left (the most common type of float), the element goes all the way to the left of its container unless there is another left-floated element in the way. Normally you float a number of elements to the left and use the clear attribute to set up rows. This is a good way to simulate a table-style layout without having to use the table tags. (Keep reading if this is confusing. I show an example next.)

✔ clear: This rule is used to specify that a floated element is supposed to occupy a certain area. If you set clear to left, the element tries to move to the left-hand side of the container. If you set clear to both, the element should be on the line by itself.

✔ padding: The padding attribute allows extra padding between the contents of an element and the border. Padding is similar to margin, but padding is inside the border and margin is outside the border. If you have no visible border, padding and margin act pretty much the same. Like margin, you can set padding to particular sides: padding-right and padding-bottom.

✔ display: The display rule is used to change the basic behavior of an element. You can use it to make a normally inline element (like a button) act like a block-level element. You can also set display to none to make an element disappear altogether.

Creating a style for the form

You can use the style rules to create an external style sheet to make your form look nice. Remember that `form.html` had a reference to a style sheet called `form.css`. Here's my text for `form.css`:

```css
h1 {
    text-align: center;
}

fieldset{
  width: 600px;
  margin: auto;
}

label {
  width: 15em;
  float: left;
  clear: left;
  text-align: right;
  padding-right: 1em;
}

input {
  float: left;
}

button {
  display: block;
  clear: both;
  margin-left: auto;
  margin-right: auto;
}

#output {
  text-align: center;
}
```

This code arranges the various CSS elements to make the page look a lot better. Here's how you clean up the form:

1. **Center the headline.**

   Apply `text-align: center` to the h1 tag. This causes the headline to be centered for a nice look.

2. **Center the** `fieldset`.

   The `fieldset` is a block-level element, so you can center it by giving it a fixed width and setting the margins to automatic.

3. **Float the labels.**

   The labels should all line up on the left-hand side of the form. Set `float` to `left`. Whenever you float an element, you should also set the width. I set the width to 15em, which is the width of 15 capital Ms in the current font.

4. **Arrange the label text.**

   The standard text alignment for a label is left-justified, which makes the labels seem far away from the input elements. Setting `text-align` right moves the labels closer to the text elements, but it's too close. Give a `padding-right` of 1 em to make a nice space between the label and the input field.

5. **Adjust the input elements.**

   The only thing you need to do to the `inputs` is float them to the left. That snuggles them up against the corresponding labels.

6. **Center the button.**

   Typically, you want a button to be centered. That's a little tricky until you know how to do it. The easiest way is to force the button into block mode so you can use the `margin:  auto` trick.

7. **Format the output.**

   I think it looks best if the output is also centered, so I add a little code to the output. Note that if you know the `id` of a page element, you can use the # sign to refer to it, so `#output` modifies the element that has `output` as its `id`.

CSS rules can be a little daunting. If you need a more careful explanation of what's going on here, please look into the much more complete discussion of CSS in my book *HTML, XHTML & CSS All-In-One For Dummies*. Even if you don't exactly understand what's happening with this style sheet, you can still copy it and use it for your own forms. Just add the `link` reference to your HTML page.

Outsourcing your JavaScript code

Programmers love the idea of breaking up big problems into smaller problems. It's nice to separate the CSS from the HTML because these are different tools for solving different problems. It's also possible to put the JavaScript code in a separate file. As your programs get more complicated, you'll want to be able to do this. Here's one more version of the greeting program. (I won't show a screen shot because it looks identical to the user.)

```
<!DOCTYPE HTML>
<html lang="en-US">
<head>
    <meta charset="UTF-8">
    <title>greetName.html</title>
    <link rel = "stylesheet"
          type = "text/css"
          href = "form.css" />
    <script type = "text/javascript"
            src = "greet.js"></script>
</head>
<body>
    <form>
        <fieldset>
            <label for="txtName">Please type your name</
            label>
            <input type="text"
                    id = "txtName"/>
            <button type = "button"
                    onclick = "greet()">
                submit
            </button>
        </fieldset>
    </form>
    <div id = "output">empty</div>
</body>
</html>
```

The HTML code hasn't changed at all. The only difference is the reference to the external JavaScript code. Here's how it works:

1. **Copy all of the JavaScript code.**

    Take all the JavaScript code out of the `script` tags.

2. **Create a new file.**

    I called my file `greet.js`. This is just a plain text file.

3. **Paste all the code into the new file.**

    The new file contains all the JavaScript code. (I show you the file next.)

4. **Add a `src` attribute to the `script` tag.**

    You can attach a `src` attribute to a script tag. This tells the browser to extract the JavaScript code from an external file. It's generally best to keep the file in the same directory as the main HTML page.

5. **Leave the script element empty.**

    You still need a `</script>` tag, but you don't need any code between `<script>` and `</script>`.

The `greet.js` file contains nothing but the code used to make the program work. There is no need to change any of the code:

```
function greet(){
    var txtName = document.getElementById("txtName");
    var userName = txtName.value;
    var output = document.getElementById("output");
    output.innerHTML = "Hi, " + userName + "!";
} // end greet
```

Building the Word Story Game

If you know how to build form elements, write a little JavaScript code, and format a form, you're ready to build the Word Story game described at the beginning of this chapter. (If you're a little fuzzy on any of these areas, you may want to go back through the chapter and review them.)

Games are complicated, so you need to think carefully about how you're going to build this thing. The best way to solve complex problems is to break them into smaller steps. The multiple file system makes this a bit easier. Here's how to make your own Word story game:

1. **Design the game on paper.**

   The most important programming happens before you turn on the computer. Plan out your game. I show you my plan for this game in the next section.

2. **Build your framework.**

   The web page forms the essential infrastructure of the page. This is done in HTML. If you've planned your project well, this isn't difficult to create.

3. **Add style details.**

   Use CSS to make your page look how you want. Most of the details can wait, but you'll at least want to add enough CSS to ensure your page is usable.

4. **Build the code.**

   Add the JavaScript code to make your program do what it does.

5. **Test.**

   Check the program to see if it does what you want. You should also have others test your game.

Designing the game

This game doesn't take a lot of work to design, but there are two components. First is the *data design*, which helps you understand what data the program is about. The data design for this game can simply be the story. In this example, I start with a classic nursery rhyme and add placeholders for the user input, like this:

> *<boy> and <girl> went up the <geol> to <verb>*
>
> *a <container> of <liquid>.*
>
> *<boy> fell down and broke his <bodyPart> and*
>
> *<girl> came <gerund> after.*

From this document, you can figure out what variables you need, which gives you the information you need to build your user interface.

It's generally best to sketch out your user interface on paper first. Figure 2-10 shows my sketch for the interface.

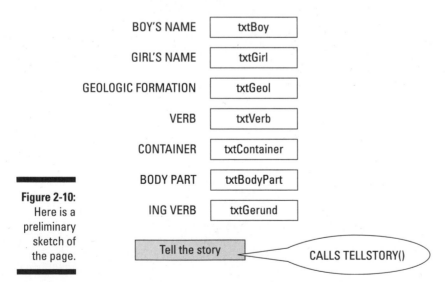

WORD STORY

BOY'S NAME	txtBoy
GIRL'S NAME	txtGirl
GEOLOGIC FORMATION	txtGeol
VERB	txtVerb
CONTAINER	txtContainer
BODY PART	txtBodyPart
ING VERB	txtGerund

Tell the story — CALLS TELLSTORY()

Figure 2-10:
Here is a
preliminary
sketch of
the page.

A sketch should have a number of features:

- ✓ **All the labels:** Make sure you know all the elements you need before you start coding. It's much easier to write the code if you already know what you need.

✔ **Names for all the components:** You'll need to know the name of every text element. It's easy to write the code using these elements if they're already listed in a document.

✔ **Any buttons you'll need:** You don't need to specify the name of every button, but you should indicate what will happen when the button is clicked.

✔ **The general layout:** The sketch should give you a sense what you're trying to accomplish with the layout. You won't be able to create a layout if you don't know how it's supposed to look.

Building the HTML foundation

After you have the design figured out, begin with the HTML foundation. Everything else in the project depends on solid HTML code, so write it well. Here's my HTML:

```
<!DOCTYPE HTML>
<html lang="en-US">
<head>
    <meta charset="UTF-8">
    <title>wordStory.html</title>
    <link rel = "stylesheet"
          type = "text/css"
          href = "wordStory.css" />
    <script type="text/javascript"
            src = "wordStory.js">
    </script>
</head>
<body>
    <h1>Word Story</h1>
    <form action="">
        <fieldset>
            <label for = "txtBoy">Boy's name</label>
            <input type = "text"
                   id = "txtBoy" />

            <label for = "txtGirl">Girl's name</label>
            <input type = "text"
                   id = "txtGirl" />

            <label for = "txtGeol">Geologic formation</
            label>
            <input type = "text"
                   id = "txtGeol" />

            <label for = "txtVerb">Verb</label>
            <input type = "text"
```

```
                           id = "txtVerb" />

              <label for = "txtContainer">Container</label>
              <input type = "text"
                           id = "txtContainer" />

              <label for = "txtLiquid">Liquid</label>
              <input type = "text"
                           id = "txtLiquid" />

              <label for = "txtBodyPart">Body Part</label>
              <input type = "text"
                           id = "txtPart" />

              <label for = "txtGerund">ing verb</label>
              <input type = "text"
                           id = "txtGerund" />

              <button onclick = "tellStory()"
                      type = "button">
                 tell the story
              </button>

          </fieldset>
      </form>

      <div id = "output">

      </div>
</body>
```

The page is much like greet.html, if a bit longer. It has a number of sections:

- ✔ **An external style sheet:** The style sheet is stored in an external file. One primary advantage of an external style sheet is how it lets you ignore the style for now. As long as you have a reference to the style, you can make the page look however you want later.

- ✔ **External JavaScript:** The JavaScript code is also stored in an external file. This practice allows you to let the HTML page focus on the web code and worry about the programming later. That's a great way to handle complex tasks like building games.

- ✔ **A form:** The main purpose of this HTML page is to provide a form. I've created a form asking for a number of terms. The form's button refers to the tellStory() function that is developed in wordStory.js.

- ✔ **An empty div for output:** The results of the story are placed in a div called output.

Adding the CSS style

With the HTML code in place, you'll have all the elements you need, but the page looks ugly unless you add some CSS. The `wordStory.css` file handles this duty. It's basically identical to the form CSS described earlier in the chapter:

```css
h1 {
   text-align: center;
}

fieldset {
   width: 600px;
   margin-left: auto;
   margin-right: auto;
}

label {
   float: left;
   width: 250px;
   clear: left;
   text-align: right;
   padding-right: 1em;
}

input {
   float: left;
}

button {
   display: block;
   clear: both;
   margin-left: auto;
   margin-right: auto;
}

#output {
   font-size: 150%;
   text-align: center;
   width: 400px;
   margin-left: auto;
   margin-right: auto;
}
```

Writing the code

The only task left is to write the JavaScript code. Although this may seem daunting, it is pretty easy because of the level of planning you've put into the game. Here's the general plan of the code:

Create a variable for each input element

Extract the text for each variable

Compile the story in a variable

Create a variable to represent output

Write the story to the output div

The actual code is nothing new. It simply uses the skills taught throughout this chapter to read the form elements and create a fun story:

```
function tellStory(){
    //gather form elements
    var txtBoy = document.getElementById("txtBoy");
    var txtGirl = document.getElementById("txtGirl");
    var txtGeol = document.getElementById("txtGeol");
    var txtVerb = document.getElementById("txtVerb");
    var txtContainer = document.getElementById("txtContainer");
    var txtLiquid = document.getElementById("txtLiquid");
    var txtPart = document.getElementById("txtPart");
    var txtGerund = document.getElementById("txtGerund");
    var output = document.getElementById("output");

    //create variables for input
    var boy = txtBoy.value;
    var girl = txtGirl.value;
    var geol = txtGeol.value;
    var verb = txtVerb.value;
    var container = txtContainer.value;
    var liquid = txtLiquid.value;
    var part = txtPart.value;
    var gerund = txtGerund.value;


    //write the story
    var story = boy + „ and „ + girl + „ went up the „;
    story += geol + „ to „ + verb + „ a „ + container;
    story += „ of „ + liquid + „. <br / > <br />";
    story += boy + „ fell down and broke his „ + part;
    story += „ and „ + girl + „ came „ + gerund + „ after.";

    //copy story to output
    output.innerHTML = story;
} // end tellStory
```

Although the code is nothing new, here are a few things you should notice about it:

- ✔ **Lots of comments:** Good coders use plenty of comments. I added comments to explain everything that was happening. I'm also a big fan of comments for right braces (to tell what's ending) because all right braces look the same, and this is a common place to get confused.

- ✔ **Careful variable names:** I used thoughtful and consistent variable names throughout. This was easy because the variable names were determined during the sketch portion of the process.

- ✔ **Good organization:** The code was carefully organized to flow in an easy-to-follow pattern. Note the use of indentation and white space to make the code easier to read.

Designing your code well leads to less frustration and much better programs. Enjoy the game. You'll be able to write even more amazing games soon.

Chapter 3

Coding Like a Pro

· ·

· ·

Computer games are complex. They are about a lot of information: scores, maps, characters, and all the data they represent. You also have complicated instructions. Even simple games are complicated enough that you'll need to break them into smaller segments. You'll also find that some of your code is repetitive. You'll also want the computer to make decisions so the enemy characters will appear to think and the game will respond to different circumstances in different ways.

The basic ideas of programming are the same in any language. Programs are about data, which is stored in variables. You'll sometimes have a chunk of code that you'll want to combine into functions. Your program needs to do different things in different situations, and sometimes it needs to be able to repeat things. Sometimes you'll also need more advanced ways to think about information and instructions. Game programming shares these characteristics with every other programming language.

All of these things require the basic elements of programming:

✔ **Variables:** These are the basic data elements. Everything in your game is housed in one or more variables.

✔ **Conditions:** A condition is a true or false statement. Conditions are critical in loops and branches.

✔ **Branches:** Your code can appear to make decisions. A number of tools help you make decisions well.

✔ **Loops:** Loops are useful when you have repetitive tasks to perform.

✔ **Arrays:** These are "super-variables" that can contain a huge amount of information.

✔ **Functions:** A function is a group of code lines with a single name. Functions help you organize your code.

Working with Variables

Variables are a really important part of computer programming. Although JavaScript makes variables pretty easy to use, you still need to keep some very important things in mind when you use a variable:

✔ **The `var` statement is preferred but not required.** It's generally considered best to use the `var` statement to define a variable. Throughout this book, I use the `var` statement to build every major variable.

✔ **Just mentioning a variable creates it.** If you leave out the `var` statement, JavaScript tries to create a variable for you. For example, `user-Name = "Andy";` is similar to `var userName = "Andy":`.

✔ **The variable type is automatically determined by JavaScript.** Different kinds of information are stored differently in the computer's memory. Integers (counting numbers), real numbers (with a decimal point), and text are all stored differently in memory. JavaScript tries to automatically create the right type of variable based on the context.

You're just my type: Handling different data types

The point about variable types is really important. Different kinds of data are stored in different ways in the computer. Some languages (like C++ and Java) are extremely picky about variable types and require you to think carefully about what type of data goes into what variable. JavaScript is much more easy-going about data types, but it still must figure out how to store the data. When you assign a value to a JavaScript variable, JavaScript turns it into one of these main types:

✔ **Integers:** Integers are the counting numbers, zero, and negative numbers. Integers do not have a decimal point. They are pretty easy for the computer to work with and rarely cause problems, so they are a favorite data type.

✔ **Floating point:** Numbers with a decimal point are often called `floats`. (Some languages have more than one floating type, but JavaScript just has `floats`.) Floating data requires a lot more memory than integers and can introduce some crazy errors, so JavaScript only stores values with the float mechanism if needed (that is, if a numeric value has a decimal part).

✔ **Strings:** Text data is a special case. Text is really stored as a bunch of integers in contiguous memory cells. This reminded early programmers of beads on a string, so programmers never say *text* data, but call text *strings* instead. Almost all user input and output is done through strings.

✔ **Boolean:** Boolean value is another special case. A Boolean data element only contains the values `true` or `false`. Simple as they are, Booleans are extremely useful.

✔ **Objects:** JavaScript supports an advanced programming idea called *object-oriented programming*. A JavaScript object can be a very complex element containing variables and functions. Any element on the web page can be converted into a JavaScript object, and JavaScript supports a rich framework of other types of objects as well.

Using a computer program to do bad math

Although JavaScript tries to shield you from worrying about data types, you still have to think about this issue because sometimes it causes you problems. For example, consider the code in `typeConv.html` (shown in Figure 3-1).

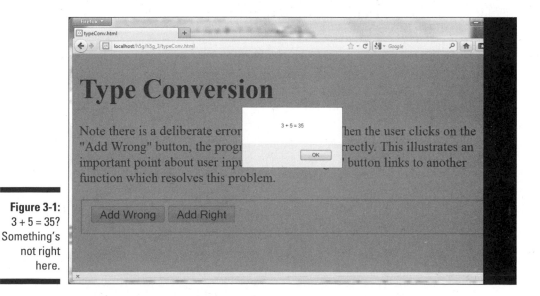

Figure 3-1:
3 + 5 = 35?
Something's
not right
here.

This program asks the user for two numbers and then tries to add them together. However, it doesn't do it correctly. If the user inputs 3 and 5, the result is 35. The Add Wrong button calls the cleverly named `addWrong()` function. Here's the code for `addWrong()`:

```
function addWrong(){
  //from typeConv.html
  //input two numbers
  var x = prompt("X");
  var y = prompt("Y");
  var sum = x + y;
  alert(x + " + " + y + " = " + sum);
} // end addWrong
```

The code for `addWrong()` looks perfectly reasonable. Here's what you're doing with it:

1. **Ask the user for** x **and** y.

   Use the prompt statement to ask the user for two numbers. Store these two numbers in the variables x and y.

2. **Add** x **and** y **and put the result in** sum.

   Make a new variable called sum that will contain the sum of x and y.

3. **Output the value of** sum.

   Use the standard `alert()` statement to output the result.

This code seems completely straightforward, and it ought to work. However, it doesn't do what you want. It reports that 3 plus 5 equals 35. And here we thought computers were good at math.

Managing data types correctly

The key to fixing the `addWrong` problem is to understand how the computer is misinterpreting the data. Here's the underlying problem: The `prompt()` command is asking for *text* from the user. That text is stored in a string variable because JavaScript assumes any input from the user is a string. So, the value 3 isn't stored as the *number* 3, but as a text variable with the value '3.' (The quotes are important because text values are always encased in quotes and numeric values are not.) The plus sign combines two string values, so if x is '3' and y is '5', x + y means 'concatenate (or combine) '3' and '5', resulting in an answer of '35'. That is not what we want at all.

The way to fix this is to tell the computer that x and y should be interpreted as integers, like this:

```
function addRight(){
  //from typConv.html
  //input two numbers
  var x = prompt("X");
  var y = prompt("Y");

  //force values to integer format
  x = parseInt(x);
  y = parseInt(y);

  var sum = x + y;
  alert(x + " + " + y + " = " + sum);

} // end addRight
```

This code is very similar to the `addWrong()` function, but it adds a new section. The `parseInt()` function accepts a string and converts it to an integer. If it cannot convert the value, it returns the special value `NaN` (Not a Number).

There are similar functions for converting data to other types. Use `parseFloat()` to convert a string value to a floating point (decimal) value. The `toString()` method can be used to convert a number to a string:

```
x = 5;
alert(x.toString());
```

However, JavaScript usually converts numbers to strings automatically, so it isn't usually necessary to use this technique.

This improved version of the adding code still pulls in the values as strings, but it converts them to integer values before doing any calculation. The exact same code is used to add the values (`sum = x + y`), but this time the values are integers, so the computer knows that the plus sign really means *add*.

Figure 3-2 illustrates the `addRight` function working as expected.

Experienced programmers (especially Java programmers) might be horrified at the cavalier way JavaScript lets you just create and change variable types on the fly. However, it really works pretty well most of the time, so you might just have to relax and appreciate that different languages have different goals. JavaScript tries to do as much automatically as it can, which is nice for beginners. Java (which is an entirely different language) is more focused on protecting you from various kinds of mistakes often brought on by sloppy coding. Java has much stricter rules, but when you follow those rules, you tend to make fewer mistakes.

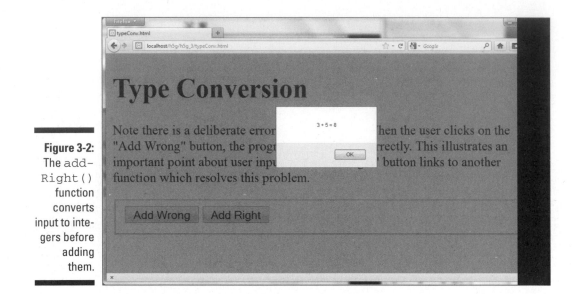

Figure 3-2:
The add-
Right()
function
converts
input to inte-
gers before
adding
them.

Making Choices with if

Sometimes you'll need your code to make decisions. For example, if some-body famous typed their name in your website, you might want to create a custom greeting for them. (I know this is a goofy example, but stay with me.) Take a look at the ifElse.html site in Figures 3-3 and 3-4.

As you can see, the program looks at the input in the text box and changes behavior based on the value of the text field. The code is quite similar to the code in the hiUser page. The only difference is the way the function is writ-ten. Here's the checkName() function called in ifElse.html:

```
function checkName()
  // from ifElse.html
  lblOutput = document.getElementById("lblOutput");
  txtInput = document.getElementById("txtInput");

  userName = txtInput.value;
  if (userName == "Tim Berners-Lee"){
    lblOutput.innerHTML = "Thanks for inventing HTML!";
  } else {
    lblOutput.innerHTML = "Do I know you?";
  } // end if
} // end function
```

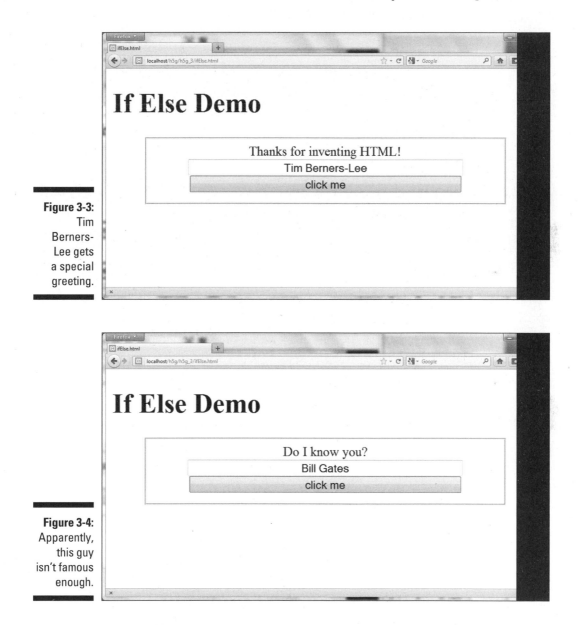

Figure 3-3:
Tim
Berners-
Lee gets
a special
greeting.

Figure 3-4:
Apparently,
this guy
isn't famous
enough.

Changing the greeting with if

This code uses an important idea called a *condition* inside a construct called an `if` statement. Here's what's happening:

1. **Set up the web page as usual.**

   The HTML code has elements called `lblOutput` and `txtInput`. It also has a button that calls `checkName()` when it's clicked.

2. **Create variables for important page elements.**

   You're getting data from `txtInput` and changing the HTML code in `lblOutput`, so create variables for these two elements.

3. **Get `userName` from `txtInput`.**

   Use the `txtInput.value` trick to get the value of the input element called `txtInput` and place it in the variable `userName`.

4. **Set up a condition.**

   The key to this program is a special element called a *condition* — an expression that can be evaluated as `true` or `false`. Conditions are often (as in this case) comparisons. Note that the double equals sign (`==`) is used to represent equality. In this example, I'm asking whether the `userName` variable equals the value `"Tim Berners-Lee"`.

5. **Place the condition in an `if` structure.**

   The `if` statement is one of a number of programming constructs that use conditions. It contains the keyword `if` followed by a condition (in parentheses). If the condition is `true`, all of the code in the following set of braces is executed.

6. **Write code to execute if the condition is `true`.**

   Create a set of squiggly braces after the condition. Any code inside these braces executes if the condition is `true`. Be sure to indent your code and use the right squiggle brace (`}`) to end the block of code. In this example, I give a special greeting to Tim Berners-Lee (because he *is* just that awesome).

7. **Build an `else` clause.**

   You can build an `if` statement with a single code block, but often you want the code to do something else if the condition is `false`. Use the `else` construct to indicate you will have a second code block that will execute only if the condition is `false`.

8. **Write the code to happen when the condition is `false`.**

   The code block following the `else` clause executes only if the condition is false. In this particular example, I have a greeting for everyone except Tim Berners-Lee.

The different flavors of if

If statements are extremely powerful, and there are a number of variations. You can actually have one, two, or any number of branches. You can write code like this:

```
if (userName == "Tim Berners-Lee"){
  lblOutput.innerHTML = "Thanks for inventing HTML"
} // end if
```

With this structure, the greeting occurs if `userName` is `"Tim Berners-Lee"` and nothing happens if the `userName` is anything else. You can also use the `if-else` structure (this is the form used in the actual code):

```
if (userName == "Tim Berners-Lee"){
  lblOutput.innerHTML = "Thanks for inventing HTML!";
} else {
  lblOutput.innerHTML = "Do I know you?";
} // end if
```

One more alternative lets you compare as many results as you wish by adding new conditions:

```
if (userName == "Tim Berners-Lee"){
  lblOutput.innerHTML = "Thanks for inventing HTML!";
} else if (userName == "Al Gore") {
  lblOutput.innerHTML = "Thanks for inventing the Internet";
} else if (userName == "Hakon Wium Lie") {
  lblOutput.innerHTML = "Thanks for inventing CSS";
} else {
  lblOutput.innerHTML = "Do I know you?";
} // end if
```

Conditional operators

The `==` operator checks to see if two values are identical, but as Table 3-1 shows, JavaScript supports a number of other operators as well.

Table 3-1	Conditional Operators
Operator	*Meaning*
a == b	a is equal to b.
a < b	a is less than b.
a > b	a is greater than b.
a <= b	a is less than or equal to b.
a >= b	a is greater than or equal to b.
a != b	a is not equal to b.

If you're coming from another programming language like Java, C++, or PHP, you might wonder how string comparisons work because they require different operators in these languages. JavaScript uses exactly the same comparison operators for types of data, so there's no need to learn different operators. Yeah JavaScript!

Managing Repetition with for loops

Computers are well known for repetitive behavior. It's pretty easy to get a computer to do something many times. The main way to get this behavior is to use a mechanism called a *loop*. The for loop is a standard kind of loop that is used when you know how often something will happen. Figure 3-5 shows the most basic form of the for loop.

For loops

count to ten | count backwards | count by fives

1
2
3
4
5
6
7
8
9
10

Figure 3-5:
This program counts from one to ten.

Setting up the web page

The same web page is used to demonstrate three different kinds of `for` loops. As usual, the HTML code sets everything up. Here's the HTML code that creates the basic framework:

```
<body onload = "init()">
  <h1>For loops</h1>
  <form action = "">
    <fieldset>
      <button type = "button"
              onclick = "count()">
        count to ten
      </button>

      <button type = "button"
              onclick = "back()">
        count backwards
      </button>

      <button type = "button"
              onclick = "byFive()">
        count by fives
      </button>

    </fieldset>
  </form>

  <div id = "output">Click a button to see some counting...</div>
</body>
</html>
```

Although the HTML is pretty straightforward, it does have some important features:

1. **The body calls an initialization function.**

   Often you'll want some code to happen when the page first loads. One common way to do this is to attach a function call to the `onload` attribute of the `body` element. In this example, I call the `init()` function as soon as the `body` is finished loading. I describe the contents of the `init()` function in the next section.

2. **The page is mostly an HTML form.**

   The most important part of this page is the form with three buttons on it. Each button calls a different JavaScript function.

3. **A special `div` is created for output.**

   It's a good idea to put some default text in the `div` so you can see where the output should go and so you can ensure the `div` is actually changing when it's supposed to.

From this example, it's easy to see why it's a good idea to write the HTML first. The HTML code gives me a solid base for the program, and it also provides a good outline of what JavaScript code I'll need. Clearly this page calls for four JavaScript functions, `init()`, `count()`, `back()`, and `byFive()`. The names of all the functions are pretty self-explanatory, so it's pretty easy to see what each one is supposed to do. It's also clear that the `div` named `output` is intended as an output area. When you design the HTML page well, the JavaScript code becomes very easy to start.

Initializing the output

This program illustrates a situation that frequently comes up in JavaScript programming: All three of the main functions refer to the same output area. It seems a waste to create a variable for `output` three different times. Instead, I make a single global `output` variable available to all functions and attach the variable to that element once when the page loads.

In order to understand why this is necessary, it's important to discuss an idea called *variable scope*. Generally, variables are created inside functions. As long as the function is running, the variable still exists. However, when a function is done running, all the variables created inside that function are instantly destroyed. This prevents functions from accidentally changing the variables in other functions. Practically, it means you can think of each function as a separate program.

However, sometimes you want a variable to live in more than one function. The `output` variable in the `forLoop.html` page is a great example because all of the functions will need it. One solution is to create the variable *outside* any functions. Then all the functions will have access to it.

You can create the `output` variable without being in a function, but you can't attach it to the actual `div` in the web page until the web page has finished forming. The `init()` function is called when the `body` loads. Inside that function, I assign a value to the global `output` variable. Here's how the main JavaScript and the `init()` method code looks:

```
  var output;

function init(){
  output = document.getElementById("output");
} // end init
```

This code creates `output` as a global variable, and then attaches it to the `output` `div` after the page has finished loading.

Creating the basic for loop

The standard `for` loop counts the values between 1 and 10. The Count to Ten button triggers the `count()` function. Here's the code for `count()`:

```
function count(){
  output.innerHTML = "";
  for (i = 1; i <= 10; i++){
    output.innerHTML += i + "<br />";
  } // end for loop
} // end count
```

Although the `count()` function clearly prints ten lines, it only has one line that modifies the `output` div. The main code repeats many times to create the long output.

1. **You can use the** `output` **var immediately.**

   Because `output` is a global variable and it has already been created, you can use it instantly. There's no need to initialize it in the function.

2. **Clear the output.**

   Set `output.value` to the empty string (`" "`) to clear the output. This destroys whatever text is currently in the `div`.

3. **Start a** `for` **loop.**

   The `for` loop is a special loop used to repeat something a certain number of times. For loops have three components: initialization, comparison, and update.

4. **Initialize your counting variable.**

   A `for` loop works by changing the value of an integer many times. The first part of a `for` loop initializes this variable (often called `i`) to a starting value (usually zero or one).

5. **Specify a condition for staying in the loop.**

   The second part of a `for` statement is a condition. As long as the condition is `true`, the loop continues. As soon as the condition is evaluated as `false`, the loop exits.

6. **Change the variable.**

   The third part of a `for` statement somehow changes the counting variable. The most common way to change the variable is to add one to it. The `i++` syntax is shorthand for "Add one to i."

7. **Build a code block for repeated code.**

   Use braces and indentation to indicate which code repeats. All code inside the braces repeats.

8. **Inside the loop, write to the output.**

   On each iteration of the loop, add the current value of i to the output div's innerHTML. Also add a break (<br />) to make the output look better. When you add to an innerHTML property, you're writing HTML code, so if you want the output to occur on different lines, you need to write the HTML to make this happen. (See the next section on operator shortcuts for an explanation of the += statement.)

9. **Close the loop.**

   Don't forget to end the loop, or your program won't run correctly.

Introducing shortcut operators

You might have noticed a couple of new operators in the code for for-Loops.html. These are some shortcut tools that allow you to express common ideas more compactly. For example, consider the following code:

```
i = i + 1;
```

This means "Add one to i and store the result back in i." It's a pretty standard statement, even if it does drive algebra teachers bananas. The statement is so common that it is often abbreviated, like this:

```
i += 1;
```

This statement means exactly the same as the last one: Add one to i. You can use this to add any amount to the variable i. Because the + sign is used to concatenate (combine) strings, you can use the += shortcut with string manipulation, so consider this variation:

```
var userName = "Andy";
userName += ", Benevolent Dictator for Life";
```

The second statement appends my official (I wish) title to the end of my name.

You can also use the -= operator to subtract from a variable. It's even possible to use *= and /=, but they are not commonly used.

Moving back to numbers — adding one is extremely common. Here's another shortcut that's even more brief:

```
i++;
```

This statement also means "Add one to `i`." In the standard `for` loop, I use that variation because it's very easy.

When programmers decided to make a new variation of C, they called the new language C++. Get it? It's one better than C! Those guys are a hoot!

Counting backward

After you understand basic `for` loops, it's not difficult to make a loop that counts backward. Here's the `back()` function (called by the Count Backwards button):

```
function back(){
  output.innerHTML = "";
  for (i = 10; i > 0; i--){
    output.innerHTML += i + "<br />";
  } // end for loop
} // end back
```

When the user activates this function, she gets the code shown in Figure 3-6.

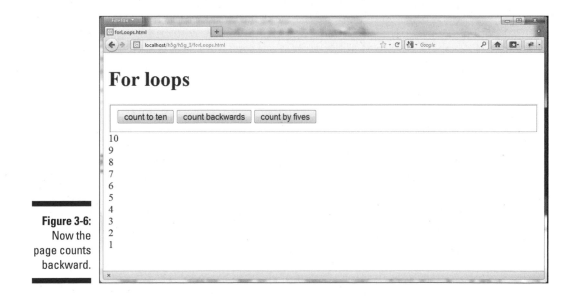

Figure 3-6: Now the page counts backward.

This code is almost exactly like the first loop, but look carefully at how the loop is created:

1. **Initialize** i **to a high value.**

   This time I want to count backward from ten to one, so start i with the value 10.

2. **Keep going as long as** i **is greater than 0.**

   It's important to note that the logic changes here. If i is greater than 0, the loop should continue. If i becomes 0 or less, the loop exits.

3. **Subtract one from** i **on each pass.**

   The -- operator works much like ++, but it subtracts one from the variable.

Counting by fives

Counting by fives (or any other value) is pretty trivial when you know how for loops work. Here's the byFive() code called by the Count by Fives button:

```
function byFive(){
  output.innerHTML = "";
  for (i = 5; i <= 25; i += 5){
    output.innerHTML += i + "<br />";
  } // end for loop
} // end byFive
```

It is remarkably similar to the other looping code you've seen:

1. **Initialize** i **to 5.**

   The first value I want is 5, so that is the initial value for i.

2. **Continue as long as** i **is less than or equal to 25.**

   Because I want the value 25 to appear, I set the condition to be less than or equal to 25.

3. **Add 5 to** i **on each pass.**

   Each time through the loop, I add 5 to i using the += operator.

The Count by Fives code is shown in action in Figure 3-7.

Figure 3-7:
Now the
page counts
by fives.

Building While Loops

for loops are useful when you know how often a loop will continue, but sometimes you need a more flexible type of loop. The while loop is based on a simple idea. It contains a condition. When the condition is true, the loop continues; if the condition is evaluated as false, the loop exits.

Making a basic while loop

Figure 3-8 shows a dialog box asking for a password. The program keeps asking for a password until the user enters the correct password.

```
function getPassword(){
  //from while.html
  var correct = "HTML5";
  var guess = "";
  while (guess != correct){
    guess = prompt("Password?");
  } // end while
  alert("You may proceed");
} // end getPassword
```

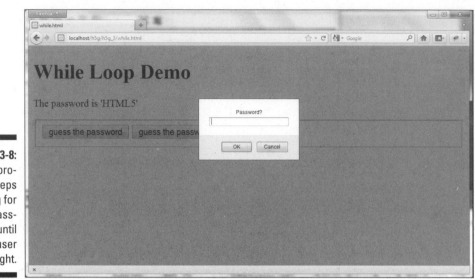

A while loop for passwords is not hard to build:

1. **Store the correct password in a variable.**

   Variable names are important because they can make your code easier to follow. I use the names correct and guess to differentiate the two types of passwords. Beginners often call one of these variables pass-word, but that can be confusing because there are actually *two* passwords (the correct password and the guessed password) in play here.

2. **Initialize the** guess **to an empty value.**

   The key variable for this loop will be guess. It starts as an empty string. It's critical to initialize the key variable before the loop begins.

3. **Set up the** while **statement.**

   The while statement has extremely simple syntax: the keyword while followed by a condition, followed by a block of code.

4. **Build the condition.**

   The condition is the heart of a while loop. The condition must be con-structed so the loop happens at least once (ensure this by comparing the condition to the variable initialization). When the condition is true, the loop continues. When the condition is evaluated to false, the loop exits. This condition compares guess to correct. If guess is not equal to correct, the code continues.

5. **Write the code block.**

   Use braces and indentation to indicate the block of code that will be repeated in the loop. The only code in this particular loop asks the user for a password.

6. **Add code to change the key variable inside the loop.**

   Somewhere inside the loop, you need code that changes the value of the key variable. In this example, the prompt statement changes the password. As long as the user eventually gets the right password, the loop ends.

Getting your loops to behave

While loops can be dangerous. It's quite easy to write a while loop that works incorrectly, and these can be an exceptionally difficult kind of bug to find and fix. If a while loop is incorrectly designed, it can refuse to ever run or run forever. These endless loops are especially troubling in JavaScript because they can crash the entire browser. If a JavaScript program gets into an endless loop, often the only solution is to use the operating system Task Manager (Ctrl+Alt+Delete on Windows) to shut down the entire browser.

The easy way to make sure your loop works is to remember that while loops need all the same features as for loops. (These ideas are built into the structure of a for loop. You're responsible for them yourself in a while loop.) If your loop doesn't work, check that you've followed these steps:

- ✔ **Identify a key variable.** A while loop is normally based on a condition, which is usually a comparison (although it might also be a variable or function that returns a Boolean value). In a for loop, the key variable is almost always an integer. While loops can be based on any type of variable.

- ✔ **Initialize the variable before the loop.** Before the loop begins, set up the initial value of the key variable to ensure the loop happens at least once.

- ✔ **Identify the condition for the loop.** A while loop is based on a condition. Define the condition so the loop continues while the condition is true and exits when the condition is evaluated to false.

- ✔ **Change the condition inside the loop.** Somewhere inside the loop code, you need to have statements that eventually make the condition false. If you forget this part, your loop never ends.

This example is a good example of a while loop, but a terrible way to handle security. The password is shown in the clear, and anybody could view the source code to see the correct password. There are far better ways to handle security, but this is the cleanest example of a while loop I could think of.

Managing more complex loops

It won't take long before you find situations where the standard `for` or `while` loops do not seem adequate. For example, consider the password example again. This time, you want to ask for a password until the user gets the password correct or guesses incorrectly three times. Think about how you would build that code. There are a number of ways to do it, but here's the cleanest approach:

```
function threeTries(){
  //continues until user is correct or has three
  //incorrect guesses
  //from while.html

  var correct = "HTML5";
  var guess = "";
  var keepGoing = true;
  var tries = 0;

  while (keepGoing){
    guess = prompt("Password?");
    if (guess == correct){
      alert("You may proceed");
      keepGoing = false;
    } else {
      tries++;
      if (tries >= 3){
        alert("Too many tries. Launching
      missiles...");
        keepGoing = false;
      } // end if
    } // end if
  } // end while
} // end threetries
```

This code is a little more complex, but it uses a nice technique to greatly simplify loops:

1. **Initialize** `correct` **and** `guess`.

   As in the previous example, initialize the `correct` and `guess` passwords.

2. **Build a counter to indicate the number of tries.**

   The `tries` variable counts how many attempts have been made.

3. **Build a Boolean sentry variable.**

   The `keepGoing` variable is special. Its entire job is to indicate whether the loop should continue. It is a Boolean variable, meaning it only contains the values `true` or `false`.

4. **Use** `keepGoing` **as the condition.**

   A condition doesn't have to be a comparison. It just has to be `true` or `false`. Use the Boolean variable as the condition. As long as `keepGoing` has the value `true`, the loop continues. Any time you want to exit the loop, set `keepGoing` to `false`.

5. **Ask for the password.**

   You still need the password, so get this information from the user.

6. **Check to see if the password is correct.**

   Use an `if` statement to see if the password is correct.

7. **If the password is correct:**

   Provide feedback to the user and set `keepGoing` to `false`. The next time the `while` statement is executed, the loop ends. (Remember, you want the loop to end when the password is correct.)

8. **If the password is incorrect:**

   If the `(guess == correct)` condition is `false`, that means the user did not get the password correct. In this case, add one to the number of tries.

9. **Check the number of tries.**

   Build another `if` statement to check the number of tries.

   If it's had three tries, provide feedback (threatening global annihilation is always fun) and set `keepGoing` to `false`.

The basic idea of this strategy is quite straightforward: Create a special Boolean variable with the singular job of indicating whether the loop continues. Any time you want the loop to exit, change the value of that variable.

If you change most of your `while` loops to this format (using a Boolean variable as the condition), you'll generally eliminate most `while` loop issues. Most beginners (like me, and I've been doing this for 30 years) make their loops *way* too complicated. Using a Boolean variable in your loop can solve a lot of logic problems.

Managing bugs with a debugger

When you're writing loops and conditions, things can go pretty badly in your code. Sometimes it's very hard to tell what exactly is going on. Fortunately, modern browsers have some nice tools that help you look at your code more carefully.

A *debugger* is a special tool that allows you to run a program in "slow motion," moving one line at a time so you can see exactly what is happening. Google Chrome has a built-in debugger, so I begin with that one.

To see how a debugger works, follow these steps:

1. **Load a page into Chrome.**

   You can add a debugger to most browsers, but Chrome has one built in, so start with that one. I'm loading the `forLoops.html` page because loops are a common source of bugs.

2. **Open the Developer Tools window.**

   If you right-click anywhere on the page and choose Inspect Element, you get a wonderful debugging tool that looks like Figure 3-9.

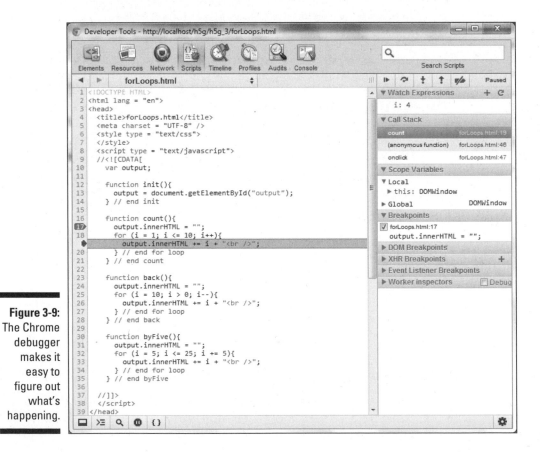

Figure 3-9:
The Chrome debugger makes it easy to figure out what's happening.

3. Inspect the page with the Elements tab.

The default tab shows you the page in an outline view, letting you see the structure of your page. If you click on any element in the outline, you can see what styles are associated with that element. The actual element is also highlighted on the main page so you can see exactly where everything is. This can be very useful for checking your HTML and CSS.

4. Look at the Console tab.

Any time your code is not working as expected, look at the Console tab. Often there will be an error message here that explains what is going wrong.

5. Move to the Scripts tab.

The developer tool has a separate tab for working with JavaScript code. Select the Scripts tab to see your entire code at once. If your page pulls in external JavaScript files, you'll be able to select them here as well.

6. Set a breakpoint.

Typically, you let the program begin at normal speed and slow down right before you get to a trouble spot. In this case, I'm interested in the `count()` function, so click on the first line (17) of that function in the code window. (It's more reliable to click on the first line of the function than the line that declares it, so click line 17 instead of line 16.)

7. Refresh the page.

In the main browser, click the Reload button or press the F5 key to refresh the page. The page may initially be blank. That's fine — it means the program has paused when it encountered the function.

8. Step into the next line.

On the developer tool are a series of buttons on top of the right column. Click the Step into the Next Line button, which looks like a down arrow with a dot under it. You can also press the F11 key to activate the command.

9. Your page is now running.

If you look back over the main page, you should see it is now up and running. Nothing is happening yet because you haven't activated any of the buttons.

10. Click the Count button.

The Count button should activate the code in the `count` function. Click this button to see if that is what happens.

11. Code should now be paused on line 17.

Back in the code window, line 17 is now highlighted. That means the browser is paused, and when you activate the Step button, the highlighted code executes.

12. **Step a few times.**

    Use the F11 key or the Step into the Next Line button to step forward a few times. Watch how the highlight moves around so you can actually see the loop happening. This is very useful when your code is not behaving properly because it allows you to see exactly how the processor is moving through your code.

13. **Hover over the variable** i **in your code.**

    When you are in debug mode, you can hover the mouse over any variable in the code window, and you'll see what the current value of that variable is. Often when your code is performing badly, it's because a variable isn't doing what you think it is.

14. **Add a watch expression to simplify looking at variables.**

    If you think the loop is not behaving, you can add a *watch expression* to make debugging easier. Right under the step buttons you'll see a tab called `watch expressions`. Click the plus sign to add a new expression. Type **i** and press Enter.

15. **Continue stepping through the code.**

    Now you can continue to step through the code and see what is happening to the variable. This is incredibly useful when your code is not performing like you want it to.

I personally think the debugger built into Chrome is one of the best out there, but it's not the only choice. If you're using Firefox, the excellent Firebug extension adds the same functionality to Firefox (`http://getfirebug.com`). Safari has a similar Web Inspector tool built in, and even IE9 finally has a decent debugger called F12. All work in roughly the same way. Usually, though, a JavaScript error crashes any browser, so pick one you like for initial testing and then use other browser-specific tools only when necessary.

Sending Data to and from Functions

Functions make your code safe because variables created inside a function are destroyed when the function dies. Sometimes, though, you want data to move from one function to another. One solution is the global variable, but it's kind of a crude option. A better solution is to allow data to pass into and out of functions. As an example, look at the program in Figure 3-10.

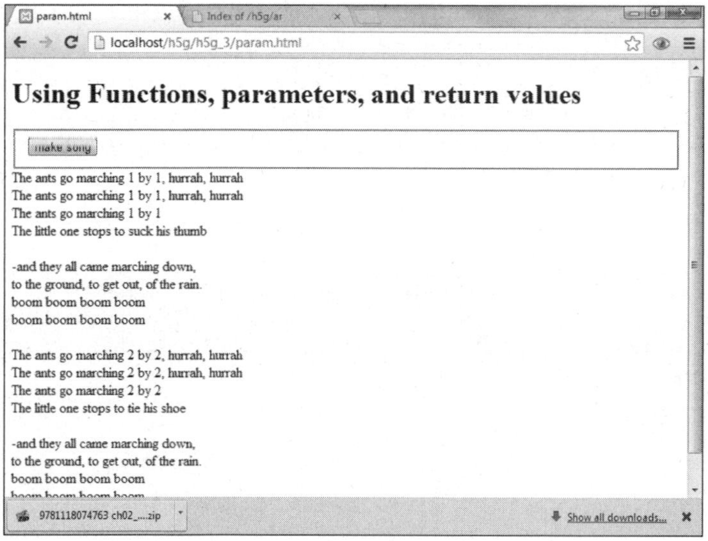

Figure 3-10:
This
program
presents
the lyrics to
a popular
song.

Of course, this program could be written by creating a really long string variable and then copying it to the `innerHTML` attribute of the `output` div, but that would be quite inefficient. Instead, I used functions to simplify the work. Begin by looking over the main function: `makeSong()`.

```
function makeSong(){
  //create output variable
  //from param.html

  var output = document.getElementById("output");

  output.innerHTML = "";

  output.innerHTML += verse(1);
  output.innerHTML += chorus();
  output.innerHTML += verse(2);
  output.innerHTML += chorus();
} // end makeSong
```

This code demonstrates one of the primary advantages of functions; they allow you to break a complex problem into a series of smaller problems. A number of interesting things are going on here:

- ✔ **The program writes to a** `div` **called** `output`. I make a variable called `output` that corresponds to a `div` called `output` on the page.

- ✔ **I'm writing text to** `output`. That's not surprising, but it is interesting because there are no text variables or values in the `makeSong()` function.

✔ **All the text is created by other functions.** There are two other functions in this program: `verse()` and `chorus()`. Both of these functions create string values.

✔ **Verse can be "fed" a numeric value.** The `verse` function is especially important because it can be passed a value. The verse changes behavior based on the value passed to it.

Returning a value from a function

To truly understand what's happening here, begin with the `chorus()` function (because it's a little simpler than `verse()`).

```
function chorus(){
  //from param.html
  var result = "-and they all came marching down, <br />";
  result += "to the ground, to get out, of the rain. <br
          />";
    result += "boom boom boom boom <br />";
    result += "boom boom boom boom <br />";
    result += "<br />";
    return result;
} // end chorus
```

The `chorus()` function is extremely simple:

1. **Create a variable called** `result`**.**

   This variable holds the result of the function's work (which will be a string value containing the chorus of the song).

2. **Append HTML code to the** `result` **variable.**

   This code has several lines that build up the result. Note that I'm using HTML formatting because this code will be printed in an `HTML div`.

3. **Return** `result`**.**

   The last statement of the function is special. The `return` statement allows you to specify a value that the function returns to whatever code called it.

4. **Use the function like a variable.**

   When a function has a return value, you can treat it like a variable. Because this function returns a string, you can use the function like a string variable in the `makeSong()` function. In that function, I said `output.innerHTML += chorus()`. That means "run the `chorus()` function and then add whatever comes out of that function to the `innerHTML` of the `output` element."

Sending arguments to a function

The `verse()` function also returns a value, but it has another trick up its sleeve. Although the chorus is always the same, the verse changes a bit each time. The little one (who appears to have attention issues) gets distracted in a different way on every verse.

The `verse()` function uses an important idea called *parameter-passing* to allow this variation in behavior. Begin by looking at the code for the function:

```
function verse(verseNumber){
  //from param.html
  var distraction = "";
  if (verseNumber == 1){
    distraction = "suck his thumb";
  } else if (verseNumber == 2){
    distraction = "tie his shoe";
  } else {
    distraction = "there's a problem here...";
  } // end if

  var result = "The ants go marching ";
  result += verseNumber + " by " + verseNumber + ", ";
  result += "hurrah, hurrah <br />";
  result += "The ants go marching ";
  result += verseNumber + " by " + verseNumber + ", ";
  result += "hurrah, hurrah <br />";
  result += "The ants go marching ";
  result += verseNumber + " by " + verseNumber + "<br />";
  result += "The little one stops to ";
  result += distraction + "<br /> <br />";

  return result;
} // end verse
```

The `verse()` function is very similar to the `chorus()` function, except it is more flexible because it can accept a parameter.

1. **Call the function with a value inside the parentheses.**

   When a function is intended to accept a parameter, it must be called with a value inside the parentheses. In `makeSong()`, you see calls to `verse(1)` and `verse(2)`, but never `verse()`. That's because `verse` is designed to always accept a single integer value.

2. **Define the function with a variable name inside the parentheses.**

   If you look at the function definition for `verse()`, you see it contains the variable `verseNumber` between the parentheses. Whenever the `verse()` function is called, it must be fed a value, and that value is placed in the special variable `verseNumber`.

3. **Use** `verseNum` **to find the distraction.**

   Analyze the `verseNumber` variable and use it to find the appropriate distraction. Put this in a variable named `distraction`.

4. **Build the verse.**

   Incorporate the `verseNumber` and `distraction` variables in the `result` variable.

5. **Return the result.**

   The main function uses the returned value as a string, printing out the verse.

Using Arrays to Simplify Data

Computer programs are about data. Often, you're working with a *lot* of data. Programmers have a number of tools for managing large amounts of data, but the most basic is the array. JavaScript supports a simple yet very powerful and flexible array mechanism that lets you do plenty with arrays. To see arrays in action, look at Figure 3-11.

An array is actually a very simple idea; it's simply a list. You've already used lists many times in HTML coding, but in programming, lists are called arrays, and have special characteristics. This example features two arrays — a list of books written by a certain charming and devilishly handsome author, and some of the topics said author writes about.

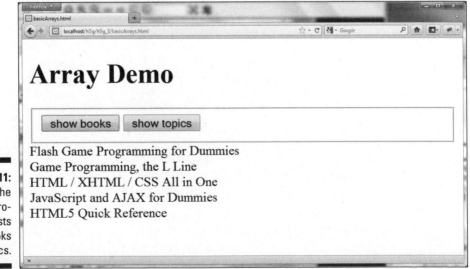

Figure 3-11: Clicking the button produces lists of books and topics.

- **HTML structure:** It has a form with two buttons. The body calls an initialization function when it loads, and each button calls its own function. The page also has a div named output.

- **An init() function:** This function provides access to the output div, and it also loads up the two arrays described in this example. Arrays usually require some kind of initialization.

- **The** showBooks() **function:** You'll be amazed and surprised that this function displays a series of book titles.

- **The** showTitles() **function:** This function demonstrates another way to walk through the elements of an array.

Building the arrays

Arrays are frequently created as global variables because they are often used throughout the program (and in some languages, passing an array as a parameter can be kind of complicated).

In this program, I create a number of variables in the global space and initialize them all in the init() function called with body.onload.

```
var output;
var books;
var topics;

function init(){
  //initialize output and arrays
  //from basicArrays.html
  output = document.getElementById("output");
  books = Array("Flash Game Programming for Dummies",
                "Game Programming, the L Line",
                "HTML / XHTML / CSS All in One",
                "JavaScript and AJAX for Dummies",
                "HTML5 Quick Reference");

  topics = Array(5);
  topics[0] = "HTML5";
  topics[1] = "CSS3";
  topics[2] = "JavaScript";
  topics[4] = "AJAX";
} // end init
```

Setting up the arrays is the most important part of the process:

1. **Create variables for the arrays.**

   I have two arrays in this example, `books` and `topics`. Each is created just like any other variable, with the `var` statement. I also create an `output` variable to hold a reference to the `output div`.

2. **Build an `init()` function to initialize variables.**

   As programs become more complex, it is common to have an initialization function to set everything up. This function is called with `body.onload`.

3. **Build the `output` variable.**

   Because all the other functions will use `output`, I create it in `init()`.

4. **Use the `Array()` function to create the array of books.**

   This special function is used to create an array of elements. Note that it uses an uppercase `A`. (If you must be technical, this is a constructor for an `Array` object, but in JavaScript, that's a function, too.)

5. **Simply list each book as a parameter in the `Array()` function.**

   If you feed the `Array` function a series of values, they become the values of the array. This technique is great if you already know what will go into each element when you build the array.

6. **Build the topics array differently.**

   The `topics` array is build with a different technique. In this array, I specified a single integer, which is the number of elements the array will contain.

7. **Use the index operator to add elements to the array.**

   All array elements have the same name, but they have a different number (corresponding to where they fit on the list). Use square braces with an integer to refer to a specific element in the array. Note that array elements always begin with element `zero`.

If you've used arrays in other programming languages, you'll find JavaScript arrays to be very forgiving. Be careful, though, because arrays are one of those features that every language supports, but they all work a little bit differently. You'll actually find the JavaScript arrays are more like the `ArrayList` in Java or the `Vector` class in C++ than the traditional array in either of these languages.

Stepping through the books array

Arrays are wonderful because they allow you to pack a lot of data into a single variable. Very often when you have an array, you'll want to do something with each element in the array. The most common structure to do this is a `for` loop. Look at `showBooks()` for an example:

```
function showBooks(){
  //from basicArrays.html
  output.innerHTML = "";
  for (i = 0; i < books.length; i++){
    output.innerHTML += books[i] + "<br />";
  } // end for loop
} // end showBooks
```

This function steps through the list of books and prints the name of each one in the output area:

1. **Clear the** `output` **div.**

   `Output` has already been defined in the `init()` function, so it's pretty easy to clear out its value in the function.

2. **Build a loop for the length of the array.**

   Arrays and `for` loops are natural partners. In this loop, I have `i` count from zero to the number of elements in the array.

3. **Begin with zero.**

   Array indices always begin with zero, so your counting variable should also start at zero (in most cases).

4. **Use the length property to determine how long the array is.**

   When you build a `for` loop to step through an array, what you really want to know is how many elements are in the array. Use *arrayName*.`length` to determine the number of elements in the current array, where *arrayName* is the name of the current array. This way, even if the number of elements in the array changes, the loop still works correctly.

5. **Process data inside the loop.**

   If the counting variable is `i`, each element of the array is *arrayName*`[i]` inside the loop. You can do what you want with the data. In my example, I'm simply printing it out.

Using the for . . . in loop to access array elements

The showTopics() function uses a special variation of the for loop to print out the contents of an array.

```
function showTopics(){
  //from basicArrays.html
  output.innerHTML = "";
  for (topicID in topics){
    output.innerHTML += topics[topicID] + "<br />";
  } // end for
} // end showTopics
```

Because loops and arrays are so commonly linked, JavaScript provides a special shortcut version of the for loop just for working with array elements.

1. **Clear the output area.**

   If there's already data in the output div, clean it out before printing anything new there.

2. **Use the for . . . in loop variant.**

   The for loop in this function is quite a bit simpler than most. It simply has a variable and an array. This loop repeats once per element in the list.

3. **Use the topicID variable to refer to each element in the loop.**

   The topicID variable contains each index used in the array. Use this index to determine the value associated with that index.

The for . . . in loop is really great, and if you know PHP, it looks at first glance just like the PHP foreach loop. However, they are not exactly the same. The JavaScript version returns the *key*, and the PHP version returns the associated *value*. I get confused every time I switch between the two languages.

I've added another variation of the Ants program to the website that uses arrays. Look over this code (antsArray.html) if you want to see an example of how arrays can further simplify that program.

This chapter covers the basic ideas of JavaScript, but if you're interested in more depth, please check my book *JavaScript & AJAX For Dummies*.

Chapter 4

Random Thoughts: Building a Simple Game

*I*f you can build an HTML page and write some JavaScript code, you're almost ready to write a game. (If you aren't comfortable with those skills, you may want to glance over Chapters 1–3.)

However, a game is more than just code. This chapter explains how to build a complete (if basic) game that involves real-time interaction with the user.

Creating Random Numbers

Random numbers are a key part of game programming. Often you want some kind of random behavior. This is used to mimic the complexity and unpredictability of the universe. Most languages have a random number generator built in. This special function produces some sort of semi-random number. Often you'll have to do some manipulation to make the number fit the pattern you want.

Figure 4-1 shows a simple page that generates random numbers between 1 and 100.

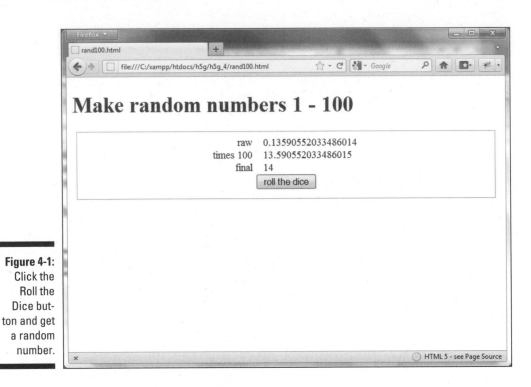

The page in Figure 4-1 seems a little complex, but it describes a powerful and flexible system, once you know how to use it. Here's what's happening:

1. **JavaScript generates a random number.**

   Different languages do this in different ways, but JavaScript has a function that creates a random floating point value between 0 and 1. That value is shown in the raw box.

2. **Multiply the raw value by 100.**

   In this example, you want a number between 1 and 100. If you multiply a 0-to-1 by 100, you'll get 0 to 99.9999 (with a lot of nines) value. That's getting closer. The times 100 box shows the raw value after it has been multiplied by 100.

3. **Convert the large number into an integer.**

   The user is never going to guess a number with 17 places after the decimal, so you need an integer. JavaScript has a number of ways to convert a float to an integer. To get the 1 to 100 behavior you're looking for, you use a method called `Math.ceil`. (Don't worry, I explain this weird name and how it works in the next section.) The final result is shown in the final box.

When you look over the code for the rand100.html page, you'll see that it basically does what I just said. Here's the code in its entirety:

```
<!DOCTYPE HTML>
<html lang="en-US">
<head>
    <meta charset="UTF-8">
    <title>rand100.html</title>
    <style type = "text/css">
    fieldset {
        width: 600px;
        margin-right: auto;
        margin-left: auto;
    }
    label {
        float: left;
        width: 250px;
        text-align: right;
        margin-right: 1em;
        clear: left;
    }
    span {
        float: left;
    }
    button {
        display: block;
        clear: both;
        margin: auto;
    }
    </style>
    <script type = "text/javascript">
    function roll(){
        //create variables for form elements
        var spnRaw = document.getElementById("spnRaw");
        var spn100 = document.getElementById("spn100");
        var spnFinal = document.
            getElementById("spnFinal");

        //get random number
        var raw = Math.random();
        spnRaw.innerHTML = raw;

        //multiply by 100
        var times100 = raw * 100;
        spn100.innerHTML = times100;

        //get the ceiling
        var final = Math.ceil(times100);
        spnFinal.innerHTML = final;
    } // end roll
```

```
        </script>
</head>
<body>
    <h1>Make random numbers 1 - 100</h1>
    <form>
        <fieldset>
            <label>raw</label>
            <span id = "spnRaw">0</span>
            <label>times 100</label>
            <span id = "spn100">0</span>
            <label>final</label>
            <span id = "spnFinal">0</span>
            <button type = "button"
                    onclick = "roll()">
                roll the dice
            </button>
        </fieldset>
    </form>
</body>
</html>
```

Seriously, math can be fun

To make this program work, you need to call in the ultimate weapon of geekiness: Math. (You know, now I'm going to have to write an adventure game just so I can include an "ultimate weapon of geekiness.")

JavaScript has a wonderful library called *Math* (I know, I used the words *math* and *wonderful* in the same sentence. Keep programming, and you will too, eventually.) The Math library has some really geeky goodness buried in it, like a number of commonly used math functions (you know, cosine, square root, and all that great stuff) as well as constants (like pi) and a few other utility functions for working with numbers. It turns out this library has some features that are extremely useful for the problem at hand (generating random numbers).

First, of course, is the function that generates random numbers. It's called (wait for it . . .) Math.random().

You really need to say Math.random(). If you call random() all by itself, JavaScript won't know what you're talking about. That's because the random() function is not part of the main body of JavaScript, but part of the special Math library. This is actually a vestige of the object-oriented scheme that underlies JavaScript. Just remember, you need to specify Math. random() to invoke a random number.

The Math.random() function produces a semi-random number. (It isn't really random but is produced through a complex formula from another number.) The random number will be a floating-point value between 0 and 1.

This doesn't seem helpful, but with a little math, you can convert the 0 to 1 value to any other range you wish.

In addition to the `random()` function, the `Math` object has a number of functions that allow you to convert a floating point value (that is, a number with a decimal point) to an integer (you got it — a number *without* a decimal point). The standard `parseInt()` method is built into JavaScript, but sometimes you want to do a fancier conversion. The Math library has a number of these tools:

- `Math.round()`: Converts a number using the standard rounding algorithm. If the decimal part is .5 or less, the smaller integer is chosen; if the decimal part is greater than .5, the larger integer is chosen. This means that 3.1 rounds to 3 and 3.8 rounds to 4.

- `Math.floor()`: This function always rounds down, so 3.1 and 3.8 both become 3. The `parseInt()` function is identical to `Math.floor()`.

- `Math.ceil()`: This function (get it — the ceiling function) always rounds up, so 3.1 and 3.8 both end up as 4.

The function you need depends on the specific circumstances. I show why `Math.ceil()` makes sense in this project as I discuss the actual code.

Making the HTML form

As always, HTML forms the foundation of any JavaScript program. The main thing here is the form that provides the user interface. This form has some predictable features:

- **A span to hold the raw data:** There's really nothing for the user to type, so I'm using a span for the various output elements. Spans are a generic inline tag. They're super for situations like this where you need some simple output element that can be inline with the main flow of the page. The raw data span is called (here you go . . .) `spnRaw`.

- **Another span for the** `times100` **data:** As the program does the calculations, it will display the output. (Normally, you won't need to show the user every detail, but this example is really about the calculations, so I want everything to be explicitly displayed.)

- **A third span for the final output:** After all the calculations are finished, you need some way to display your brilliant work. `spnFinal` will serve this purpose.

- **Labels to make everything clear:** Without labels explaining what's happening, there will just be a bunch of numbers on the screen. Don't forget to add labels even to simple examples so the user can figure out what's going on.

> ✔ **A button to start all the action:** Nothing will happen until the user asks for it, so add a button to the form. When the button is clicked, have it call the `roll()` function to roll a number.
>
> ✔ **CSS to make it all look good:** HTML without CSS is ugly, so add enough CSS to make the HTML form look decent. If you need a refresher on the CSS used in this example, please refer to Chapter 3.

Writing the roll() function

When the user clicks the button, the program will do something magical. (Okay, it only *looks* magical. You know exactly what's happening.) The code in the `roll()` function creates a random number in exactly the form you want.

Building the Number Guesser

With random numbers, you can now make interesting games.

Figure 4-2 illustrates a simple game that uses HTML, CSS, and JavaScript together.

This game has a number of interesting features:

> ✔ **It uses the web page as the interface.** Like many JavaScript programs, it uses a web page as the user interface. An input element is used for input, a `div` is the main output element, and a button triggers all the actions.
>
> ✔ **It uses CSS for styling.** The various parts of the page are formatted with CSS. The CSS is stored in an external style sheet for convenience and reusability.
>
> ✔ **It tells the user how many turns she has taken.** On each pass, the computer reminds the user how many turns have happened.
>
> ✔ **When the user has guessed correctly, a Restart button appears.** This button is hidden at first, and appears only when it is needed.
>
> ✔ **The right answer is available to programmers through a special debugging feature.** While testing the program, the developer can see what the correct answer is, but this information is hidden from the user.
>
> ✔ **An `init()` function begins the game.** The `init()` function initializes the game. It is called when the program first begins and again when the user wants to start over.
>
> ✔ **Another function is attached to the button.** When the user clicks the Check Your Guess button, the current user's guess is compared to the right answer, and a hint is returned to the user.

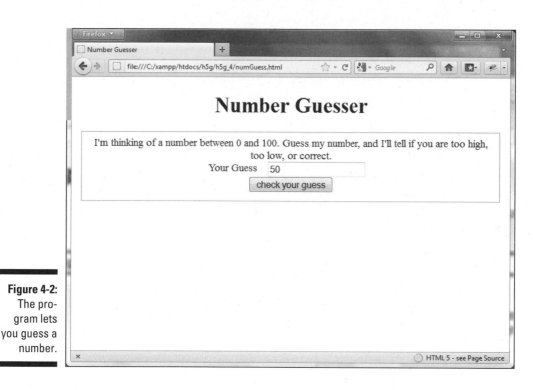

Figure 4-2:
The program lets you guess a number.

Designing the program

When you build a complex program, you need to begin with a design plan. Figure 4-3 shows the design for this game.

Much of the work in game development happens before you begin programming. If you design the game well, the programming is much easier to do. A game design helps you understand many things about the game before you begin writing code:

- ✔ **General layout:** While the layout isn't completely decided by this drawing, it's easy to see the general look I'm going for.

- ✔ **Named elements:** Every element that needs to have a name has been determined, and the names are written on the document. Some elements (like the first button) do not need names because they won't be referred to in code.

- ✔ **Button functions:** Each button will call a function. The diagram indicates which function each button will call.

- ✔ **Function plans:** Every function is planned out with an English-language description of what the function will do.

✓ **Global variables:** The variables that will need to be shared between functions are described.

It's actually difficult to create a good design document, but doing so makes the programming quite a bit easier. It's hard to figure out what you're trying to do, and it's also hard to figure out how to do it. Having a design document separates those two processes so you can first concentrate on *what* you're doing, and then worry about *how* you're going to do it.

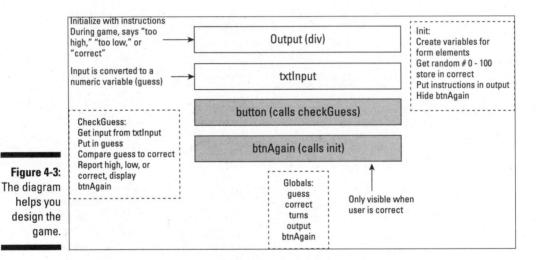

Figure 4-3: The diagram helps you design the game.

Building the HTML for the game

The HTML code for the number-guessing game is pretty easy to write if you've designed the game on paper first. Here's the code:

```
<!DOCTYPE HTML>
<html lang="en-US">
<head>
  <meta charset="UTF-8">
  <title>Number Guesser</title>
  <link rel = "stylesheet"
        type = "text/css"
        href = "numGuess.css" />
  <script type = "text/javascript"
          src = "numGuess.js"></script>
</head>

<body onload = "init()">
  <h1>Number Guesser</h1>
  <form>
    <fieldset>
```

```
      <div id = "output">
        I'm thinking of a number between 0 and 100.
        Guess my number, and I'll tell if you are
        too high, too low, or correct.
      </div>
      <label for = "">Your Guess</label>
      <input type = "text"
             id = "txtGuess">
      <button type = "button"
              onclick = "checkGuess()">
        check your guess
      </button>

      <button type = "button"
              id = "again"
              onclick = "init()">
        try again
      </reset>
    </fieldset>
  </form>
</body>
</html>
```

It's nice to separate HTML, CSS, and JavaScript because this practice allows you to "divide and conquer" a big problem into a number of smaller problems. Here are the main features of the HTML document:

1. **Link to the CSS in an external file.**

   At the moment, the CSS isn't critical, so you move it off into a separate file so you can work with it later.

2. **Outsource the JavaScript code.**

   You also move the JavaScript code into an external file so you don't have to worry about it yet. In the HTML code, simply make the linkages to the external files.

3. **Build a form as the main component of the page.**

   The most important aspect of this page is the form. Like most forms, it will have a fieldset, labels, input elements, and buttons.

4. **Create a** div **for output.**

   The output div is just an ordinary div. You put it inside the fieldset so it will maintain a visual link to the rest of the form. You can put default text inside the div (though you will probably change this text later). Because the div will be referred to through code, it needs an id attribute.

5. **Make an input area for the user's guess.**

The user will need to type some sort of numeric input. Use an input element for this purpose. Refer to your documentation to remember the id of this element. (You *did* make a design document, right?) It's nice to add a label to the input so the user knows what's expected there.

6. **Build a button for checking the guess.**

The user doesn't commit a guess until she clicks the Check Your Guess button. So, you really need to have such a button. This button doesn't need a name, but it will call the checkGuess() function.

7. **Build a second button to start again.**

One interesting feature of this program is a button that allows the user to restart. This second button is available only when the user has correctly guessed the answer. You create it with ordinary HTML and use CSS and JavaScript tricks to make it disappear and appear on demand.

Writing the CSS for the number guesser

The HTML provides the foundation, but it needs some CSS code to make it have the look you're aiming for. The CSS isn't just for beauty's sake. It also adds some functionality to the page. Specifically, one of the buttons will appear and disappear on command. The visibility of the button is controlled with a CSS style, which is changed through JavaScript code.

Here is how to build the CSS for the game:

1. **Center the headline.**

Most of the content of this page will be centered, so center the h1 element. Set the text-align to center.

2. **Format the fieldset.**

The page consists of a form with a fieldset. Change the fieldset's width to a fixed size and set the margins to auto. This will center the fieldset in the page.

3. **Format the** output div.

There is a special div called output that will contain the instructions to the user. The only formatting necessary is to center the text with text-align: center. (Remember, you center the contents of an element with text-align. Center the element itself with margin: auto.)

4. Float the labels and input elements.

This will be a standard form with the label on the left and input elements to the right. Assign the necessary attributes to float and input elements. (Please refer to Chapter 3 for more information on applying float styles.)

5. Center the buttons.

The buttons will look best if they're centered on the page. Convert buttons to block-level and set the margins to auto for this effect.

The complete CSS code is available here:

```css
h1 {
    text-align: center;
}

fieldset {
    width: 600px;
    margin-left: auto;
    margin-right: auto;
}

#output {
    text-align: center;
}

label {
    float: left;
    width: 250px;
    clear: left;
    text-align: right;
    padding-right: 1em;
}

input {
    float: left;
}

button {
    display: block;
    clear: both;
    margin-left: auto;
    margin-right: auto;
}
```

Note that the Play Again button is visible. Although CSS code is used to hide and display the button, that code will be generated through JavaScript.

Thinking through the game's data

Games are ultimately about data. Before writing any code, you should think through the various data elements you'll need to make the program work. If you did a good job of the design document, you've already thought this through. The first few lines of numGuess.js create the variable elements that will be shared throughout the rest of the code.

```
//from numGuess.js
//page-level variables
var guess;
var correct;
var turns;

//components
var output;
var txtGuess;
var btnAgain;
```

In JavaScript programming, you typically have two types of page-level variables. Some of these indicate data about the *game*, and others refer to *interface elements*. Both are important. First, think through the game variables:

✔ guess: This will be the number that comes from the user. Remember that data that comes from form elements is usually in string format, and you'll need an integer.

✔ correct: This is another integer, but this one is randomly generated by the computer. The random number will need to be in the range from 1 to 100.

✔ turns: This variable represents the number of guesses the user has made already. A smart user should be able to guess a number between 1 and 100 in 7 or fewer turns.

You'll also need to create a variable for every form component that will be manipulated through code. This is easy to determine from the diagram:

✔ output: The output element is the div that will contain instructions and feedback for the user.

✔ txtGuess: This is a textbox that will hold the user's name.

✔ btnAgain: This is a button that will be hidden most of the time. It will be visible only when the user has guessed the correct answer.

Setting up the initialization routine

If you look over the game design document again, it's clear that the game has two distinct phases: Initialization will happen when the game first begins, and when the user chooses to go again. Another set of actions should happen when the user clicks the Check Your Guess button.

Begin with the code that will happen as part of initialization:

```
function init(){
  //from numGuess.js
  //initialize components
  output = document.getElementById("output");
  txtGuess = document.getElementById("txtGuess");
  btnAgain = document.getElementById("again");

  //hide again button
  btnAgain.style.display = "none";

  //initialize counter
  turns = 0;

  //initialize output
  output.innerHTML = "I'm thinking of a number between 0
        and 100. ";
  output.innerHTML += "Guess my number, and I'll tell if
        you are ";
  output.innerHTML += "too high, too low, or correct.";

  //generate random for correct answer
  correct = parseInt(Math.random() * 100);
  console.log(correct);

  //make sure input text gets focus
  txtGuess.focus();

}  // end init
```

There is a lot of code in this section, but most of it is pretty obvious from the documentation. Initialization routines are almost always about *setting up the data* that a game will be about. This one is no different:

- **Initialize the components.** Build JavaScript variables to represent any form elements that will be referred to in code. Normally, these are input fields and output divs. The btnAgain button will be referred to by code, so it also needs a variable associated with it.

- **Hide the Play Again button.** In this particular program, the Play Again button should appear only when the game is over. Hide the button for now, so you can make it visible at the appropriate time. Set the display property to none to hide any HTML element.

✔ **Initialize the turn counter.** You'll want to indicate the number of turns the user required. The turn counter is just an integer variable that starts at 0.

✔ **Initialize the output.** The `output div` will contain opening instructions to the user. Put the instructions in the `div` with JavaScript code so that when the game is reset, the instructions reappear.

✔ **Generate a random number.** The correct answer will be randomly generated once per game. (See the upcoming sidebar about the `console.log()` command for information on how the log can be used for debugging.)

✔ **Make sure the** `input` **text element has the focus.** When the user begins the game, she will probably want to type a number. It's a good idea to ensure that any numbers typed right away will go to the text box. The `focus()` method is an easy way to place the focus on any form element (as though the user clicked on the text field with the mouse).

Responding to the Button

As in most HTML forms, the real action happens when the user clicks a button. This form has two buttons, but one of them is hidden most of the time. For now, concentrate on the code that happens when the user clicks on the Check Your Guess button.

```
function checkGuess(){
  //from numGuess.js
  //increment turns
  turns++;

  response = turns + ") ";
  //get guess from user
  guess = parseInt(txtGuess.value);
  if (guess < correct){
    response += "Too low";
  } else if (guess > correct){
    response += "Too high";
  } else if (guess == correct){
    response += "Correct!";
    //show again button
    btnAgain.style.display = "block";
  } else {
    response += "Please enter a number between 1 and
        100";
  } // end if
  output.innerHTML = response;
}  // end checkGuess
```

Cheat codes and console.log

There's a particularly interesting line in the `init()` code that looks like this:

```
console.log(correct);
```

This line prints the correct answer! It might surprise you that the game actually gives out its own answer key, but that's a very common mechanism in game programming. Two interesting things are actually happening here: using a console and adding a cheat feature to a game.

The `console.log()` command is a special function that allows you to print results to a secret console supported by some browsers. If you right-click on the page in Chrome and choose Inspect Element, you'll be taken to a special developer's view. On any other browser, you can use Firebug. (Use the Firebug extension for Firefox or the Firebug Lite for other browsers — all available for free at http://www.getfirebug.com.) The console is a hidden text area simply for programmers. Ordinary users don't even know it exists, so it's perfect for putting quick debugging code. The `console.log()` command does nothing unless there is a console available. If the browser has a console, anything after the `console.log()` command is printed to the console.

The question is, why would you want to do such a thing? The answer is play testing. You'll need to play this game a lot while you're testing it, and in testing, you really want to look for the main cases: What happens when the guess is too large, too small, or perfect? To do this, you need to know what the correct answer is. `console.log()` prints the answer in a place only the programmer can see, so it's easier to test your code. Sneaky, huh? The following figure shows the program running in Firefox with the Firebug extension running.

Incidentally, this was the original motivation for cheat codes in games. Most games have mechanisms built in for the convenience of programmers and testers. For example, a special code can allow you to jump directly to a certain level or be invulnerable to damage. Programmers use these features to test the game. Early in the history of gaming, players learned about the existence of these codes. Now the practical test codes are still included in many games, and additional cheat codes are often also included. Today, game companies sometimes hide such features and leak them after a period of time to extend interest in a game.

This function is a real powerhouse, but it isn't much of a mystery. Again, everything this function does was predicted by the design document. Here are the details:

1. **Increment the turn counter.**

   Every time the user clicks the button, she's taken a turn, so begin by adding one to the turn counter.

2. **Begin building the response.**

   The main purpose of the `checkGuess()` function is to get input from the user and return some sort of output. That output will be stored in a string variable called `response`. Response begins with the turn number and a parenthesis.

3. **Get the guess from the text field.**

   The user should have entered some value in the text box. Grab that value, convert it to an integer, and store it in the `guess` variable.

4. **Check to see if the guess is too low.**

   Use an `if` statement to determine if the guess is less than the correct answer. Note how careful variable names make this a very easy line of code to understand. Just tell the user that the guess is too low by adding the message to `response`.

5. **Check to see if the guess is too high.**

   If the guess is too high, all that's necessary is to inform the user.

6. **Check for a correct guess.**

   If the user guesses correctly, there's a little more work to do, but none of it is very difficult.

7. **Tell the user she is correct.**

   Add a congratulation message to the `response` variable.

8. **Show the Play Again button.**

   If the game is over, you need a way to reset it so the user can play again. Simply show the Play Again button. When this button is clicked, it calls `init()`, which restarts the entire game (and rehides the Play Again button).

9. **Check for errors.**

   You might think the user's guess would be too high, too low, or correct, but those aren't the only options. If the user does something crazy (like types the word "three" or hits the guess button before entering anything at all), the program should do something. The `else` clause catches any condition that wasn't caught by the previous tests. Just gently remind the user what input is required, and count it as a turn.

Part II
Basic Game Development

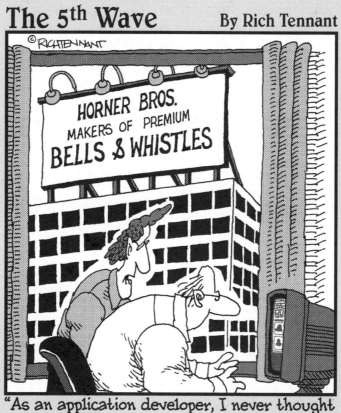

In this part . . .

This part introduces the `simpleGame` engine, which gives you the ability to make fun and powerful games right away.

Chapter 5 introduces the `simpleGame` engine. It walks you through how to build a basic game or animation. It then provides a template you can use for your own games. I show how to add basic keyboard input to convert an animation to an interactive experience.

Chapter 6 focuses on those game engine elements that are the foundation of any game. You find out how you can use object-oriented programming to create your own new sprite types. You add properties and methods to give your sprites new features and behavior. You manage sound effects and basic collision-detection, and you discover how to use the timer object in your games.

Chapter 7 takes you from the idea stage to the delivery of a complete game. It highlights a game design document as well as a strategy for working on the game project. I show the various elements of my game, how to build a library of components, and how to bring them together. You also find out how to convert a single element into a group of elements and how to design a game with variable difficulty levels.

Chapter 5

Introducing simpleGame.js

In This Chapter

▶ Using the `simpleGame` engine

▶ Building a game with `simpleGame`

▶ Understanding properties and methods

▶ Sprite motion methods

▶ Reading the keyboard

*G*ames are a lot of fun to play, and they can be even more fun to create. However, game programming is often considered one of the more difficult forms of programming to learn. Game development might seem a bit intimidating, but there's good news. It's more manageable to learn how to build games when you have a library that simplifies all various features you need.

This chapter introduces you to a simple game engine and library called… `simpleGame`. Along the way you'll also learn about object-oriented programming and one of the most important types of objects you'll use: the sprite.

Using a Game Engine

Games often use sophisticated programming techniques, and often require a great deal of math knowledge. Eventually, you'll learn these things, but even experienced programmers frequently use some sort of gaming library to simplify the task.

Essential game engine features

Game engines normally have a few important features:

- ✔ **A game/animation loop:** Most games use a coding structure called the game and animation loop. This is code that executes very quickly (usually 20 to 30 times per second). Game engines usually have some automated way to create and control this structure.

- ✔ **Sprite objects:** The various elements that bounce around on the screen (zombie robot banana slugs or whatever) are called *sprites*. The player is usually a sprite and so are the enemies, bullets, and sometimes even scoreboards and the background itself. A game engine needs some way to manage sprites. Most sprites are based on one or more images.

- ✔ **Movement system:** Sprites need some way to move around. Often you can set the position directly, but also often you can modify the position of each sprite a number of ways. Some systems allow you to set the speed and direction of a sprite, which simplifies many types of games.

- ✔ **Collision detection:** When sprites start moving around on the screen, they will bonk into each other. Game engines need some mechanism for detecting these collisions, because most of the interesting stuff that happens in a game occurs when sprites have crashed into each other.

- ✔ **Event detection:** Games are about events. Somehow, the user will need to provide input to the game. This can be through the keyboard, joystick, mouse, or other elements. For web-based gaming, you will mainly use the mouse and keyboard. In Chapter 9, I demonstrate how to use the touch screen on mobile devices for user input.

- ✔ **Audio support:** Sound effects are more than a final touch. They can add important feedback to the user. Game engines usually have some mechanism for loading and playing sounds.

- ✔ **Advanced features:** Often a game engine will contain other advanced features, like a physics system (which allows more realistic motion and gravity effects), a tile-based system (which simplifies building large map-based games), and a state system that allows sprites to have different animations and behaviors in different circumstances.

Gaming on the web

JavaScript by itself is not an ideal platform for game development. This is why most game development on the web has been based on Adobe's Flash environment (in fact, I wrote a book about creating games with Flash). Although Flash is a great tool, it can be expensive, and it isn't supported on all platforms. HTML5 now has some very interesting features that make it a viable tool for game development.

The most important of these tools is a new HTML element called the *canvas* tag. The canvas is a piece of the page that can be changed with programming code. You can draw images on the canvas and change the rotation and scale of each image. It's not difficult to draw an image on the canvas, but transformations (moving, rotating, and resizing the image) are a bit more challenging.

The canvas tag does not directly support sprites or collisions, but it's possible to make a special object that can add these features.

HTML5 has support for new audio elements that can be controlled through JavaScript code. Although this is easy enough to use, it isn't integrated tightly with the canvas element.

JavaScript has long supported a behavior called `setTimeOut`, which allows you to specify a function to run on intervals. See Chapter 12 for an example of a program that uses the `setTimeOut` mechanism.

Building an Animation with simpleGame.js

It's possible to build a library that simplifies all of these various features discussed in the previous section. Such a library can provide abstractions to make everything work without worrying about the details.

Of course, I've provided exactly such a library: `simpleGame.js`. This library is easy to use and is fully capable of sophisticated game development. It uses a notion called *object-oriented programming* to simplify the complexity of game development. This idea (object-oriented programming) is not really new because you've been using objects all along. (The document is an object, and form elements are objects, for example.) Building a game with the library involves creating objects and using them. To get started, you really need to understand only two objects:

- ✔ **The scene:** This object starts with an HTML canvas object and adds the main loop. The scene is the unifying object that controls the game.

- ✔ **Sprites:** These objects are the elements that move around on the screen. Most of the game elements are sprites. Each sprite must belong to a single scene, but you can have as many sprites as you want. A sprite is based on an image.

Take a look at Figure 5-1, and you see a simple program that uses this library.

Figure 5-1:
It looks like
a rectangle
with a ball,
but it's
much more
than that.

This code is actually a lot more sophisticated than it looks. Here's what it does:

- ✔ **It adds a canvas to the page.** The gray rectangle is actually a canvas tag that's been automatically added to the page.

- ✔ **It begins a game loop.** This program has a game loop already running at 20 frames per second.

- ✔ **It contains a sprite.** The ball image is much more than an image. It's a sprite, which has the capability to move any speed in any direction and other interesting features like collision detection built in.

- ✔ **The ball is moving.** I know you can't see this on a screen shot, but the ball is moving on the screen. It automatically wraps to the other side of the screen when it leaves one side.

With all the interesting stuff happening under the hood, you may be surprised at how simple the code is. Here's the entire code listing:

```
<!DOCTYPE HTML>
<html lang="en-US">
<head>
    <meta charset="UTF-8">
    <title>redBall.html</title>
    <script type="text/javascript"
```

```
        src = "simpleGame.js"></script>
<script type="text/javascript">
//simple game with a single moving ball
var scene;
var ball;

function init(){
  scene = new Scene();
  ball = new Sprite(scene, "redBall.png", 50, 50);
  ball.setMoveAngle(180);
  ball.setSpeed(3);

  scene.start();
} // end init

function update(){
  scene.clear();
  ball.update();
} // end update

</script>
</head>
<body onload = "init()">

</body>
</html>
```

The surprising thing about this code is how simple it is. The game engine takes a very complex process and makes it pretty easy to understand. You begin with a basic HTML5 page and add a few features to turn it into a gaming environment.

Building your page

Begin by building the underlying page:

1. **Begin with an HTML5 page.**

    You can use the same tools you've been using for your other web development. Build a basic HTML5 template like you do for any other HTML5 document.

2. **Import the** simpleGame.js **library.**

    This library is available for free from my website (www.aharrisbooks. net). Use a <script> tag to import the library. Set the src property to the name of the library (simpleGame.js). It's generally easier to keep a copy in the same directory as your page.

3. **Keep the HTML simple.**

   You can put whatever HTML you want on the page, but you don't need much. The game engine will create a canvas containing the scene. You might put a title, instructions, or other tools like scoreboards on the page, but the game engine will do most of the work.

4. **Call** `init()` **when the body loads.**

   It's very common to have a function called when the body loads. Add `onload = "init()"` to the body tag to call the `init()` method.

5. **Create a second script tag to contain your code.**

   You need to have a second script tag for custom code. Place this after the tag that imports the library.

6. **Place two functions in your script.**

   All `simpleGame` programs will have at least two functions: `init()` happens on startup, and `update()` happens once per frame.

Initializing your game

The initialization part of the game happens as the page loads. It's mainly taken up with setting up sprites and other resources. Here's the code:

```
var scene;
var ball;

function init(){
  scene = new Scene();
  ball = new Sprite(scene, "redBall.png", 50, 50);
  ball.setMoveAngle(180);
  ball.setSpeed(3);
} // end init
```

Most games will use a similar style of initialization. Here's how you set up the game:

1. **Define a variable to contain the scene.**

   Every `simpleGame` game will have at least one scene object. Define the scene outside any functions, so it is available to all of them. You will actually create the scene inside the `init()` function.

2. **Define a variable for each sprite.**

   Every sprite in your game will need to belong to a global variable as well. You'll create the sprites in the `init()` function, but you need to make the variable available to all functions.

3. **Build the** `init()` **function.**

   This function is called by `body onload`. It will run after the page has loaded into memory.

4. **Create the scene.**

   To build the scene, create an instance of the scene class. What you're really saying is "Make me a Scene object and call this particular instance 'scene.'" (See the later section "Making instance pudding" on class and instance for more details.) The scene doesn't require any parameters.

5. **Create the ball sprite.**

   The ball is a `Sprite` instance. To make a sprite, you need a few more bits of information. You need a scene, an image filename, width, and height.

6. **Set the ball's movement angle.**

   You can change the angle the ball moves. The angles are measured in degrees like on a map (0 is North, 90 is East, and so on).

7. **Set the ball's movement speed.**

   You can also determine the speed of the ball (in pixels per frame).

8. **Start the scene.**

   When you're done setting everything up, tell the scene to start.

Updating the animation

After you start the scene, a timer will begin. Twenty times a second, it will call a function on your page called `update()`. So, you need to have such a function, and it needs to have some code for your game to run.

The `update()` function is not terribly difficult either.

```
function update(){
  scene.clear();
  ball.update();
} // end update
```

The `update()` function typically does three things:

✔ **Clears the previous screen:** The first order of business is to clean up any mess caused by the last screen. The `Scene` object has a `clear()` function for exactly this purpose.

✔ **Checks for events:** Usually in a game, things will happen (or it isn't much of a game). Typically, you check for these types of events, like user input, sprites crashing into each other, sprites leaving the screen, or whatever. For this simple animation, the only event is a sprite leaving the screen, and I've automated the behavior associated with this action.

✓ **Updates each sprite:** The final part of the screen update is updating the sprites. When you update a sprite, it will draw in its new position (taking into account any changes you've made to the sprite's speed or direction).

In this case, it isn't necessary to check for any events. All the program does is clear the screen and update the `ball` sprite.

Figure 5-2 shows what happens if you don't clear the screen. All the sprite motion will be drawn on the canvas, and it looks like a big smear rather than a moving ball.

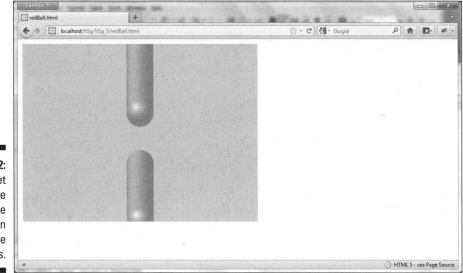

Figure 5-2: If you forget to clear the scene, the animation will look like this.

It might seem like a lot of work, but a similar version of this animation without the `simpleGame` library would be much more complex, and would take well more than 100 lines of code to write. (And that's nothing. It would be easily more than 200 lines in C++.)

Starting from a template

Almost every game in the rest of the book will begin with exactly the same code. If you want, you can start from this template, but really you should just type it yourself a few times until you can do it from memory:

```
<!DOCTYPE HTML>
<html lang="en-US">
<head>
    <meta charset="UTF-8">
    <title>template for simple games</title>
    <script type="text/javascript"
            src = "simpleGame.js"></script>
    <script type="text/javascript">
        var scene;
        var sprite1;

        function init(){
            scene = new Scene();
            sprite1 = new Sprite(scene, "image.png", 30,
        30);

            scene.start();
        } // end init

        function update(){
            scene.clear();

            //handle events here

            //update all the sprites
            sprite1.update();
        }
    </script>
</head>
<body onload = "init()">

</body>
</html>
```

You can download this template from my website or type it in. Here are a few things to remember:

✔ **You'll probably have several sprites.** I just put one sprite in the template, but most games will have several: One for the user and one for each enemy or target. Use better names than `sprite1` so you can remember what things are.

✔ **You'll need some other files.** Be sure your directory contains some suitable sprite images and the `simpleGame.js` file.

✔ **Define variables outside the functions.** The variables for the sprites and the scene will need to be defined outside all the functions.

✔ **Create the scene and the variables inside the** `init()` **function.** The main purpose of the `init()` function is to build all the various elements that will be populating your game.

✔ **Don't forget to start the scene.** The last line of the init() function should be scene.start(). This command begins the animation loop that gets the whole ball rolling. If your game isn't doing anything, check to be sure this line is here.

✔ **You need to have an** update() **function.** The update() function is not optional. All the game action is controlled by this function.

✔ **Clear the scene every frame.** The first thing to do in the update() function is to clear the screen with scene.clear(). If you forget to do this, you'll have very strange trail effects.

✔ **Check for events in the** update() **function.** The update() function is where you look for events (key presses, collisions, leaving the screen, and so on).

Considering Objects

The idea of object-oriented programming is really important in game programming because it's natural to think of games in terms of objects. You can do more interesting things with the game engine, but you need to have a grasp of how objects work. The game itself is an object (called a scene in simpleGame). The things that move around on the screen are also objects, called *sprites*. When a programming language allows you to think about your code as objects, it's called an *object-oriented* language. The simpleGame library makes heavy use of object-oriented techniques, so it's important to understand a few terms.

First, an *object* is simply a combination of code and data. Just like functions can be used to combine code statements and arrays can combine data elements, an object can combine functions and variables to make something bigger and cooler. With explosions.

Making instance pudding

When you create an object, you're essentially creating a new data type. First, you need to define what the object is and how it works. This is called a *class definition*. A class is essentially the instructions or blueprint for an object. Sprite and Span are the main objects in the simpleGame library. (There are others, but these are by far the most important.) Note the capital letters. It's customary to capitalize class names.

A class is like a recipe, but you wouldn't eat the recipe. Instead, you use a recipe to make cookies. (Okay, I've made some cookies that aren't much better to eat than the recipe, but you get my drift.) The actual cookies are *instances* of the class. The distinction is important because sometimes you're talking about a particular object, and sometimes you're talking about a whole class of objects. Instance names are not usually capitalized. Now look back at this line of code:

```
ball = new Sprite(scene, "redBall.png", 50, 50);
```

What it's really saying is the variable `ball` will now contain an instance of the `Sprite` class, with all the various characteristics indicated by the parameters. Now you can also see why the capitalization is so important in this line:

```
scene = new Scene();
```

It isn't as redundant as it seems. It means that the variable `scene` will contain an instance of the `Scene` class. It's common to give instances and classes the same name (but with different capitalization) when there's only one instance of the class, but different names when there are several. There are usually many sprites in a scene, and it's helpful to give them useful variable names like `ball` so you can tell what they are.

Adding methods to the madness

Objects are like variables, but they have a lot of other features ordinary variables don't have. For one thing, an object can have *properties*. These are like sub-variables attached to a primary variable. For example, `input` elements in ordinary JavaScript have a `value` property. You can often read and change a property directly. Properties usually describe something about an object.

Objects also have *methods*, which are things the object can do. If properties are essentially variables, methods are functions attached to an object. You've seen this before, too. The `document` is the primary object of a web page, and it has a method called `getElementById()` that is commonly used to get access to that element as a JavaScript variable.

Custom-built objects like the `Scene` and `Sprite` classes in `simpleGame` also can have properties and methods. Generally, however, I'll stay away from properties and mainly use methods instead. (This practice is a bit safer because properties can cause problems if you're not careful.) Look at the `simpleGame` documentation to see all the methods of the various objects, but don't worry if you don't understand them all.

Bringing Your Game

Animations and object-oriented theory are nice and all, but we're here to build a *game.* The biggest difference between a game and an animation is user interaction. If you want to make it a game, you need the user to get involved. Figure 5-3 shows a new game with a car driving around on the screen.

It really doesn't make sense to view an interactive program on a static book page. Please go to my website (www.aharrisbooks.net) and see the program run in your own browser. It's kind of fun, even if it isn't a real game yet.

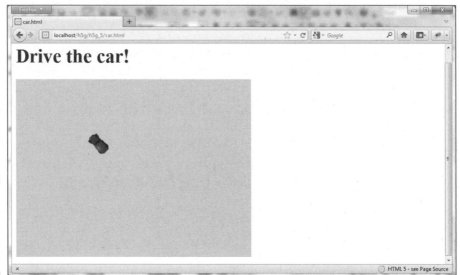

Figure 5-3:
The user
can steer
this car with
arrow keys!

The car game is similar to the ball animation, but it has some slightly different behaviors:

✓ **It's a car, not a ball.** I'll get the obvious stuff out of the way first. I can make a sprite out of any web-capable image, so this time I'll make the sprite a car by basing it on a car image. (See Chapter 11 for tips on building graphics for your games.)

✓ **Up and down arrows change the speed.** You can change the speed of the car with the up and down arrows. (You'll need a keyboard for this example. If you're on a mobile device, please look at Chapter 9 for more on using a virtual joystick or keypad solution.)

✓ **Left and right keys change the direction.** Pressing the left- or right-arrow key changes the direction the car is going. Turning even works correctly when going into reverse!

The code is actually not much more complicated than the ball animation.

```html
<!DOCTYPE HTML>
<html lang="en-US">
<head>
    <meta charset="UTF-8">
    <title>car.html</title>
    <script type="text/javascript"
            src = "simpleGame.js"></script>
    <script type="text/javascript">
    var scene;
    var car;

    function init(){
        scene = new Scene();
        car = new Sprite(scene, "car.png", 50, 30);
        car.setAngle(270);
        car.setSpeed(0);
        scene.start();
    } // end init

    function update(){
        scene.clear();
        //check keys

        if (keysDown[K_LEFT]){
            car.changeAngleBy(-5);
        } // end if

        if (keysDown[K_RIGHT]){
            car.changeAngleBy(5);
        } // end if

        if (keysDown[K_UP]){
            car.changeSpeedBy(1);
        } // end if

        if (keysDown[K_DOWN]){
            car.changeSpeedBy(-1);
        } // end if

        car.update();
    } // end update
    </script>
</head>
<body onload = "init()">
    <h1>Drive the car!</h1>
</body>
</html>
```

Checking the keyboard

Somehow the user needs to interact with the page. The keyboard is one of the easiest input elements to use. `simpleGame` provides a couple ways to check the keyboard, but the most powerful technique uses a special variable called `keysDown`. Here's how it works:

✔ `keysDown` **is a global array.** This variable is automatically created when you build a scene. It is an array of Boolean values — that means each element can be only true or only false.

✔ **There is a constant defined for each key.** Each key on the standard keyboard has a special constant already defined. For example, `K_A` represents the A key, and `K_B` represents the B key. See the chart for the names of special characters like the arrow keys and space bar.

✔ `keysDown` **tells the status of every key.** If the A key is currently pressed, `keysDown[A]` will contain the value `true`. If the A key is not pressed, `keysDown[A]` will contain the value `false`. See Table 5-1 for a rundown of the keyboard constants.

✔ **You can determine the current status of any key.** Just check the `keysDown[]` array to determine the current status of any key.

✔ **You can have multiple keys down at once.** The primary purpose of this technique is to allow for multiple keys to be pressed at once. In normal computing, it's unusual to have more than one key at a time (except special keys like Shift and Ctrl). In gaming, it's very common to press more than one key at a time, so you need a mechanism that can support this expectation.

Table 5-1	Keyboard Constants in `simpleGame`
simpleGame Constant	*Key*
K_A – K_Z	Standard character keys (capitalization is irrelevant)
K_UP	Up arrow
K_DOWN	Down arrow
K_LEFT	Left arrow
K_RIGHT	Right arrow
K_SPACE	Spacebar

See Chapter 12 for information on using other keys and defining new constants for them.

Moving the sprite

Sprites have a number of interesting built-in methods that allow you to change the position, angle, and speed of your sprite. Table 5-2 shows the highlights.

Table 5-2	Sprite Movement Methods	
Method	*Description*	*Parameters*
setPosition (x, y)	Places the sprite at the indicated position.	x: horizontal position y: vertical position
setX(x)	Sets the X position to a specific value.	x: new x position of sprite
setY(y)	Sets the Y position to a specific value.	y: new y position of sprite
changeXby(dx)	Changes the X position by some amount one time.	dx: amount to change x (positive values move right)
changeYby(dy)	Changes the Y position by some amount one time.	dy: amount to change y (positive values move down)
setChangeX(dx)	Sets an ongoing change in X (keeps going until you change it).	dx: amount to change x
setChangeY(dx)	Sets an ongoing change in Y (keeps going until you change it).	dy: amount to change y
setAngle(angle)	Sets both visual and motion angle of sprite.	angle: angle in degrees (standard map format)
changeAngleBy (dAngle)	Changes both visual and motion angle by some amount.	dAngle: degrees to change (positive is clockwise)
setImgAngle (angle)	Sets only the visual angle (does not affect motion).	angle: angle in degrees (standard map format)
changeImgAngle (angle)	Changes only the visual angle (does not affect motion).	dAngle: degrees to change (positive is clockwise)

(continued)

Table 5-2 *(continued)*

Method	Description	Parameters
setMoveAngle (angle)	Sets only the movement angle (does not affect appearance).	angle: angle in degrees (standard map format)
changeImgAngle (angle)	Changes only the movement angle (does not affect appearance).	dAngle: degrees to change (positive is clockwise)
setSpeed(speed)	Sets the speed of the car (in pixels / frame).	speed: new speed (can be negative for backward motion)
changeSpeedBy (dSpeed)	Changes the speed of the car.	dSpeed: positive values to speed up, negative values to slow down

There's a lot of information in Table 5-2, but it's not as complicated as it might look. Essentially, a sprite has a position, which is controlled by X and Y properties. If you remember from math class, X represents horizontal values, and Y is for vertical location. The *origin* (0, 0) is the top-left corner of the screen.

X coordinates work just like you remember from math class. As X values get larger, the sprite moves to the right. In computer graphics, Y acts a little different than it did in math class. Most display hardware scans from top to bottom, so Y is 0 at the top of the screen and increases as you move downward. This can be confusing at first, but I promise, you'll get used to it.

Figure 5-4 shows the coordinate system for a scene. Note that the maximum height and width are stored in variables: scene.height and scene.width. (The default scene is 400px by 300px, but you can change it if you want.)

All of the various movement methods are really about manipulating X and Y. You can set these values manually (setPosition(), setX(), and setY()), or you can change the values (changeXby(), changeYby()). Each of these methods acts immediately, so you can use them to direct the position or motion of the sprite.

Some of these functions seem similar to each other. For example, changeXby() looks a lot like setChangeX(). These functions have a subtle but important difference. The changeXby() function changes the value of X one time. If you want the change to continue, you have to keep calling this function. The `setChangeX()` function is more powerful because you can call it one time, and it repeatedly changes x by whatever value you determine until you call `setChangeX()` again (or something else that affects the car's speed).

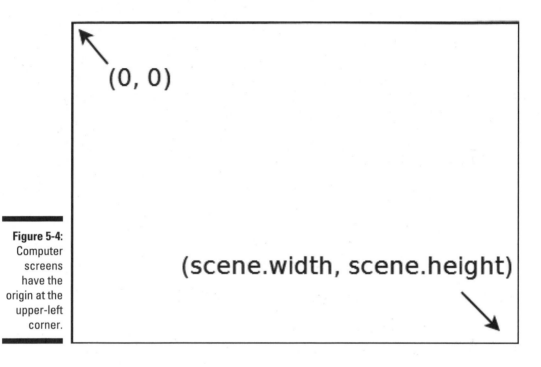

Figure 5-4:
Computer
screens
have the
origin at the
upper-left
corner.

It's fine if all this is a little lost on you right now because you're not going to use any of these techniques yet. The whole point of a game engine is to provide *abstraction*, which allows the programmer to think in a less mathematical way.

For most sprites, you really want to simply give the sprite an angle and a speed, and let it go. The `sprite` object has exactly the methods you need for this behavior. `setAngle()` allows you to determine the direction the sprite will go, and `setSpeed()` lets you specify the speed to go in that direction. Like most motion functions, there are also `changeAngle()` and `changeSpeed()` methods.

Note that for basic examples, I'm assuming that the sprite goes in the direction it's pointing, but that's not always the case. Sometimes, you'll want a car that skids or a spaceship that drifts sideways. It's possible to separate the movement angle from the visual angle with the provided methods.

Using the speed and angle to control a sprite is a really big deal. It vastly simplifies your game programming, but what's really going on under the hood? Well, it's math. The speed and angle are used to calculate a new change in X and change in Y every frame, using a mathematical technique called *vector projection* (which in turn uses basic trigonometry). I explain the technique in Chapter 12. For now, you can consider it magic, but I absolutely promise you're going to use math in game programming, so it might be time to break out those math books. When will you use math in real life? How about today?

Baby, you can drive my car

The `keysDown` mechanism can be combined with the motion methods to easily control your car. Here's the relevant code from `update()` again:

```
function update(){
    scene.clear();
    //check keys

    if (keysDown[K_LEFT]){
        car.changeAngleBy(-5);
    } // end if

    if (keysDown[K_RIGHT]){
        car.changeAngleBy(5);
    } // end if

    if (keysDown[K_UP]){
        car.changeSpeedBy(1);
    } // end if

    if (keysDown[K_DOWN]){
        car.changeSpeedBy(-1);
    } // end if

    car.update();
} // end update
```

The actual coding is pretty easy to understand:

1. **Clear the scene.**

   As usual, the first order of business in the `update()` function is to clean up the playroom. Make sure you've erased the previous frame before you do anything else.

2. Check for a left-arrow press.

Use the `keysDown` mechanism to determine whether the left arrow is currently pressed. (Of course, you can use WASD or some other control scheme if you prefer.)

3. If the left arrow is pressed, turn the car left.

If the user is currently pressing the left-arrow key, turn the car five degrees counter-clockwise (which will turn its nose to the car's left). Use the `changeAngleBy()` method to change the car's visual appearance as well as the direction it's travelling.

4. Repeat for the right arrow.

The right arrow check is similar, but this time turn the car five degrees clockwise (a positive angle turns the car's nose to the car's right).

5. Use the up arrow to accelerate.

If the user presses the up arrow, change the car's speed. Use a positive value to accelerate the car. It won't take much because this code is being checked 20 times a second.

6. Slow the car down with the down arrow.

Use a similar mechanism for the down arrow. Change the speed by a negative value to slow down the car. This approach allows for negative values, and the car will back up if you want.

7. Draw the car in its new position.

It's critically important to remember that calling the sprite's motion functions *does not change the location of the car!* It only changes internal data in the game's memory. You must call the car's `update()` method to see these changes in action.

You've got a pretty good start. Try building your own. Create an image, build a control system, and get it going. If you're ready for a challenge, see if you can figure out how to make your sprite go in the direction you pressed. For example, if you press the right arrow, the car goes right. If you press the up arrow, the car goes up.

Chapter 6

Creating Game Elements

Games have things moving around, crashing into each other, and making noise. Obviously, to have a game, you'll need these elements. You can build objects with the `Sprite` element built into the `simpleGame` library (refer to Chapter 5 if you need a review of building simple games with this library).

Building Your Own Sprite Objects

To make very powerful games, you'll want to be able to build your own sprites that do exactly what you want them to do.

In this chapter, you find out how to build your own new types of objects based on existing objects. After you make an object, you can give it characteristics and behavior.

Making a stock sprite object

To get started, take a look at this simple object:

```
<!DOCTYPE HTML>
<html lang="en-US">
<head>
    <meta charset="UTF-8">
    <title>critter</title>
    <script type="text/javascript"
            src = "simpleGame.js">
    </script>
    <script type="text/javascript">
        var game;
        var critter;
        function init(){
            game = new Scene();
            critter = new Sprite(game, "critter.gif",
          30,30);
            critter.setSpeed(0);
            game.start();
        }

        function update(){
            game.clear();
            critter.update();
        }
    </script>
</head>
<body onload = "init()">

</body>
</html>
```

This is an extremely simple program. It creates a scene and a single sprite called *critter*. Right now, the critter doesn't do much. Figure 6-1 shows what it looks like, but it's just an object that sits there and does nothing.

Building your own sprite

Sprite objects are great, but wouldn't it be awesome if the critter itself were an object and even better if it were a new object based on the sprite? It could start with all the basic features of the sprite, but you could add new capabilities to differentiate critters from other sprites.

Figure 6-1:
This is a
sprite right
out of the
box with no
modifica-
tions.

Take a look at `CritterConstructor.html` to see a way to do so:

```
<!DOCTYPE HTML>
<html lang="en-US">
<head>
    <meta charset="UTF-8">
    <title>critter</title>
    <script type="text/javascript"
            src = "simpleGame.js">
    </script>
    <script type="text/javascript">
        var game;
        var critter;

        function Critter(){
            tCritter = new Sprite(game, "critter.gif", 30,
          30);
            tCritter.setSpeed(0);
            return tCritter;
        }

        function init(){
            game = new Scene();
            critter = new Critter();
            game.start();
        }

        function update(){
            game.clear();
```

```
            critter.update();
      }
   </script>
</head>
<body onload = "init()">

</body>
</html>
```

This program works exactly like the last one, but it's organized a bit differently.

- ✔ **There is a function called** `Critter()`**.** It's important that the function is the name of an object and it's also capitalized. This is a very special function, because it's used to define a `Critter()` object.

- ✔ **The** `Critter()` **function creates a temporary sprite object.** Inside the `Critter()` function, you see a temporary sprite object called `tCritter()`. This is a new sprite.

- ✔ **Modify the temporary sprite as much as you want.** To make a new type of object in JavaScript, you essentially make a new object and then modify it to get exactly the behavior you want. In this case, I set the critter's default speed.

- ✔ **Return the temporary** `Critter` **object.** The end of the special `Critter()` function returns the sprite, but now it's not just a sprite, but a critter.

The point of this mechanism is to have new kinds of objects available. The `Critter` is much like a `Sprite`, but it can have new behavior and characteristics. This is an incredibly powerful feature.

The technical term for making a sprite act like it's descended from another sprite is *inheritance.* JavaScript's inheritance model is usually done in a different way (using a mechanism called *prototyping*). After much consideration, I chose to use this simpler approach to inheritance for this book. It is not the way formal JavaScript inheritance is done, but the mechanism shown here is easier to understand than the "right" way, and it's similar to how inheritance is done in many other languages. There is nothing at all wrong with this approach, but you'll sometimes see other approaches to inheritance in JavaScript.

Using your new critter

The `Critter()` function gives you the ability to create new critter objects. This changes the way you write your `init()` function:

```
function init(){
    game = new Scene();
    critter = new Critter();
    game.start();
}
```

The only thing that's really new is the way the critter is created. Now that you have a Critter() function, you can use it to build new critters. This special type of function (one that's designed to return a new class) is called a *constructor*. When there's only one critter to build, this may not seem like a big deal, but building objects with constructors is the key to building large and complex games with many kinds of interrelated objects.

Note that critter and Critter (watch the capitalization) are different things. Object definitions are normally written with the first letter shown in uppercase (the term is capitalized), and variables normally begin with a lowercase letter. In this situation, you're creating a variable called critter that is of the new type Critter. When you've got only one copy of a custom type, you often use this lower-upper trick for naming.

If you already know something about object-oriented programming (OOP) in another language, like C++ or Java, you're probably pretty confused. JavaScript seems to be object-oriented, but not in a way you're familiar with. That's true. JavaScript does have a form of OOP, but the mechanisms are different. Don't get too hung up on the details. The important ideas (inheritance, encapsulation, and polymorphism) are all there, but it may not look exactly like what you've already seen. Don't panic, and see if it all falls together as the examples become more involved.

Adding a property to your critter

One of the most interesting things about objects is that they are variables that can contain other variables. When a variable exists in the context of an object, the variable is called a *property*. Properties are the characteristics of an object, such as its speed or its size. As an example, please look at the following variation of the critter code:

```
<!DOCTYPE HTML>
<html lang="en-US">
<head>
    <meta charset="UTF-8">
    <title>critterSpeed.html</title>
    <script type="text/javascript"
            src = "simpleGame.js">
    </script>
```

```
<script type="text/javascript">
    var game;
    var critter;

    function Critter(){
        tCritter = new Sprite(game, "critter.gif", 30,
      30);
        tCritter.speed = 3;
        tCritter.setSpeed(tCritter.speed);
        return tCritter;
    }

    function init(){
        game = new Scene();
        critter = new Critter();
        game.start();
    }

    function update(){
        game.clear();
        critter.update();
    }
</script>
</head>
<body onload = "init()">

</body>
</html>
```

A property is simply a special variable associated with an object. Normally, you use `object.property` to designate that a particular property is associated with a particular object. For this example, I added a `speed` property to the `Critter` object.

1. **Build a property by referring to it.**

   In JavaScript, you can simply refer to a variable, and it will be created. This is also true in objects. Simply make a reference to `Critter.speed`, and the `Critter` object magically has a `speed` property.

2. **Create properties in the constructor.**

   You can technically create or refer to a property anywhere, but normally they're created in the constructor.

3. **Use the property like any other variable.**

   The property acts like any other variable, so you can use it to actually change the speed of the object.

Yes, I know this is more work than you need here because you could simply pass a number or ordinary variable to the `setSpeed()` method. However, I'm setting up the next example, which creates a custom behavior for the `Critter` class.

Adding methods to classes

If properties describe the characteristics of an object, *methods* describe the behavior. A method is a function associated with an object. You build methods very much like creating a property, but rather than adding a simple value, you assign an entire function to a name.

For example, the next version of the critter has a `changeSpeed()` method. When the user presses the up arrow, the critter will speed up, and when the user presses the down arrow, the critter will slow down (and eventually go the other direction). Here's the code for the critter with its new method in place:

```
<!DOCTYPE HTML>
<html lang="en-US">
<head>
    <meta charset="UTF-8">
    <title>critterChangeSpeed.html</title>
    <script type="text/javascript"
            src = "simpleGame.js">
    </script>
    <script type="text/javascript">
        var game;
        var critter;

        function Critter(){
            tCritter = new Sprite(game, "critter.gif", 30,
          30);
            tCritter.speed = 0;
            tCritter.checkKeys = function(){
                if (keysDown[K_RIGHT]){
                    this.speed++;
                }
                if (keysDown[K_LEFT]){
                    this.speed--;
                }
                tCritter.setSpeed(this.speed);
            } // end method
            return tCritter;
        }

        function init(){
            game = new Scene();
            critter = new Critter();
            game.start();
```

```
            }

        function update(){
            game.clear();
            critter.checkKeys();
            critter.update();
        }
    </script>
</head>
<body onload = "init()">

</body>
</html>
```

Note that I'm not showing a screen shot of this program because it looks exactly like the previous critter programs, except that it moves when the user presses the keys. For this and most examples, a static image will not be enough to help you see what's going on. You really need to see this program in action on my website: www.aharrisbooks.net.

In this new version of the program, the Critter object has a new behavior identified. Essentially, a method is nothing more than a function defined inside a class (which is also a function — my head is hurting here). Don't panic. It's really not that difficult to figure out. You're telling the system what to do if the user ever asks the Critter object to change speed.

1. **Create a new property called** checkKeys.

   In JavaScript, a property and a method are exactly the same thing. If you attach a regular variable to an object, it's a property. If you attach a function to it, it's a method. (Property names are normally nouns. Method names are normally verbs or verb phrases.)

2. **Build a new method to contain the behavior.**

   changeSpeed isn't an ordinary property, but a method, so you'll attach a function to it. (For the Computer Science majors out there, building an anonymous function on the fly like this is an example of a *lambda* function. Watch for it on the midterm exam!)

3. **Check for keyboard input.**

   Use the mechanism described in Chapter 5 to check to see whether the user presses the left or right arrow. The only difference is this: When you make a Critter object, it will already know how to look for its own key presses.

4. **Change the speed based on keyboard input.**

   If the user presses right, increase the speed (at the default direction, positive speeds move the sprite to the right). If the user presses left, decrease the speed.

5. Use the `setSpeed()` **method to change the actual speed.**

The `Sprite` object that provides the blueprint for critter already has a `setSpeed()` method. Use this method to make the object move at the indicated speed.

6. Inside a method, use the `this` **keyword.**

When you create a method inside a constructor, the computer can get a bit confused about the names of things. For the most part, you're adding stuff to a temporary critter called `tCritter`. However, when you're done, the actual critter you create will normally be called something else. To eliminate confusion, if you need to refer to other properties or methods of the object you're modifying, use the general keyword `this` rather than the actual name of the object (which will probably change by the time the method is being called).

7. Modify the `update()` **function so the critter checks the keyboard.**

Remember, the main `update()` function happens once per frame. Anything you want to happen once per frame should be called in `update()`. Add a call to `critter.checkKeys()`. This will remind the critter to check the keyboard every frame and change its speed as needed.

Sound Programming Principles

Sound effects have long been one of the biggest weaknesses of the web as a gaming platform. Web browsers had very inconsistent and troublesome audio capabilities. Fortunately, HTML5 solves the sound issue (at least at some level).

The `simpleGame` library makes it very easy to build new sounds by adding a `Sound` object. Here's a very simple program that plays a sound effect:

```
<!DOCTYPE HTML>
<html lang="en-US">
<head>
    <meta charset="UTF-8">
    <title>sound.html</title>
    <script type="text/javascript"
            src = "simpleGame.js"></script>
    <script type="text/javascript">
        var scene;
        var ribbit;

        function init(){
```

```
        scene = new Scene();
        owMP3 = new Sound("ow.mp3");
        owOgg = new Sound("ow.ogg");
        scene.start();
    } // end init

    function update(){
        if (keysDown[K_SPACE]){
            owMP3.play();
            owOgg.play();
        } // end if
    } // end update

    </script>
</head>
<body onload = "init()">
    <div>DO NOT press the space bar!!</div>
</body>
</html>
```

Sound effects are easy to manage with the `simpleGame` library:

1. **Create your sound effect.**

   Look over Chapter 11 for information on building and modifying sound effects, or find an audio file. The best formats are mp3 and ogg. Put your audio file in the same directory as your program.

   To maximize browser compatibility, continue to Step 2.

2. **Make a variable to hold your sound effect.**

   Like every game asset, you'll have a variable containing your sound. Define the variable outside any functions.

3. **Build a `Sound` object to initialize your sound effect.**

   The `simpleGame` library has a `Sound` object. Create an instance of this object to build your sound. The object requires one parameter: the name of the file containing your sound effect. Normally, you'll do this in the `init()` function of your game.

4. **Play the sound with the `play()` method.**

   Once you've defined a sound effect, you can play it back easily with the sound object's `play()` method.

This program is shown in Figure 6-2, but understandably, it won't be very interesting in the book. You really need to view it at www.aharrisbooks. net to get the full effect.

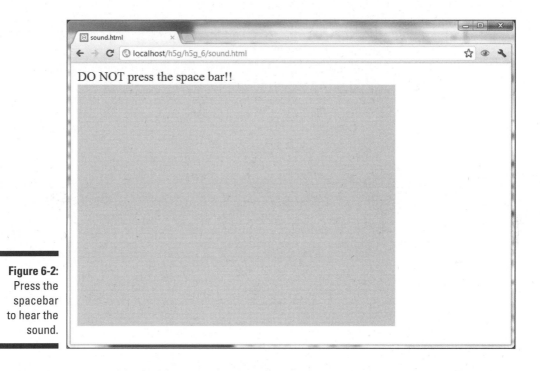

Figure 6-2:
Press the
spacebar
to hear the
sound.

Getting sound effects

Sound effects add a lot to your game. It used to be quite difficult to work with sound effects in web pages, but HTML5 has a wonderful new `<sound>` tag that finally gives the browser access to sound effects without third-party plug-ins. The `Sound` object in the `simpleGame` library is based on the HTML5 `<sound>` tag.

Great as the sound element is, there are some problems. Although all HTML5-compliant browsers play audio files, they do not play the same file types. The mp3 format is very well known, but not all browsers support it. Many browsers prefer the newer (and open source) Ogg format. If this isn't confusing enough, the support changes from version to version of the same browser.

My suggestion is to use both mp3 and Ogg formats and let the browser play whichever one it can. That will resolve most issues.

Of course, it isn't easy to find the same sound effect in both formats. I recommend you use the free audio editor, Audacity (`http://audacity.sourceforge.net`). This tool allows you to record and edit sound effects in multiple formats. Depending on the version of Audacity you get, you may also need the LAME plug-in (`http://lame.sourceforge.net`). With these tools, you can easily record your own sound effects and save them in both Ogg and mp3 formats. Please see Chapter 11 for more information on recording your own audio.

Game Programming's Greatest Hits!

The most interesting things in video games happen when sprites conk into each other. Game engines normally have some sort of tool for testing whether two sprites are overlapping. This is called *collision detection*, and it can be done a number of ways. For this example, I'll use the standard *bounding rectangle* scheme. It's not perfect, but it's very easy to implement and is commonly used.

Setting up bounding rectangle collisions

Take a look at `colTest.html` as shown in Figure 6-3, and you'll see a simple example.

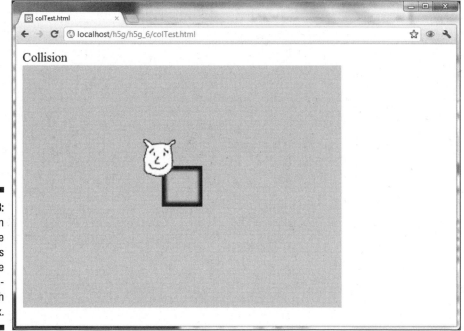

Figure 6-3: A Collision message appears when the critter collides with the box.

In the `colTest.html` example, the user moves the critter with the mouse, and you'll get a message when the critter is touching the box in the middle of the screen.

```html
<!DOCTYPE HTML>
<html lang="en-US">
<head>
    <meta charset="UTF-8">
    <title>colTest.html</title>
    <script type-"text/javascript"
            src = "simpleGame.js"></script>
    <script type="text/javascript">
        var game;
        var box;
        var critter;
        var output;

        function init(){
            game = new Scene();
            game.hideCursor();
            box = new Sprite(game, "simpleBox.png", 50,
          50);
            critter = new Sprite(game, "critter.gif", 50,
          50);
            output = document.getElementById("output");

            //give box fixed position
            box.setPosition(200, 150);
            box.setSpeed(0);


            //critter controlled by mouse
            critter.setPosition(100, 100);
            critter.setSpeed(0);
            critter.followMouse = function(){
                this.setX(document.mouseX);
                this.setY(document.mouseY);
            } // end followMouse

            game.start();
        } // end init

        function update(){
            game.clear();
            critter.followMouse();
            checkCollisions();
            box.update();
            critter.update();
        } // end update;

        function checkCollisions(){
            if (box.collidesWith(critter)){
                output.innerHTML = "Collision";
            } else {
```

```
                output.innerHTML = "No collision";
            } // end if
        } // end checkCollisions

    </script>
</head>
<body onload = "init()">
    <div id = "output">empty</div>
</body>
</html>
```

A number of interesting things are happening in this code:

1. **Hide the normal mouse cursor.**

   When you're going to have some other object follow the mouse, you normally want to hide the normal arrow cursor. In `simpleGame`, use the `game.hideCursor()` method to hide the mouse cursor inside the game screen.

2. **Create more than one sprite.**

   It takes two to tango, or collide. In this example, I have a box that will remain stationary, and a critter that follows the mouse.

3. **Give the critter a `followMouse()` method.**

   In this example, you have the critter follow the mouse. Begin by creating a `followMouse()` method.

4. **Determine the mouse's position.**

   The mouse position is determined (in `simpleGame.js`) with the `document.mouseX` and `document.mouseY` properties.

5. **Copy the mouse position to the critter position.**

   Use the mouse's x position to set the critter's x position, and repeat with y.

6. **Call the critter's `followMouse()` method every frame.**

   As usual, the `update()` function is where you put code that should happen repeatedly.

If you play around with the `colTest.html` page, you'll probably notice that the collisions are not exact. It's possible to have a collision register even when the critter isn't actually touching the box. This is important because `simple Game` uses a scheme called *bounding box collisions*. This means you're not actually checking to see whether the images collide but whether the rectangles around the images collide. In this example, the difference is minor, but you'll sometimes see significant errors with this mechanism, especially with elements that are long and thin. Figure 6-4 illustrates the problem with bounding rectangles. As a sprite rotates, the size of the bounding rectangle can change.

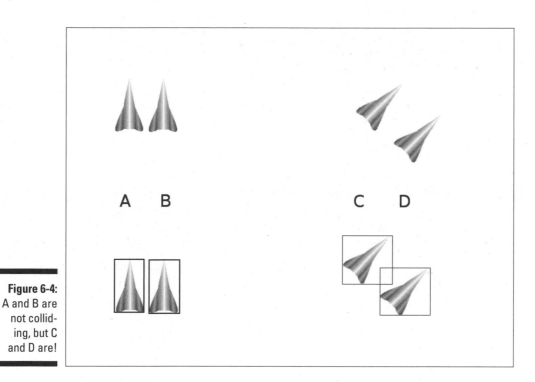

Figure 6-4:
A and B are not colliding, but C and D are!

Distance-based collisions

An alternative form of collision detection, called *bounding circle* collisions, is available. With this mechanism, you simply calculate the distance between the center of two sprites, and if that value is smaller than some threshold, you consider it a collision. This approach has two advantages:

- ✔ **The collision distance is constant.** The distance between image centers will not change when images are rotated, even if the images change size.

- ✔ **The collision threshold can be varied.** You can set any sensitivity you want. Set a large collision radius for easy collisions and a smaller one when you want collisions to be triggered only when the sprites are very close to each other.

The `simpleGame` library `Sprite` object has a `distanceTo()` method, which calculates the distance from one sprite to another. You can see an example of this code in the `distance.html` example:

```
<!DOCTYPE HTML>
<html lang="en-US">
<head>
```

```
<meta charset="UTF-8">
<title>distance.html</title>
<script type="text/javascript"
        src = "simpleGame.js"></script>
<script type="text/javascript">
    var game;
    var box;
    var critter;
    var output;

    function init(){
        game = new Scene();
        game.hideCursor();
        box = new Sprite(game, "simpleBox.png", 50,
    50);
        critter = new Sprite(game, "critter.gif", 50,
    50);
        output = document.getElementById("output");

        //give box fixed position
        box.setPosition(200, 150);
        box.setSpeed(0);
        critter.setPosition(100, 100);
        critter.setSpeed(0);

        //critter controlled by mouse
        critter.followMouse = function(){
            this.setX(document.mouseX);
            this.setY(document.mouseY);
        } // end followMouse

        game.start();
    } // end init

    function update(){
        game.clear();
        critter.followMouse();
        checkDistance();
        box.update();
        critter.update();
    } // end update;

    function checkDistance(){
        dist = box.distanceTo(critter);
        if (dist < 50){
            output.innerHTML = "Collision: " + dist;
        } else {
            output.innerHTML = "No collision: " +
    dist;
        } // end if
```

```
        } // end checkDistance

    </script>
</head>
<body onload = "init()">
    <div id = "output">empty</div>
</body>
</html>
```

The distance-based collision method is very similar to the bounding-rectangle version. Create a checkDistance() function that will act just like the old checkCollisions(). Here are the steps for what happens in check-Distance:

1. **Find the distance between the two sprites.**

   Use the sprite's distanceTo() method to determine the distance between the two sprites.

2. **If the distance is less than some threshold, count it as a collision.**

   Generally I use the width of the smaller sprite as a starting point for a collision threshold, but you can adjust this to make collisions more or less likely.

3. **Report the collision status.**

   In this example, I simply print "collision" or "no collision," but in a real game, collisions are triggers for other actions: increasing the score, decreasing the number of lives, changing the speed or position of the collided elements, or whatever. (Hopefully, it involves explosions.)

I'm not showing a screen capture of the distance-based collision program because to the user it looks exactly like the earlier collision routine. Please run it in your own browser to see how these collision schemes compare.

Collisions are more complicated than I'm letting on

The two basic forms of collision described in this book (bounding box and distance-based) are adequate for most basic games, but collision detection gets far more complicated than this. If the two objects have a very high relative speed, they might pass right through each other without ever actually overlapping. Also, neither scheme really takes into account the actual shapes of the sprites, but approximates the sprite shapes. There are more complex collision-detection schemes that resolve these issues (usually by creating more complex shapes for comparison), but these schemes often slow down the game, so they should not be used until necessary. Stick with bounding-rectangle and distance-based collision for now, and you should be fine.

It's All About Timing . . .

Often the passage of time will be an element in your games. Racing games are all about speed, or you may have a time limit for performing some task. The simpleGame library includes a very handy timer object that allows you to manage time easily. The Timer object is created like any other JavaScript object. It has three methods:

- ✔ reset(): This function initializes the timer and starts the elapsed time counter.

- ✔ getCurrentTime(): This function returns the current system time at the moment it's called. (Note that the time is in a special integer format, and it will not be recognizable by human readers.)

- ✔ getElapsedTime(): Returns the number of seconds since the timer was created or the last reset (whichever is more recent).

In JavaScript and most other languages, date and time information is generally stored in a special integer format. Time is actually counted as a huge integer showing the number of milliseconds since midnight January 1, 1970. Although this may seem like a really complicated scheme, it's actually perfect for your use because what you really want to know is how much time has elapsed between two events. If you want to actually get the current date and time in a human-readable format, look up the JavaScript Date object. I actually used this object to create the Timer object in the simpleGame library.

For an example of timing, look at timerDemo.html:

```
<!DOCTYPE HTML>
<html lang="en-US">
<head>
    <meta charset="UTF-8">
    <title>timerDemo</title>
    <script type="text/javascript"
            src = "simpleGame.js"></script>
    <script type="text/javascript">
        var timer;
        var output;
        var game;

        function init(){
            game = new Scene();
            output = document.getElementById("output");
            timer = new Timer();
            timer.reset();
            game.start();
        } // end init
```

```
         function update(){
             game.hide();
             currentTime = timer.getElapsedTime();
             output.innerHTML = currentTime;
         } // end update

         function reset(){
             timer.reset();
         } // end reset
    </script>
</head>


<body onload = "init()">
    <div id="output">empty</div>
    <button onclick = "reset()">
      reset timer
    </button>
</body>
</html>
```

This example (illustrated in Figure 6-5) demonstrates a simple timer. It displays the number of seconds the page has been running. The timer can be reset with the (cleverly named) Reset Timer button.

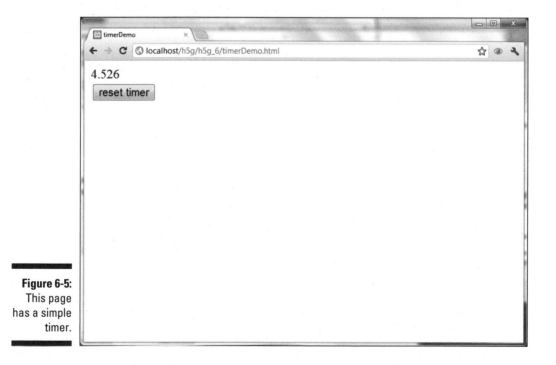

Figure 6-5:
This page
has a simple
timer.

This program is relatively simple, but it illustrates some very powerful ideas. Use this process to build your own time-sensing game:

1. **Create a variable for the timer.**

   This should be getting familiar. All the interesting elements are objects, and the timer is no exception. Create a variable called `timer` that will be an object of type `Timer`.

2. **Reset the timer.**

   Be sure the timer starts out at zero.

3. **Get the elapsed time in every frame.**

   In the `update()` function, call the timer's `getElapsedTime()` method to find out how much time has passed and copy this value to the output area.

4. **Reset the timer when the user presses the button.**

   When the user presses the `reset` button, call the timer's `reset()` method to reset the elapsed time back to zero.

5. **Hide the main scene.**

   This program uses the main loop from `simpleGame`, but it doesn't really need to display the scene. For this reason, the `Scene` object has a `hide()` method. You can also display the scene later with its `show()` method.

Chapter 7

Getting to a Game

*I*f you know how to boil and stir, you've got some of the mechanics of cooking, but you're still not a chef. It's great to know how to build a sprite, how to add sound effects and timers, and how to read the keyboard. But you're here to make a game. You're here to find out how to design a game and then to actually build and implement that game design. This chapter walks you through the process of building a real game from beginning to end.

Building a Real Game

If you can build a sprite that moves under user control, you're getting very close to a real game, but you still need a little more. A game really needs these elements:

✔ **Some sort of plot:** The plot doesn't have to be complicated (PAC-MAN), but there has to be some kind of theme or setting.

✔ **Some kind of goal:** The player must have a goal to achieve. Often a large goal requires a number of smaller goals, but the player is always trying to achieve something, whether it is capturing an enemy, getting to the end of a level, or completing a race in first place.

✔ **Some kind of obstacle:** To make the game interesting, something needs to be in the player's way. It can be things the player is trying not to hit, things shooting at the player, or even simple things like time or gravity.

In addition to these game elements, you need to add a few more mechanical concepts:

- **Collisions:** The interesting part of any arcade game often happens when things crash into each other. You need some mechanism to manage this action.

- **Sound effects:** Sound effects add tremendously to a game. They not only add to the general atmosphere of the game, but also they often provide important user feedback.

- **Text feedback:** It can be nice to explain to the user exactly what's going on in the game. This can be useful for scorekeeping, displaying the number of lives left, and so on.

- **A replay button:** At some point, the game will end. You need a mechanism to restart the level or move to a new one.

In this chapter, I take you through the process of adding all these features. Along the way, you will build a working game.

Planning Your Game

The first part of game creation is planning. It's pretty hard to program a game in the best of circumstances, and it's nearly impossible if you don't know exactly what you're trying to accomplish.

For that reason, the first thing you need to do when you build a game is to turn off the computer. Get out paper and pencil, and come up with a plan for your game. The plan should be detailed enough that you know how you're going to code everything. Here's what your diagram needs to include:

- **Setting and theme:** What does the game look like? What is the overall theme? What is the general style?

- **Environment:** Are there any special environmental rules? For example, is the player always moving forward in an endless scrolling world? Is gravity a feature of the game (for example, do things fall)?

- **Avatar:** What is the role of the player in the game? Does the player control a particular sprite, or is the player an omniscient presence (as in most puzzle games)?

- **Player control:** How does the player control things? Is it mouse-based? Keyboard? Touch screen? Are there limitations to motion?

- **Goals:** What is the player trying to do? Touch something? Avoid something? Gather things? Shoot something? Go somewhere?

✔ **Obstacles:** What is preventing the user from accomplishing this? Are there things the player should avoid?

✔ **Artificial intelligence:** If there are sprites on the screen that are not controlled by the player, how do they behave? Do they move? How? What happens when they leave the screen?

✔ **Collision management:** What happens when things crash into each other?

✔ **Scorekeeping:** Will the game have a scorekeeping mechanism? This can include points, but it can also incorporate a set number of lives or a time limit.

✔ **Game end state:** What causes the game to end? What will happen when the game ends? How do you motivate the user to play again?

As the primary example for this chapter, I developed a game called *Frog Lunch.* Figure 7-1 illustrates the main points of this game.

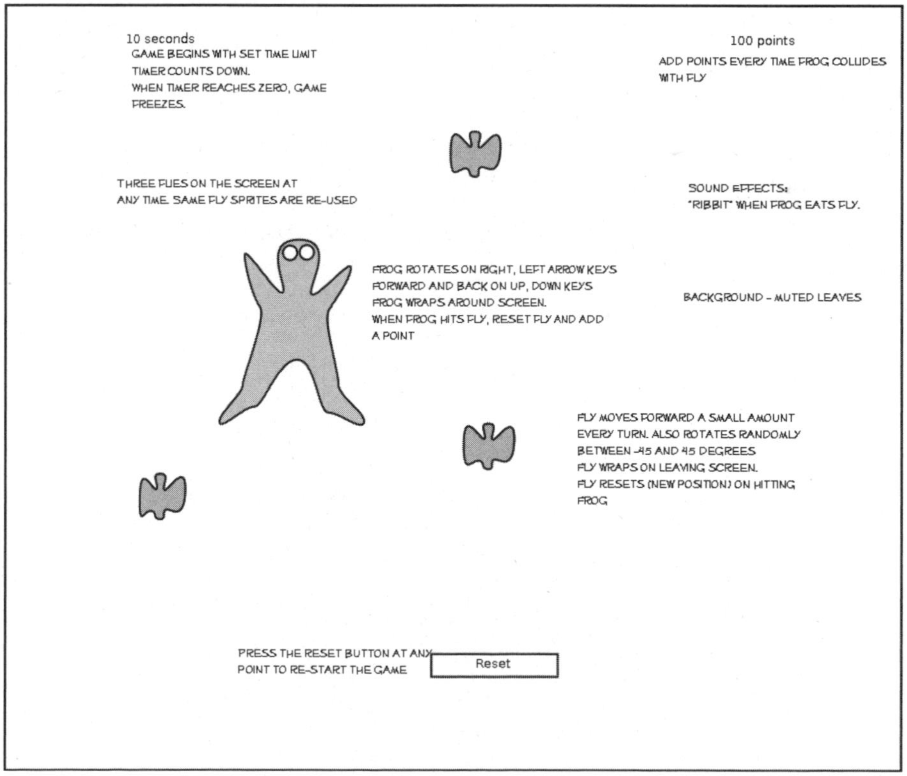

Figure 7-1:
The Frog Lunch planning diagram.

Even this very simple game has a number of details. If you think about the details in the design phase, programming the game becomes much easier to accomplish. Here are the highlights of this game's design:

- ✔ **The player is a hungry frog.** I don't know if there was a kissing princess involved, but somehow, you're a frog. Live with it.

- ✔ **Control the frog with the keyboard.** The frog is controlled with the arrow keys. Turn left and right to, well, turn left and right.

- ✔ **The forest is filled with flies.** There are tasty flies running around, acting like flies. You know what to do . . .

- ✔ **Gain points by eating flies.** Run into a fly to eat it.

- ✔ **Eat the most flies in a set time to win.** The main obstacle is time. After a short time period, the game will end and you can no longer control the frog.

The game is very simple, and that's a good thing. At this stage, it already requires a number of techniques you might not know, so I explain some of these techniques as you go.

Programming On the Fly

Often I begin a game with the avatar, but in this case, I begin with the fly because it's one of the easiest objects in the game, and it illustrates some really interesting new points. Figure 7-2 illustrates the fly on the screen.

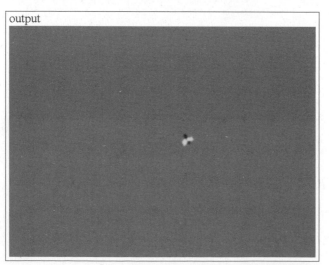

Figure 7-2: There is a bug in this program.

Of course, the most interesting thing about the fly is how it moves. No self-respecting fly would go in a straight, predictable pattern. Instead, it wanders all around the screen, randomly turning a bit at every opportunity (looking for coleslaw to land on). If you want to see this for yourself (and I know you do), you need to view the program on my website: www.aharrisbooks.net.

The code for the fly follows the very standard framework for simpleGame programs. It has a simple HTML page with some basic JavaScript code: an init() and an update(). Here's the code:

```html
<!DOCTYPE HTML>
<html lang="en-US">
<head>
    <meta charset="UTF-8">
    <title>fly.html</title>
    <script type="text/javascript"
            src = "simpleGame.js"></script>

    <script type="text/javascript">
        var scene;
        var fly;
        var output;

        function Fly(){
            tFly = new Sprite(scene, "fly.png", 20, 20);
            tFly.setSpeed(10);
            tFly.wriggle = function(){
                //change direction by some random amount
                newDir = (Math.random() * 90) - 45;
                this.changeAngleBy(newDir);
            } // end wriggle
            return tFly;
        } // end Fly

        function init(){
            scene = new Scene();
            scene.setBG("green");
            output = document.getElementById("output");
            //createCar();
            fly = new Fly();
            scene.start();
        } // end init

        function update(){
            scene.clear();
            fly.wriggle();
            fly.update();
        } // end update

    </script>
```

```
</head>
<body onload = "init()">
    <div id = "output">output</div>
</body>
</html>
```

There seems to be a bug in this program

For the most part, this program is like the ones in Chapter 5, but there's something new: A fly is moving around on the stage by itself. There are really two changes. First, you build a fly object. Second, you figure out a way to make it act like a fly, wriggling around on the screen in a somewhat random way.

This function creates a special version of the sprite called a fly. Refer to Chapter 6 if you need a refresher on building custom objects, but here's how this one works:

1. **Name the function the same as the object.**

   You make a function called `Fly()` to build a `Fly` object. It's traditional to capitalize object names, so that's what you do here.

2. **Build a temporary sprite.**

   Flies are sprites, so begin by making a sprite. This one has an appropriately entomological picture. This temporary fly is called `tFly`. You're going to make a few more changes to it before releasing it to the wild.

3. **Set the sprite's speed.**

   Use the standard `setSpeed()` method to change the fly's speed.

4. **Add a new method to the fly.**

   It turns out you can add new properties and behaviors to an object quite easily. Just create a property called `wriggle` and assign a function to it.

5. **Change the fly's direction.**

   To get the seemingly random pattern of a fly, change the fly's direction by a random value between 45 and -45 degrees. (Pick a random number between 0 and 90; then subtract 45.) If you change the fly's direction according to this pattern, you'll get surprisingly convincing fly behavior.

6. **Use `this.changeAngleBy()` to change the fly's direction.**

   Within the context of defining a method (that is, a function that belongs to an object), use the keyword `this` to refer to the currently defined object.

7. **Return the newly created temporary fly.**

   The point of this function is to manufacture a new `Fly` object based on the `Sprite` pattern. When the programmer runs this function, she'll get a fly — and who doesn't love bugs?

Fly, fly! fly!

The `init()` function of the main program builds all the standard elements, but this time, rather than making a stock `Sprite`, you make a `Fly()` object.

```
function init(){
    scene = new Scene();
    scene.setBG("green");
    output = document.getElementById("output");
    //createCar();
    fly = new Fly();
    scene.start();
} // end init
```

Now that you've created the fly, you can manipulate it in the `update()` function. Take a look at how that works:

```
function update(){
    scene.clear();
    fly.wriggle();
    fly.update();
} // end update
```

This is a simple function, but it outlines something profound. Your fly has an `update()` method because the fly is also a sprite, and sprites have `update()` methods. It also has a `wriggle()` method. If you want the fly to wriggle every frame, you need to call the `wriggle()` method from the main `update()` function.

Clearly, We Need an Amphibian

When you built the fly object, you not only described how a fly will work, you made it possible to build a *lot* of flies easily, just like in real life. Skip ahead to the section "Working with Multiple Flies" to see how that works. Obviously, before you start adding flies indiscriminately, you're going to need some pest control.

The `frog.html` page (demonstrated in Figure 7-3) shows a page much like the fly, but this time with a frog object.

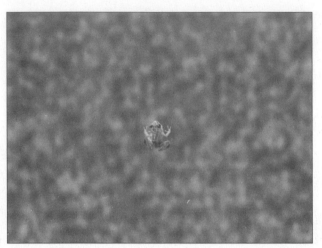

Figure 7-3:
This pro-
gram has
a frog. And
leaves.

The code is similar to `fly.html`, but of course, it has a lot more frogs and fewer flies.

```html
<!DOCTYPE HTML>
<html lang="en-US">
<head>
    <meta charset="UTF-8">
    <title>Frog</title>
    <script type="text/javascript"
            src = "simpleGame.js"></script>
    <script type="text/javascript">
        var scene;
        var frog;
        var leaves;

        function init(){
            scene = new Scene();
            scene.setBG("green");
            frog = new Frog();
            leaves = new Sprite(scene, "leaves.png", 640,
            480);
            leaves.setSpeed(0);
            scene.start();
        }

        function update(){
            scene.clear();
            leaves.update();
            frog.checkKeys();
            frog.update();
        }
```

```
            function Frog(){
                tFrog = new Sprite(scene, "frog.png", 50, 50);
                tFrog.maxSpeed = 10;
                tFrog.minSpeed = -3;
                tFrog.setSpeed(0);
                tFrog.setAngle(0);
                tFrog.checkKeys = function(){
                    if (keysDown[K_LEFT]){
                        this.changeAngleBy(-5);
                    } // end if
                    if (keysDown[K_RIGHT]){
                        this.changeAngleBy(5);
                    } // end if
                    if (keysDown[K_UP]){
                        this.changeSpeedBy(1);
                        if (this.speed > this.maxSpeed){
                            this.setSpeed(this.maxSpeed);
                        } // end if
                    } // end if
                    if (keysDown[K_DOWN]){
                        this.changeSpeedBy(-1);
                        if (this.speed < this.minSpeed){
                            this.setSpeed(this.minSpeed);
                        } // end if
                    } // end if
                } // end checkKeys
                return tFrog;
            } // end Frog

    </script>
</head>
<body onload = "init()">

</body>
</html>
```

Making a frog

The code for making a frog is similar to the fly code. It basically outlines the creation of a frog. The frog code is a bit different than the fly because it's meant to be controlled by the user. Just follow these steps:

1. **Create a temporary sprite.**

   As with the fly, you begin with a temporary Sprite object and hang the various new features on it to make the sprite into a frog. Begin with a frog image, pointing to the right. (See Chapter 11 for information on modifying images, if necessary.)

2. **Add some properties.**

   The frog needs a couple of properties to keep the speed under control. `maxSpeed` is the upper speed limit, and `minSpeed` is the lower speed limit. You allow a negative speed, meaning the frog can back up, but slowly.

3. **Add a `checkKeys()` method.**

   The frog is user-controlled, so it will need to respond to key presses. You add a `checkKeys()` method for this purpose.

4. **Turn the frog on left or right key press.**

   If the user presses the left or right arrow, use the built-in `changeAngleBy()` method to change the direction the frog is pointing. (This will also affect the direction of travel.)

5. **Change the frog's speed on up or down key press.**

   If the user presses the up or down arrow, use the built-in `changeSpeedBy()` method to change the speed at which the frog moves.

As you write the `update()` function for the game, you need to tell the program when to invoke the frog's `checkKeys()` method.

Adding a background

The other obvious new feature of the frog program is the addition of a background. There are a number of ways to make a background image, but the easiest is to simply add a new large sprite. You simply make a suitable image and create a sprite to manage that image.

1. **Create a variable to hold the background.**

   Because there's a leafy forest floor as the backdrop for the game, you create a variable called `leaves`. Like all the other sprites, the variable is created at the beginning of the code:

   ```
   var leaves;
   ```

2. **Instantiate the background sprite.**

   The `leaves` sprite is pretty simple. It doesn't really need any new data or behavior, so you can use a stock `Sprite` object. Create the sprite in the `init()` function:

   ```
   leaves = new Sprite(scene, "leaves.png", 640, 480);
   ```

3. **This is a non-moving background.**

   It's possible to create a scrolling background, but that takes a little more effort. Set the leaves' speed to zero:

   ```
   leaves.setSpeed(0);
   ```

4. **Update the background.**

   In the `update()` function, be sure to call the `leaves.update()` method. Even though the leaves don't move, you need to update to ensure the leaves are drawn:

   ```
   leaves.update();
   ```

Managing updates

There are now two sprites on the screen, and the interaction of these objects is largely controlled by the `update()` function. Review that function:

```
function update(){
    scene.clear();
    leaves.update();
    frog.checkKeys();
    frog.update();
}
```

The `update()` function is the key to any game. This function describes exactly what will happen on every frame of the game. In general, you use this function to call the various methods of the sprites you've created. The order in which you do things matters. Remember that the `update()` method of each object draws that object on the screen. In general, you want to check events on an object before you run its `update()` method, so anything that happened in the frame is reflected by the screen.

Also, note that objects are drawn in the order of the `update()` method calls, so a background image (`leaves` in this case) should be drawn *before* any objects meant to be in the foreground. If you draw the large background last, it will obscure the main game elements.

Combining the Frog and the Fly

The fly is wonderful, and so is the frog. It's great to test each creature in isolation as shown in the earlier examples (that way you're focusing on one new big idea at a time), but these two objects are really meant to be together. The next version of the program puts the frog and the fly in a separate file and creates a new program to put them together.

Building a library of reusable objects

I'll be using the frog and the fly many more times in this chapter, and they're going to stay about the same. So, it makes sense to put them in a library for easy reuse. That's exactly what you're going to do. Take a look at `frogLib.js`:

```
//frogLib.js
//Objects for frog game

function Fly(){
    tFly = new Sprite(scene, "fly.png", 20, 20);
    tFly.setSpeed(10);
    tFly.wriggle = function(){
        //change direction by some random amount
        newDir = (Math.random() * 90) - 45;
        this.changeAngleBy(newDir);
    } // end wriggle
    return tFly;
} // end Fly

function Frog(){
    tFrog = new Sprite(scene, "frog.png", 50, 50);
    tFrog.maxSpeed = 10;
    tFrog.minSpeed = -3;
    tFrog.setSpeed(0);
    tFrog.setAngle(0);
    tFrog.checkKeys = function(){
        if (keysDown[K_LEFT]){
            this.changeAngleBy(-5);
        } // end if
        if (keysDown[K_RIGHT]){
            this.changeAngleBy(5);
        } // end if
        if (keysDown[K_UP]){
            this.changeSpeedBy(1);
            if (this.speed > this.maxSpeed){
                this.setSpeed(this.maxSpeed);
            } // end if
        } // end if
```

```
            if (keysDown[K_DOWN]){
                this.changeSpeedBy(-1);
                if (this.speed < this.minSpeed){
                    this.setSpeed(this.minSpeed);
                } // end if
            } // end if
        } // end checkKeys
        return tFrog;
    } // end setupFrog
```

This is an interesting document. It contains nothing but the two class definitions. It is used because several other programs will use these two classes.

If you look at `frogLib.js` on the website, you see that the `Fly` definition is a bit different than described in this section. That's because you'll be adding a new feature to the fly as a part of the collision-detection feature. For now, just look at the classes as they're currently defined.

Using a library is simplicity itself. Here's the `frogFly.html` file that puts these two elements together in a single game:

```
<!DOCTYPE HTML>
<html lang="en-US">
<head>
    <meta charset="UTF-8">
    <title>frogFly.html</title>
    <script type="text/javascript"
            src = "simpleGame.js">
    </script>
    <script type = "text/javascript"
            src = "frogLib.js"></script>
    <script type="text/javascript">
    var scene;
    var frog;
    var fly;
    var leaves;

    function init(){
        scene = new Scene();
        scene.setBG("green");
        frog = new Frog();
        fly = new Fly();
        leaves = new Sprite(scene, "leaves.png", 640,
            480);
        leaves.setSpeed(0);

        scene.start();
    } // end init

    function update(){
```

```
        scene.clear();
        frog.checkKeys();
        fly.wriggle();
        leaves.update();
        frog.update();
        fly.update();
    } // end update();

    </script>
</head>
<body onload = "init()">

</body>
</html>
```

This program doesn't introduce much that's new. It simply implements the elements defined in the library, according to these steps:

1. **Import the** `froglib.js` **library.**

   The `frogLib` file created in the last section is simply a JavaScript file. Import it in the same way you import the `simpleGame.js` file, with a separate `<script>` tag.

2. **Create the sprites.**

   The `leaves` sprite is just an ordinary sprite. Build the frog and fly just like you did before, even though they're defined in another file. (If the frog or fly doesn't get created, make sure you imported the library correctly.)

3. **Manage change.**

   The `update()` function takes responsibility for control of the game. This is where you manage all of the various sprite behaviors: Tell the frog to look for keystrokes (with the `frog.checkKeys()` method), and tell the fly to wriggle (with the `fly.wriggle()` method).

4. **Draw the sprites.**

   Once you've handled everything that caused the sprites to change, draw the sprites on the screen. Draw each sprite by invoking its `update()` method. Sprites are drawn in order, so anything you want to have in the background should be drawn before items that will display in front. (For example, the frog will appear on top of the background, so the frog should be drawn after the background on each screen update.)

You can see the frog and the fly cavorting on the screen together in Figure 7-4, but really you should check out the website for the real thing.

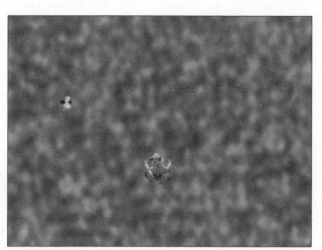

Figure 7-4:
Now the
frog and the
fly can play
together.

When Sprites Collide

The basic functionality is in place, but the interesting part of the game happens when the frog collides with the fly. It's relatively easy to add collision-detection to the game because the sprite object has a `collidesWith()` method. Of course, you need something to happen when two things collide.

For this game, you want two things to happen when the frog and the fly collide:

✔ **You want to play a satisfied "ribbit" sound.**

Nothing is tastier than a crunchy fly, so you should play some sort of sound to indicate the frog has touched the fly. This is useful for player feedback, so the player knows something happened.

✔ **You want to move the fly to a new place.**

Normally after a collision, you either destroy one of the objects or move it to a new spot. In this case, you move the fly to a new, random position on the screen.

The `collision.html` page illustrates these new features. (Note that I'm not providing a screen shot because it looks just like `frogFly.html`. To see, and hear, the new behavior, you need to run it from my website or on your own machine.)

Collisions apply to the frog and the fly

It's time to add collisions and sound effects to the frog and fly game. For the most part, it's pretty straightforward. Here's the code:

```
<!DOCTYPE HTML>
<html lang="en-US">
<head>
    <meta charset="UTF-8">
    <title>collision.html</title>
    <script type="text/javascript"
            src = "simpleGame.js">
    </script>
    <script type = "text/javascript"
            src = "frogLib.js"></script>
    <script type="text/javascript">
        var scene;
        var frog;
        var fly;
        var leaves;
        var ribbitMP3;
        var ribbitOGG;

        function init(){
            scene = new Scene();
            scene.setBG("green");
            frog = new Frog();
            fly = new Fly();
            leaves = new Sprite(scene, "leaves.png", 640,
            480);
            leaves.setSpeed(0);
            ribbitMP3 = new Sound("ribbit.mp3");
            ribbitOGG = new Sound("ribbit.ogg");

            scene.start();
        } // end init

        function update(){
            scene.clear();
            frog.checkKeys();
            fly.wriggle();
            checkCollisions();
            leaves.update();
            frog.update();
            fly.update();
        } // end update();

        function checkCollisions(){
            if (frog.collidesWith(fly)){
                ribbitMP3.play();
                ribbitOGG.play();
```

```
                fly.reset();
            } // end if
        } // end checkCollisions

    </script>

</head>
<body onload = "init()">
</body>
</html>
```

For the most part, it's just a matter of incorporating sound effects and collision-detection to the frog and fly game. Look back over the code, and you'll see that the new elements are highlighted. Here are the steps:

1. **Add a sound effect.**

   You create a `ribbit` sound and save it in both Ogg and MP3 formats. You then create a `Sound` object for each format. Refer to Chapter 6 if you need a refresher on building `Sound` objects.

2. **Make a** `checkCollisions()` **function.**

   The `checkCollisions()` function will (you're way ahead of me here) check for collisions.

3. **Play the ribbit sound when the frog touches the fly.**

   In the collision code, play both sound effects. (Remember, you created two versions to have maximum browser coverage.)

4. **Reset the fly on a collision.**

   Look to the next section for an explanation of the `fly.reset()` method.

Resetting the fly — on the fly

When two objects collide, it often means something important. You'll often want to change the score, play a sound, reduce the number of lives, or something. However, if those objects are moving slowly, they could overlap for multiple turns. Generally, game programmers avoid this by applying a simple rule: *When two things collide, move or kill one of them.* For this particular application, the fly gets eaten by the frog, and a new fly appears. Of course, that's just an illusion. The same fly gets recycled and simply appears in a new space.

You can see the `fly.reset()` method call in the `update()` function, but now you need to add that method to the fly's definition in `frogLib.js`. Take a look at the final version of the `Fly` class:

```
function Fly(){
    tFly = new Sprite(scene, "fly.png", 20, 20);
    tFly.setSpeed(10);
    tFly.wriggle = function(){
        //change direction by some random amount
        newDir = (Math.random() * 90) - 45;
        this.changeAngleBy(newDir);
    } // end wriggle

    tFly.reset = function(){
        //set new random position
        newX = Math.random() * this.cWidth;
        newY = Math.random() * this.cHeight;
        this.setPosition(newX, newY);
    } // end reset

    tFly.reset();

    return tFly;
} // end Fly
```

The `reset()` method applies a new random position to the fly. Here's how it works:

1. **Generate a random number between 0 and 1.**

   The `Math.random()` function built into JavaScript does this.

2. **Multiply that value by the canvas width.**

   The canvas width is stored in each sprite's `cWidth` property.

3. **Set the sprite's x value to the resulting random number.**

   This generates a random value between 0 and the width of the screen.

4. **Repeat for the y value.**

   Calculate a new Y position in the same way, but this time multiply by the sprite's `cHeight` property.

5. **Reset the temporary fly before returning it.**

   If you call the fly's `reset()` method before returning it, you guarantee that the fly begins in a random position.

Working with Multiple Flies

The game is coming along nicely, but it would be nice to have more than one fly. That will make the game a bit more exciting.

What good are bugs if you can't be infested with them? Figure 7-5 shows the latest version of the game, with three flies at a time.

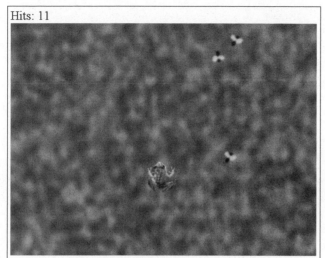

Hits: 11

Figure 7-5:
Now there
are three
flies zipping
around!

Because the game was created with object-oriented principles, it's quite easy to add multiple flies. Here's the code (with the new bits highlighted, as usual).

```
<!DOCTYPE HTML>
<html lang="en-US">
<head>
    <meta charset="UTF-8">
    <title>multiFlies.html</title>
    <script type="text/javascript"
            src = "simpleGame.js">
    </script>
    <script type = "text/javascript"
            src = "frogLib.js"></script>
    <script type="text/javascript">
        var scene;
        var frog;
        var flies;
        var leaves;
        var scoreBoard;
        var hits;
        var ribbitMP3;
        var ribbitOGG;
        //var fly;
        var NUMFLIES = 3;

        function init(){
            scoreBoard = document.
          getElementById("scoreBoard");
            hits = 0;
            scene = new Scene();
            scene.setBG("green");
```

```
        frog = new Frog();
        setupFlies();
        leaves = new Sprite(scene, "leaves.png", 640,
    480);
        leaves.setSpeed(0);
        ribbitMP3 = new Sound("ribbit.mp3");
        ribbitOGG = new Sound("ribbit.ogg");
        scene.start();
    } // end init

    function update(){
        scene.clear();
        frog.checkKeys();
        leaves.update();
        for (i = 0; i < NUMFLIES; i++){
          flies[i].wriggle();
          checkCollisions(i);
          flies[i].update();
        } // end for loop
        frog.update();
    } // end update();

    function setupFlies(){
        flies = new Array(NUMFLIES);
        for (i = 0; i < NUMFLIES; i++){
          flies[i] = new Fly();
        } // end for
    } // end setupFlies

    function checkCollisions(flyNum){
        if (frog.collidesWith(flies[flyNum])){
            flies[flyNum].reset();
            ribbitMP3.play();
            ribbitOGG.play();
            updateScore();
        } // end if
    } // end checkCollisions

    function updateScore(){
        //update the scoreboard
        hits += 1;
        scoreBoard.innerHTML = "Hits: " + hits
    } // end updateScore

    </script>

</head>
<body onload = "init()">
    <div id = "scoreBoard">Hits: 0</div>
</body>
</html>
```

Essentially, you turn a single fly into an array of flies. Every time you would have done something with a single fly, you iterate through the array of flies. Here are the highlights:

1. **Change the** `fly` **variable so it's now called** `flies`.

   Rather than a single `fly` variable, you'll be working with an array of `flies`.

2. **Create a** NUMFLIES **constant.**

   Store the number of flies in a special variable called NUMFLIES. This tracks the number of flies in the game. You can easily change this value to make the game harder or easier. Note that the value of NUMFLIES isn't expected to change during a single run of the game, so you put it all in uppercase to indicate it's a constant.

3. **Add a** `hits` **variable and a** `scoreboard` div.

   This variable will keep track of the number of fly-frog collisions. There's a corresponding `div`, which will display the score.

4. **Set up the flies.**

   The `setupFlies()` function runs through a loop NUMFLIES times. Each time through the loop, it creates a fly and appends it to the `numFlies` array:

```
function setupFlies(){
    flies = new Array(NUMFLIES);
    for (i = 0; i < NUMFLIES; i++){
      flies[i] = new Fly();
    } // end for
} // end setupFlies
```

5. **Modify the** `update()` **function.**

   Now that you have multiple flies, you need to make sure you update each element of the `flies` array. Again, use a `for` loop to go through the array. For each fly in the array, call its `wriggle()` method, check for collisions with the frog, and update:

```
function update(){
    scene.clear();
    frog.checkKeys();
    leaves.update();
    for (i = 0; i < NUMFLIES; i++){
      flies[i].wriggle();
      checkCollisions(i);
      flies[i].update();
    } // end for loop
    frog.update();
} // end update();
```

6. Modify the `checkCollisions()` **function.**

You need to make some minor changes to `checkCollisions` so it can check for a collision between the frog and the current fly. Simply pass a fly number to the function and use that index to make the collision check:

```
function checkCollisions(flyNum){
    if (frog.collidesWith(flies[flyNum])){
        flies[flyNum].reset();
        ribbit.play();
        updateScore();
    } // end if
} // end checkCollisions
```

7. Update the scoreboard.

The last step is to update the scoreboard. All this requires is to increment the number of hits and then change the `scoreboard` `div` to reflect the new number of hits:

```
function updateScore(){
    //update the scoreboard
    hits += 1;
    scoreBoard.innerHTML = "Hits: " + hits
} // end updateScore
```

Adding the Final Touches

The game is nearly complete, but it needs a couple more features. There's no real sense of urgency because the game just goes on forever. You need some sort of ending state. The simplest to implement is a basic timer. After a predetermined length of time (ten seconds in the test version, but longer in a production version of the game), the game will stop. Of course, you also need a way to restart the game. Both of these are relatively easy to add.

```
<!DOCTYPE HTML>
<html lang="en-US">
<head>
    <meta charset="UTF-8">
    <title>timing.html</title>
    <style type="text/css">
        #reset {
            position: absolute;
            left: 150px;
            top: 300px;
        }
    </style>
    <script type="text/javascript"
            src = "simpleGame.js">
```

```
</script>
<script type = "text/javascript"
        src = "frogLib.js"></script>
<script type="text/javascript">
    var scene;
    var frog;
    var flies;
    var leaves;
    var ribbitMP3;
    var ribbitOGG;
    var scoreBoard;
    var hits;
    var NUMFLIES = 3;
    var MAXTIME = 10;
    var timer;
    var time;

    function init(){
        scoreBoard = document.
      getElementById("scoreBoard");
        hits = 0;
        timer = new Timer();
        scene = new Scene();
        scene.setBG("green");
        frog = new Frog();
        leaves = new Sprite(scene, "leaves.png", 640,
      480);
        leaves.setSpeed(0);
        ribbitMP3 = new Sound("ribbit.mp3");
        ribbitOGG = new Sound("ribbit.ogg");

        setupFlies();
        scene.start();
    } // end init

    function update(){
        scene.clear();
        checkTime();
        frog.checkKeys();
        leaves.update();
        for (i = 0; i < NUMFLIES; i++){
          flies[i].wriggle();
          checkCollisions(i);
          flies[i].update();
        } // end for loop
        frog.update();
    } // end update();

    function setupFlies(){
        flies = new Array(NUMFLIES);
        for (i = 0; i < NUMFLIES; i++){
```

```
                    flies[i] = new Fly();
                } // end for
            } // end setupFlies

            function checkCollisions(flyNum){
                if (frog.collidesWith(flies[flyNum])){
                    flies[flyNum].reset();
                    ribbitMP3.play();
                    ribbitOGG.play();
                    hits += 1;
                    updateScore();
                } // end if
            } // end checkCollisions

            function updateScore(){
                //update the scoreboard
                scoreBoard.innerHTML = "Hits: " + hits + ".
              Time: " + time;
            } // end updateScore

            function checkTime(){
                time = timer.getElapsedTime();
                if (time > MAXTIME){
                    scene.stop();
                } // end if
                updateScore();

            } // end checkTime

            function restart(){
                document.location.href = "";
            } // end restart

        </script>
</head>
<body onload = "init()">
    <div id = "scoreBoard">Hits: 0</div>
    <div id = "reset">
        <button type = "button"
                onclick = "restart()">
            Play again
        </button>
    </div>
</body>

</html>
```

Figure 7-6 illustrates the final version of the program with the timer and the Play Again button.

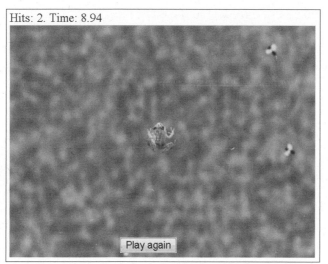

Hits: 2. Time: 8.94

Play again

Figure 7-6:
Now the
game is
ready to
play.

Adding the timer

The timer is easy to add. Refer to Chapter 6 if you need a refresher on
how timers work in the simpleGame engine. This timer will actually do
something, though. When the timer reaches a certain limit (ten seconds at
first) the game will automatically end.

Here's the process:

1. **Create a** timer **variable.**

   Use a variable to hold the timer object.

2. **Build a** MAXTIME **constant to determine the game time.**

   Constants make your code easier to read and modify. The MAXTIME constant indicates the length of the game in seconds.

3. **Initialize the timer.**

   In the init() function, create your timer.

4. **Check the time on every frame.**

   In the update() method, call the checkTime() method every frame.

5. **In** checkTime(), **get the elapsed time.**

   Use the timer's getElapsedTime() method to see how much time has
   passed since the game began.

6. **If the time has expired, stop the main loop.**

   The `Scene` object has a `stop()` method. Invoke this method to stop all gameplay. The game screen and objects will still be visible, but the event loop will no longer happen.

Resetting the game

Of course, if the game can stop, you need a way to restart it. The easiest way is to use a dirty trick. Because the game is in a web page, all you have to do is refresh the web page in the browser, and the game will restart. You can cause the browser to refresh in JavaScript by setting the `document.location.href` property to the value `""`. This will effectively reload the current page in the browser, restarting the game in the process. It's not hard to implement this feature.

1. **Add a button to your page.**

   Use an ordinary HTML button to trigger the reset. If you want, you can position the button with CSS to appear exactly where you want it to be. (Use `position: absolute` along with the `left` and `top` attributes to set the position of your button.)

2. **Tell the button to call the** `restart()` **function.**

   Every button has an `onclick` attribute. Use this to determine a JavaScript function to run when the button is clicked. In this case, you call the `restart()` function.

3. **Build a** `restart()` **function.**

   Of course, if you're going to call a `restart()` function, you need to create it.

4. **Reload the current document.**

   The easiest way to restart a JavaScript program is to reload the current page in the browser. This will not only reload the HTML code but also the JavaScript, starting all the code over from the beginning.

5. **Set** `document.location.href` **to nothing.**

   If you set the `document.location.href` attribute to the empty string (`""`) you will in effect reload the current page. This is the easiest way to restart the game.

Part III
Diving Deeper

The 5th Wave   By Rich Tennant

"I've tried every other way of debugging it. Let's just throw the chicken bones and see what happens."

In this part . . .

This part takes you into more advanced ideas in game programming. Once the basics are out of the way, you'll want to know how to make more interesting motion and how to take advantage of mobile devices.

Chapter 8 is all about motion and animation. It explains how useful basic physics concepts can be and uses a simple physics model to generate interesting behavior. It explains how to move a spacecraft, how to add drag and drifting behavior to vehicles, how to manage jumping and falling, how to create realistic orbital mechanics, how to fire bullets and other projectiles, and how to build a multi-image animation from a sprite sheet.

Chapter 9 demonstrates the mobile features of the `simpleGame` library. Use this chapter to convert your games to phone and tablet wonders. You find out how to adjust the size and position of your game scene for various mobile devices. You create full-screen games with custom icons (and the ability to be run off-line). You add buttons for input, and you learn how to use the touch screen to create a virtual joystick. Finally, you explore how to use your mobile device's accelerometer to read tilt input.

Chapter 10 is the documentation for the `simpleGame` library. Use this chapter to see all the objects provided by the library and every feature presented by each object.

Chapter 8

Motion and Animation

. . . .

In This Chapter

▶ Understanding the basic physics principles used in gaming

▶ Adding a force vector to your sprites

▶ Using a force vector for space simulation

▶ Adding drag and skidding behavior

▶ Working with gravity

▶ Building multi-image animations

. . . .

S prites move around on the screen. That's the central part of most games. But if you've looked at Chapters 6 and 7, you've seen that the sprite motion was somewhat simplistic in those chapters. Now you find out how to add more zip to your sprites. You make sprites accelerate smoothly, slow down with drag, skid around corners, and fall off cliffs.

All of these fun effects are made possible by understanding a little about how things move in the real world. In school, they called that *physics class*. Don't worry, though. This will be the most fun you've ever had with physics. We make missiles.

Physics — Even More Fun Than You Remember

In prior chapters, I explain how to build a game, how sprites and scenes work together, and how to use sprites to make all your game elements. The simpleGame.js library supports a nice form of motion using speed and direction, but often you will want more direct control of motion. When you understand a little more about how objects move in the real world, you will have a head start on making more interesting motion in your games. Understanding how real objects move will give you access to realistic acceleration, skidding, space-based motion, and gravity effects. These can add a great deal of interest to your games.

Newton without all the figs

Sir Isaac Newton would have been a terrific game programmer. He came up with a number of observations about how things move. These observations have become immortalized as *Newton's Laws of Motion*. Newton's laws do a pretty good job of describing how things move, and if you understand them, you can create a reasonable approximation of real-world motion. Of course, being an eighteenth-century scholar, Newton was a bit stuffy. I present my own version of Newton's laws of motion:

✔ **If it's moving, it's moving. If it ain't, it ain't.**

A more official version of Newton's first law goes like this: "An object in motion stays in motion, and an object at rest stays at rest." If an object is not moving, it won't start until some kind of force causes it to move. If it's currently moving, it will stay moving unless some kind of force stops it. If a ball is rolling, it will continue rolling, but (at least on earth) it will eventually stop because it will encounter wind resistance and rolling resistance. In a game, we're constantly making things start and stop moving, but so far it's been done in an unrealistic manner. Newton's first law explains that you need force to get motion.

✔ **If you want it to go farther, kick it harder.**

My version has a certain style, but Newton expressed this idea in a math formula ($f = ma$). What it really means is that there is a simple mathematical relationship between the mass (m) of an object, the force (f) applied to that object, and the acceleration (a) of the object. If you know any two variables, you can do a little algebraic magic to find the third. This second law tells how much force you need to get the motion you want (or how much motion you'll get with a given amount of force).

✔ **When you throw a ball, the ball throws you.**

Newton's third law is really useful for engineers because it explains *how* to apply a force. His original version goes something like this: "For every action, there's an equal and opposite reaction." Imagine you're in an art museum standing on a skateboard and holding a bowling ball. (I don't know how you got into this situation. Just go with me here.) If you throw the bowling ball from the front of the skateboard, a number of interesting things will happen. The ball will move forward, but you and the skateboard will move backward. Mayhem will ensue until the big guys with no sense of humor make you leave the museum. Newton predicted that applying a force in one direction automatically applies a force in the opposite direction. Presumably he did not destroy any art galleries in the process. This is useful to game programmers because it helps us see the relationship between applying a force and seeing the results.

Phuzzy physics

Don't panic. I'm not going to make you start doing all kinds of calculations. The main thing to get here is how physics relates to the gaming world. In the simpleGame library, I've provided a simple kind of motion that's really easy to understand. If you've gone through some of the earlier chapters, you've already used this basic mechanism. Every object can have a position, a speed, and a direction. This is easy to work with, but it's a little simplistic. A lot of motion doesn't work like that: Cars skid sideways, gravity pulls helicopters downward, and spacecraft often travel backward. You don't have to get all the math exactly right, but you need to understand the big ideas.

In a game, you can set an object's position to whatever you want. It's perfectly reasonable to set an object's position directly, and the setPosition() method does exactly that. However, it isn't satisfying.

In the real world, you can never actually set the position of anything. Instead, the object has a position, which is modified by a *motion vector*. The motion vector is the combination of speed and direction that determines how an object is currently moving. In the simpleGame library, you can also manage the motion vector. The setSpeed() and setAngle() methods directly set the speed and angle.

But this is also unrealistic. In the real world, you can't directly change the motion, either. Instead, you have to apply a *force vector*. A force vector influences the motion vector, which in turn influences the position. To get more realistic motion, you don't directly set position or motion; instead, you use force vectors to indirectly change the motion, which will change the position.

All of the interesting motion techniques in this chapter use this technique. Rather than changing the speed and direction directly, they apply a force vector to the sprite, which changes the sprite's motion. It's a really powerful idea.

The Sprite object has a function called addVector(degrees, speed).

This function adds a force vector to the current object in the specified direction and speed. The addVector() function is the secret to all the interesting motion effects. It expects an angle in degrees and a force in pixels per frame as parameters.

Lost in Space

Take a look at space.html. This simple game (shown in Figure 8-1) utilizes the control scheme made famous in the classic games *Asteroids* and *Spacewar!* (Though *Asteroids* is better-known, *Spacewar!* is by far the earlier and more influential game.)

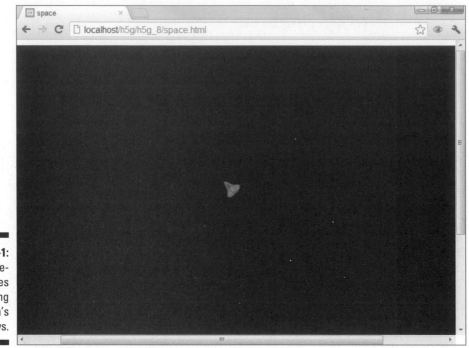

Figure 8-1:
The space-
ship moves
following
Newton's
laws.

Like all the examples in this chapter, the motion of the objects is the interesting thing, so a static screen shot is simply not adequate. You'll need to see the
example on my website (`www.aharrisbooks.net`) to get the full experience.

Becoming a space cadet

The ship is controlled by the arrow keys, but Newton's effect is easier to see
in space than on the ground (no pesky drag forces to get in the way). The left-
and right-arrow keys rotate the ship, but they do not affect the ship's motion.
The up arrow fires a rocket, which adds a force vector in the direction the
ship is currently facing.

Here's the code:

```html
<!DOCTYPE HTML>
<html lang="en-US">
<head>
    <meta charset="UTF-8">
    <title>space</title>
    <script type="text/javascript"
            src = "simpleGame.js"></script>
    <script type="text/javascript">
```

```
        var ship;
        var game;

        function Ship(){
            tShip = new Sprite(game, "ship.png", 25, 25);
            tShip.setSpeed(3);
            tShip.checkKeys = function(){
                if (keysDown[K_LEFT]){
                    this.changeImgAngleBy(-5);
                }
                if (keysDown[K_RIGHT]){
                    this.changeImgAngleBy(5);
                }
                if (keysDown[K_UP]){
                    this.addVector(this.getImgAngle(), .1);
                }
            } // end function
            return tShip;
        } // object definition

        function init(){
            game = new Scene();
            ship = new Ship();
            game.setBG("black");

            game.start();
        } // end init

        function update(){
            game.clear();
            ship.checkKeys();
            ship.update();
        } // end update

        </script>
    </head>
    <body onload = "init()">

    </body>
</html>
```

Building the space simulation

This example is similar to motion examples described in Chapters 6 and 7. Here's the rundown:

1. **Begin the example in the normal way.**

   Like most `simpleGame` demos, begin with a sprite and a scene. Because the ship will have a custom method, you make it a unique object. Check Chapter 6 if you need a refresher on how to build a custom object.

2. **Give the ship a** `checkKeys()` **method.**

   The `checkKeys()` method looks for key presses and changes the ship's behavior accordingly.

3. **Change the image angle.**

   A sprite actually has two distinct angles. It can have an angle that it's pointing (called the `imgAngle` in `simpleGame`) and the angle it's moving (called the `moveAngle`). When you change the angle (as you do in many examples throughout the book), you're changing both the movement and the image angles on the assumption that the object will simply travel in the direction it's facing. For simple examples this is fine, but many kinds of motion require decoupling the image and motion angles. The `changeImgAngleBy()` method allows you to change the direction the image is pointing without changing the motion angle. (There is a `changeMotionAngle()` method, too, but it isn't used very often.)

4. **Add a force vector to simulate thrust.**

   When the user presses the up arrow, the ship fires its main rockets. This adds a small force vector in the direction the ship is currently facing. Use the `getImgAngle()` method to determine the direction the ship is currently facing, and use this value to specify where the force should be added. Because this code is happening in the animation loop and is amplified as the arrow key is held down, only a very small force is needed.

Don't Be a Drag — Adding Drag Effects

The vector addition principle can be useful in other ways. For one, it can lead to more accurate land-vehicle behavior. Imagine my car is stuck in a bad neighborhood in the middle of the night (again). I can't simply change the position of the car directly. I can't even change its motion. What I have to do instead is add a force. When I add force (by pushing the car while murmuring affectionately to this unreliable piece of transportation), I slowly add to the motion vector. Eventually, the car starts moving. If I stop applying force, it will eventually stop as wind resistance and rolling resistance slow the car down.

Drag racing

The `drag.html` example illustrated in Figure 8-2 shows a realistic car that accelerates slowly and slows to a stop as the accelerator (in this case, the up arrow) is released.

As before, you'll really need to see the program in action to appreciate its behavior.

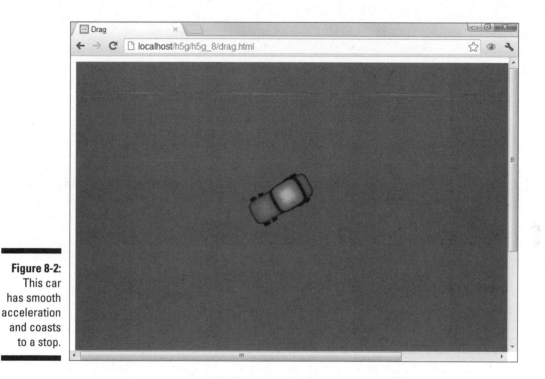

Figure 8-2:
This car
has smooth
acceleration
and coasts
to a stop.

Again, the code is probably familiar from Chapters 6 and 7:

```
<!DOCTYPE HTML>
<html lang="en-US">
<head>
    <meta charset="UTF-8">
    <title>Drag</title>
    <script type = "text/javascript"
            src = "simpleGame.js"></script>
    <script type="text/javascript">
    var game;
    var boat;

    function Car(){
        tCar = new Sprite(game, "car.png", 100, 50);

        tCar.checkKeys = function(){
            console.log(this.speed);
            if (keysDown[K_LEFT]){
                this.changeImgAngleBy(-5);
            }

            if (keysDown[K_RIGHT]){
```

```
                    this.changeImgAngleBy(5);
        }

        if (keysDown[K_UP]){
            this.addVector(this.imgAngle, 2);
        }

    //move in the current direction
        this.addVector(this.imgAngle, 2);
    } // end checkKeys

    tCar.checkDrag = function(){
        speed = this.getSpeed();
        speed *= .95;
        this.setSpeed(speed);
    } // end checkDrag

    return tCar;
} // end car def

function init(){
    game = new Scene();
    game.setBG("#666666");
    car = new Car();
    game.start();
} // end init

function update(){
    game.clear();

    car.checkKeys();
    car.checkDrag();
    car.update();
} // end update

</script>

</head>
<body onload = "init()">

</body>
</html>
```

Implementing drag

This example is similar to the critter app illustrated in Chapter 6, but this version uses a more realistic force-based motion. When the user presses the up arrow, the car builds up speed. If the user leaves the up arrow pressed, the car reaches a top speed naturally. When the user releases the up arrow, the car gradually slows and eventually stops. Force vectors are the key.

Here's how it works:

1. **Build a basic vehicle.**

   The starting place for this type of motion is very familiar if you've examined the other examples in this chapter. Create a custom sprite with a `checkKeys()` method, and check for all the normal arrow keys. The code for checking left and right arrows is exactly what you expect.

2. **Move forward with a force vector.**

   The code for moving forward is slightly different. Rather than simply modifying the speed directly, apply a force in the car's current direction. Use the sprite's `getImgAngle()` method to determine which direction the car is pointing, and add a small force in that direction.

3. **Create a `checkDrag()` method.**

   Cars don't just keep going without power. Wind and ground resistance will slow them down, and eventually they will stop. Simulate the various drag forces by adding a `checkDrag()` method to your object.

4. **Multiply the speed by a drag factor.**

   For this example, the various drag forces will rob the car of 5 percent of its speed every frame. Remember that the game is running at 20 frames per second, so the drag force is quite substantial. You can achieve the drag effect in many ways (add a force vector opposite the car's direction, for example), but the easiest way is to multiply the car's speed by some value smaller than 1.

5. **No brakes!**

   You can add brakes, but I didn't bother. What self-respecting arcade car has brakes? Seriously, you might want to add a down-arrow input, but it shouldn't be necessary because the car will slow down on its own.

6. **Season to taste.**

   This example provides a rough outline, but you can modify a number of values to get exactly the car performance you want. You can simulate a more powerful engine (or a smaller mass) by increasing the force vector when you press the accelerator. You can simulate a more responsive suspension by altering the turning rate if the user presses the right or left arrows. You can also simulate a more or less efficient car by modifying the drag ratio. Right now, the car turns at any speed, but you can prevent left- and right-arrow inputs if the car is below a certain speed.

Do You Catch My Drift?

You can use force vectors in another interesting way. Many racing games include skidding or drifting mechanisms. Getting this behavior exactly right requires very sophisticated mathematics, but you can make a reasonable approximation of this behavior without too much effort. Take a look at `drift.html`, shown in Figure 8-3.

I've said it for every example in this chapter: This image is not enough. You really need to see this as a working program because it's really cool. As you move the boat around on the screen, the boat drifts and skids. It's really fun to play with.

Burning virtual rubber

To get a simple drifting behavior, simply add a small force vector (I started with 5 percent of the boat's current speed) in the boat's current direction regardless of whether the user is currently pressing the accelerator.

Figure 8-3:
This boat has a realistic drifting mechanism.

This technique is a compromise between the space-based motion (where the force vector is added only when the accelerator is pressed) and standard car behavior (where the direction of travel is always following the vehicle's nose). Each frame has a little of each behavior.

Here's the code:

```
<!DOCTYPE HTML>
<html lang="en-US">
<head>
    <meta charset="UTF-8">
    <title>drift.html</title>
    <script type = "text/javascript"
            src = "simpleGame.js"></script>
    <script type="text/javascript">
    var game;
    var boat;

    function Boat(){
        tBoat = new Sprite(game, "boat.png", 100, 50);

        tBoat.checkKeys = function(){
            console.log(this.speed);
            if (keysDown[K_LEFT]){
                this.changeImgAngleBy(-5);
            }

            if (keysDown[K_RIGHT]){
                this.changeImgAngleBy(5);
            }

            if (keysDown[K_UP]){
                this.addVector(this.getImgAngle(), 2);
            }
            this.addVector(this.getImgAngle(), (this.speed
        / 20));
        } // end checkKeys

        tBoat.checkDrag = function(){
            speed = this.getSpeed();
            speed *= .95;
            this.setSpeed(speed);
        }
        return tBoat;
    }

    function init(){
        game = new Scene();
        game.setBG("#000066");
        boat = new Boat();
```

```
        game.start();
    } // end init

    function update(){
        game.clear();

        boat.checkKeys();
        boat.checkDrag();
        boat.update();
    }


    </script>
</head>
<body onload = "init()">

</body>
</html>
```

Adding drift to your sprites

There's really only one new line here. Most of the code is familiar from the other examples in this chapter.

1. **Build a standard vehicle model.**

   This time I made a boat, just to be different. The code is really the same as the car from the last example.

2. **Use a force vector for acceleration.**

   Again, you're manually controlling the speed, so the addVector() mechanism gives you great power. The acceleration force vector (used in the up-arrow key press) can be a literal value, but it doesn't need to be huge. Because you're actually going to be adding a second force vector, you might want to tone down the acceleration vector — but I didn't. More power!!! Muhaahaa!

3. **Add a small force vector every frame.**

   The primary force vector happens only when you accelerate, but a secondary smaller vector is added every frame. This vector goes in the direction the boat is currently facing. This small motion vector will simulate momentum. It's important that this force vector be a percentage of the speed rather than a literal value. If you always move forward one pixel, for example, the boat will never stop.

Recognizing the Gravity of the Situation

Yet another use of force vectors involves gravity. Gravity calculations have been a part of video games from the very beginning. There are actually two kinds of gravity to consider. In platform-style games, the player is close to a planet, and all gravity appears to pull everything straight down. (You calculate gravity differently in space, but that's covered in the section "Houston, We've Achieved Orbit" later in this chapter.)

When you know how to add acceleration vectors, platform-style gravity is actually easy to work with. Think of gravity as a constant force always pulling down a small amount every frame. To illustrate, take a look at `hoverCar.html` shown in Figure 8-4.

You know what I'm going to say. This example is no fun as an image in a book. You need to play with the example to see what's going on.

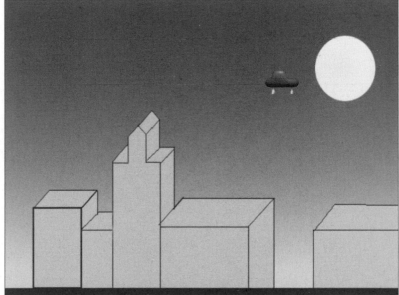

Figure 8-4:
If you press the up arrow, the car will fire rocket boosters and hover.

Adding rockets to your ride

This example has one other interesting feature. When you press the up arrow, the car image is changed to another image with flames. (I wish *my* car had booster rockets.)

The code for the `hoverCar` example is shown here in its entirety:

```html
<!DOCTYPE HTML>
<html lang="en-US">
<head>
    <meta charset="UTF-8">
    <title>hoverCar.html</title>
    <script type="text/javascript"
            src = "simpleGame.js"></script>
    <script type="text/javascript">
        var car;
        var city;
        var game;

        function Car(){
            tCar = new Sprite(game, "hoverCar.png", 70,
            50);
            tCar.setSpeed(0);
            tCar.hSpeed = 0

            tCar.checkKeys = function(){
                tCar.changeImage("hoverCar.png");
                if (keysDown[K_LEFT]){
                  this.hSpeed -= 1
                }

                if (keysDown[K_RIGHT]){
                  this.hSpeed += 1
                }

                if (keysDown[K_UP]){
                  this.addVector(0, .5);
                  this.changeImage("hoverCarThrust.png");
                }

                this.changeXby(this.hSpeed);
            } // end checkKeys

            tCar.checkGravity = function(){
                if (this.y > 580){
                    this.setPosition(this.x, 580);
                } else {
                    this.addVector(180, .1);
                } // end if
            } // end checkGravity

            return tCar;
        } // end car def

        function init(){
```

```
            game = new Scene();
            car = new Car();
            city = new Sprite(game, "city.png", 800, 600);
            city.setSpeed(0);
            city.setPosition(400, 300);

            game.start();
        } // end init

        function update(){
            game.clear();
            city.update();

            car.checkKeys();
            car.checkGravity();
            car.update();
        } // end update

    </script>
</head>
<body onload = "init()">
</body>
</html>
```

Use the force (vector), Luke

Gravity is actually pretty straightforward. It's simply a force vector. The other interesting parts of this example involve changing the horizontal motion without changing the car's image angle and adjusting the image to indicate the thruster. Here are the steps:

1. **Build two different images.**

   Use your image editor to build two different versions of the image. My two images are identical, except one has flames for the retro-rockets and the other does not.

2. **Build an ordinary sprite.**

   Like most vehicle sprites, you need a `checkKeys()` method. This one is set up in the ordinary way, but the behavior is a bit different.

3. **Set the image to default.**

   The default image has no thrusters. Use the `changeImage()` method to make this the default image. When the thrusters are turned on, the image will be changed.

4. **Use a variable to control horizontal speed.**

   I created the `hSpeed` variable to manage the horizontal speed of the car. I found this gave the performance I was looking for (easy forward and back motion with a lot of momentum).

5. **Set the left and right arrows to modify** `hSpeed`.

   The left and right arrow keys modify the `hSpeed` variable.

6. **Use** `changeXby` **to set the horizontal speed.**

   After checking all the keys, change the x value of the car to the current value of `hSpeed`.

7. **The up arrow adds a vector upward.**

   Use the now-infamous `addVector()` function to add a small force vector upward when the user presses the up arrow. Remember that 0 degrees is up. Play around with this value to get the amount of thrust you want for your game.

8. **Show the thrusters when the up** arrow **is pressed.**

   If the user is pressing the up arrow, you need to show the thrusters. Use the `changeImage()` method to set the sprite's image to the one with rocket thrusters.

9. **Build a** `checkGravity()` **method.**

   This method will be called every frame to compensate for gravity.

10. **Check to see if you're on the ground.**

    In this example, the ground is defined as a y value larger than 580.

11. **If you're not on the ground, add a gravity force vector.**

    Because it will accumulate, the gravity force vector needs to be pretty small. You'll need to balance the force of the gravity and the thrusters to get the behavior you want. If gravity is too strong, the thrusters won't work. If thrusters are too strong, the car simply flies into space.

Houston, We've Achieved Orbit

The kind of gravity described in the `hoverCar` example is fine when you're really close to a planet because when tiny things like people, cars, or buildings are interacting with huge things like planets, the world seems flat, and gravity always seems to be pulling down.

However, when you get into space, things become more complicated. A planet has a large gravitational pull that influences the smaller things moving around that planet.

Round and round she goes . . .

Play around with `orbit.html` (see Figure 8-5) to confirm that the orbit shown in this example acts like real-world orbits.

Orbits may seem difficult to program because they follow a very specific set of rules. Any orbit should have the following characteristics:

- ✔ **An orbit is actually an ellipse.** Orbits aren't perfect circles but are ellipses.

- ✔ **The planet is one focus of the ellipse.** As you may remember from math class, an ellipse is defined as a constant sum of radii from two points, called *foci.*

- ✔ **The distance from the planet predicts the speed.** When the ship is closer to the planet, it will move more quickly.

- ✔ **Accelerate on one side to influence the other.** Firing your thrusters in the current direction of travel moves the *opposite* side of the ellipse away from the planet. Firing against the direction of travel moves the opposite side of the ellipse closer to the planet.

- ✔ **Smaller orbits are faster than larger orbits.** This is an odd fact of space travel, but to speed up in orbit, you typically fire backward, bringing yourself into a tighter orbit that moves more quickly!

Figure 8-5:
Orbits follow very specific rules.

This may seem like a lot of rules that will be difficult to program, but it turns out to be really easy to generate a realistic orbit. Newton (there's that guy again; I *told* you he'd be an amazing game programmer) predicted exactly how it works in his famous law of universal gravitation. Newton's law is summarized in a somewhat dizzying formula, as shown in Figure 8-6.

$$f = \frac{m_1 * m_2}{d_2} G$$

Figure 8-6:
Newton's
law of
universal
gravitation.

f = force
m_1 = mass of object 1
m_2 = mass of object 2
d = distance between objects
G = gravitational constant

Decoding the alphabet soup

Newton's law can look a bit daunting, I know, but it's really easy to follow when you have the secret decoder ring that explains what all the variables mean. Here's what's happening:

- ✔ **It describes the length of a force vector.** Any two objects will exert some kind of gravitational force on each other. It is an attractive force, so the direction is simply the direction between the centers of the objects. The formula describes the strength of the force.

- ✔ ***f* is the force magnitude.** That is, it's the amount of force between the two objects.

- ✔ ***m1* is the mass of the first object.** For this example, the first object will be the planet. It will have a really big mass.

- ✔ ***m2* is the mass of the second object.** The second object is the space-ship, which will have a much smaller mass.

- ✔ ***d* is the distance between the objects.** It doesn't matter exactly how you measure the distance as long as you're consistent. Here, pixels are used.

- ✔ ***G* is a universal gravitational constant.** If you were doing real calculations, you would modify by a universal constant.

- ✔ **Divide the product of the masses by the distance squared.** The basic calculation is simply the product of the masses divided by the distance between the centers squared, and the whole thing is multiplied by the gravitational constant.

This isn't rocket science

Okay, it is, sort of, but it's *really* simplified. You should really take a genuine physics course to learn more about this fascinating topic. For the purposes of game programming, I'm going to simplify Newton's law in a couple of ways:

- ✔ **Mass is measured in an arbitrary unit.** It really doesn't matter exactly what the masses are as long as the planet is a lot heavier than the space-ship. I'm going with a mass of 1000 units for the planet and one unit for the ship. That gives pretty good behavior, but you can modify these values if you want.

- ✔ **Distance is measured in pixels.** This isn't genuine unit of distance measure, either. It doesn't matter how much space a real pixel represents as long as the simulation acts like you want it to.

- ✔ **You can skip *G*.** Because the mass and distance are already somewhat arbitrary, you don't really need to worry about *G* because you can just wrap that into the already-arbitrary masses without any problems.

- ✔ **Calculate in only one direction.** It's true that each object will exert a force on the other, but the ship's pull on the planet is immeasurably small, so you can just skip it in your code.

Writing the orbit code

Now you're ready to see some code. After you know what's going on, you'll be surprised at how easy the code is:

```
<!DOCTYPE HTML>
<html lang="en-US">
<head>
    <meta charset="UTF-8">
    <title>orbit</title>
    <script type="text/javascript"
            src = "simpleGame.js"></script>
    <script type="text/javascript">
    var ship;
    var planet;
    var game;

    function Ship(){
        tShip = new Sprite(game, "ship.png", 25, 25);
        tShip.setSpeed(3);
        tShip.setBoundAction(CONTINUE);
        tShip.setPosition(400, 200);
```

```
        tShip.checkKeys = function(){
            if (keysDown[K_LEFT]){
                this.changeImgAngleBy(-5);
            }
            if (keysDown[K_RIGHT]){
                this.changeImgAngleBy(5);
            }
            if (keysDown[K_UP]){
                this.addVector(this.getImgAngle(), .1);
            }
        } // end function
        return tShip;
    } // end object definition

    function init(){
        game = new Scene();
        ship = new Ship();
        planet = new Sprite(game, "planet.png", 50, 50);
        planet.setSpeed(0);
        planet.setPosition(400, 300);

        game.setBG("black");

        game.start();
    } // end init

    function update(){
        game.clear();
        ship.checkKeys();
        checkGravity();
        planet.update();
        ship.update();
    } // end update

    function checkGravity(){
        //checks gravity pull of planet on ship
        PLANET_MASS = 1000;
        SHIP_MASS = 1;
        dist = ship.distanceTo(planet);
        dir = planet.angleTo(ship);
        force = (PLANET_MASS * SHIP_MASS) / (dist * dist);
        ship.addVector(dir, force);
    } // end checkGravity

    </script>
</head>
<body onload = "init()">

</body>
</html>
```

This example begins with `space.html`. In fact, I copied that program and used it as a starting place for this one because the basic behavior is the same. Here's how I modified the space program to account for orbital gravity:

1. **Change the ship's** `boundAction` **to** `CONTINUE`.

   The default wrap behavior will be weird when you're looking at orbits. This is a good place to allow the ship to wander on forever. You might lose your ship altogether, but space travel is a lonely business.

2. **Add a planet sprite.**

   This is a pretty simple sprite. It's just a picture of a planet, with speed set to zero.

3. **Create a** `checkGravity` **function.**

   This function will calculate the planet's gravitational pull on the ship.

4. **Determine the masses of the two objects.**

   Through careful scientific measurement, I totally made up the mass of my planet and my ship. I stored the masses in capitalized variables to indicate they should be considered constant values.

5. **Calculate the distance between the objects.**

   Fortunately, `simpleGame` provides a really handy `distanceTo()` method for exactly this purpose.

6. **Determine the direction between the two objects.**

   Once again, `simpleGame` makes this easy because each sprite has an `angleTo()` method. Note that if the ship seems to be thrown away from the planet, you may have the wrong order. Determine the direction from the planet to the ship.

7. **Calculate the force magnitude.**

   Use the handy-dandy formula to figure out how strong the force pulling the ship to the planet is.

8. **Add a force vector to the ship.**

   Now just use the `addVector()` method to add the calculated force vector to the ship.

That's all there is to it. Amazingly enough, this simple calculation does all the real work, and you'll find that the orbits are strikingly realistic.

Although the math is simplified, there is still a lot of math going on here. If you want to be a game programmer, this is just the beginning of the math you'll need. For example, you may wonder how I figured the distance between the objects in `simpleGame` (I used the Pythagorean theorem) or how I calculated the angle between them (I used the arc-tangent from trigonometry).

The `simpleGame` library takes care of a lot of the math for you (you're welcome), but eventually you'll need to be able to do it yourself. If you've ever asked your math teacher when you would ever use math, I've got an answer. Today's a good day to start. You can't make games without math, but our math is fun because we blow virtual stuff up.

Does This Car Come with a Missile Launcher?

Normal car dealerships are touchy about installing weaponry in your ride, but that's exactly why we became game programmers. If I want missiles in my mini-van, I'll have missiles (at least in the virtual minivan). Lots of video games involve shooting, and that's a pretty easy effect to add. The `missile. html` example illustrated in Figure 8-7 shows how it works.

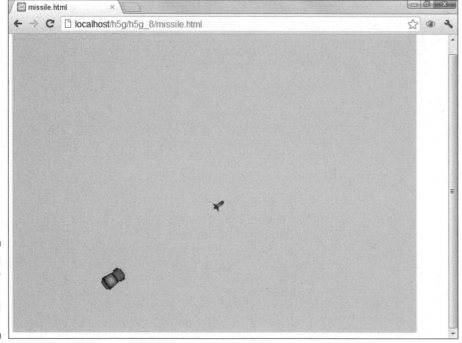

Figure 8-7: Now my car fires missiles. It's about time.

Projectiles in a nutshell

Missiles, bullets, and other projectiles are pretty easy to work with. Here are a few ideas to keep in mind:

- **The projectile is a sprite.** Make a new sprite for the projectile. You can make it a simple dot, or (as I did) draw a complete missile.

- **Make a custom sprite for the missile.** The missile will need some methods, so you might as well make it a custom sprite.

- **Missiles die when they leave the screen.** The easiest way to get this behavior is to set the missile's boundAction to DIE.

- **Add a fire() method.** The fire() method will activate when the missile is fired.

- **Reuse the same missile over and over.** Old missiles never die. They are just hidden and reused when the user shoots again. When a missile hits something, hide the missile. That will make it invisible and impervious to collisions.

It's time to launch the missiles

The code for missile.html is like much of the standard car code you've seen:

```
<!DOCTYPE HTML>
<html lang="en-US">
<head>
    <meta charset="UTF-8">
    <title>missile.html</title>
    <script type="text/javascript"
            src = "simpleGame.js"></script>
    <script type="text/javascript">
        var game;
        var car;
        var missile;

        function Car(){
            tCar = new Sprite(game, "car.png", 50, 30);
            tCar.setSpeed(3);
            tCar.setAngle(135);

            tCar.checkKeys = function(){
                if (keysDown[K_LEFT]){
                    this.turnBy(-5);
```

```
                            }
                            if (keysDown[K_RIGHT]){
                                this.turnBy(5);
                            }
                            if (keysDown[K_SPACE]){
                                missile.fire();
                            }
                    } // end checkKeys

                    return tCar;
                } // end car def

            function Missile(){
                tMissile = new Sprite(game, "missile.png", 30,20);
                tMissile.hide();

                tMissile.fire = function(){
                    this.show();
                    tMissile.setSpeed(15);
                    this.setBoundAction(DIE);
                    this.setPosition(car.x, car.y);
                    this.setAngle(car.getImgAngle());
                    this.setImage("missile.png");
                    this.setSpeed(15);
                } // end fire

                return tMissile;
            } // end missile def

            function init(){
                game = new Scene();
                car = new Car();
                missile = new Missile();
                game.start();
            } // end init

            function update(){
                game.clear();

                car.checkKeys();
                car.update();
                missile.update();
            } // end update

        </script>
    </head>
    <body onload = "init()">

    </body>
</html>
```

Projectiles are lots of fun to build, and they aren't very difficult, as shown here:

1. **Build a normal sprite to launch the projectile.**

   This isn't absolutely necessary, but normally a bullet will be fired from a gun, an arrow will be fired from a bow, and a nuclear banana rocket will be fired from whatever vehicle has that sort of thing. (I want one.)

2. **The projectile will be its own sprite.**

   The projectile works just like an ordinary sprite, but it will be created and destroyed dynamically.

3. **Add a trigger to fire the missile.**

   In my game, the spacebar fires the missile. Because my car will launch the missile, I put the trigger code in the car's `checkKeys` method.

4. **Set the missile to be hidden by default.**

   The missile is always around, but it's hidden offstage when it isn't needed. If you invoke a sprite's `hide()` method, that sprite will still be in memory, but it won't be drawn, and it won't trigger any collisions.

5. **Create a `fire()` method for the missile.**

   The missile is sitting around waiting to be activated. The `fire()` method springs the missile into action.

6. **Make the projectile visible.**

   The `show()` method is the opposite of `hide()`. It causes a sprite to be visible and trigger collisions.

7. **Give the missile a quick initial speed.**

   As you know, missiles are normally fast.

8. **Hide the missile when it hits the edge.**

   When the missile hits the edge of the screen, it needs to be hidden. Setting the missile's `boundAction` to `DIE` will make this behavior automatic.

9. **Hide the missile if it hits anything else.**

   This simple example doesn't have any other objects, but if the missile collides with something else, invoke its `hide()` method to simulate the missile being destroyed on contact.

After you have the ordinary missile behavior working, you can try a number of interesting variations:

- **Add gravity to the missiles.** If it's a side scroller, add a gravitational force to your missiles for a worm-like effect. See the `hoverCar.html` example earlier in this chapter for details.

✔ **Add other physics to missiles.** You can make the missiles have drag like any other sprite. See the `drag.html` example earlier in this chapter for more details.

✔ **Make a smart missile.** Use the `angleTo` method to determine the angle between a missile and a target, and turn the missile toward the target on every frame. This will simulate a smart missile that never misses. (A great power-up, but it makes the game too easy if you have too many.)

✔ **Make a not-so-smart missile.** If the enemy is firing a missile at the player, you don't want it quite so smart. You can do so in a few ways. First, make the missile as smart as you want but slow enough that it can be outrun. Second, put barriers that can destroy the missile in the way. Third, make the missile smart only once in a while so that it only checks for the position of the target once every five or ten frames. Use your imagination!

Building a Multi-State Animation

With all this motion going on, you're sure to want more sophisticated animations. You can use the `changeImage()` or `setImage()` function (they're two different names for the same thing) to change the image associated with a sprite any time. Sometimes, though, you want much more sophisticated animations. Take a look at `walkAnim.html` shown in Figure 8-8.

Figure 8-8:
When you press the arrows, the character walks with a realistic animation.

Your character

Like all examples in this chapter (indeed in the entire book), you really need to see it on my website and play with it to get a feel for what this example is doing.

There's a whole lot of image-swapping going on here. The walking animation is actually a series of eight different images rapidly swapped to give the illusion of walking. There are 4 different animations (one for each of the cardinal directions), so that's a total of 32 different images. However, if you look over the code, you'll see that the character sprite contains only one image. That image is pretty special, as you can see in Figure 8-9.

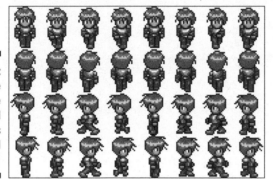

Figure 8-9:
This file has all the needed images combined into one!

This image is a composite animation. Each row represents a direction, and each row contains a cycle, or a series of images, meant to be repeated.

The rpg_sprite_walk.png image was created by Franck Dupont. He generously posted this image on the OpenGameArt.org site (http://open gameart.org), where he is known as "Arikel." He released his work under a special license called "Attribution — Share Alike." This means people can use or remix his work for free, as long as they attribute the original author. The background image is by an author named Hyptosis, who released images under the public domain on the same site. Talented and thoughtful contributors like Franck and Hyptosis are the key to the thriving creative community. Feel free to look over the open game art site for more great artwork to use in your games, but be sure to thank and attribute the authors as they deserve.

The simpleGame.js library contains a feature for making multi-image animations quite easily. Look over the code for walkAnim.html to see how it works:

```
<!DOCTYPE HTML>
<html lang="en-US">
<head>
    <meta charset="UTF-8">
```

```html
<title>walkAnim.html</title>
<script type = "text/javascript"
        src = "simpleGame.js"></script>
<script type = "text/javascript">
    var game;
    var background;
    var character;

    function init(){
        game = new Scene();
        background = new Sprite(game, "rpgMap.png",
    800, 600);
        background.setSpeed(0,0);
        background.setPosition(400, 300);
        character = new Sprite(game, "rpg_sprite_walk.
    png", 192, 128);
        character.loadAnimation(192, 128, 24, 32);
        character.generateAnimationCycles();
        character.renameCycles(new Array("down", "up",
    "left", "right"));
        character.setAnimationSpeed(500);

        //start paused
        character.setPosition(440, 380);
        character.setSpeed(0);
        character.pauseAnimation();
        character.setCurrentCycle("down");

        game.start();
    } // end init

    function update(){
        game.clear();
        checkKeys();

        background.update();
        character.update();
    } // end update

    function checkKeys(){

        if (keysDown[K_LEFT]){
            character.setSpeed(1);
            character.playAnimation()
            character.setMoveAngle(270);
            character.setCurrentCycle("left");
        }
        if (keysDown[K_RIGHT]){
            character.setSpeed(1);
            character.playAnimation()
            character.setMoveAngle(90);
            character.setCurrentCycle("right");
```

```
        }
    if (keysDown[K_UP]){
        character.setSpeed(1);
        character.playAnimation()
        character.setMoveAngle(0);
        character.setCurrentCycle("up");
    }
    if (keysDown[K_DOWN]){
        character.setSpeed(1);
        character.playAnimation()
        character.setMoveAngle(180);
        character.setCurrentCycle("down");
    }

    if (keysDown[K_SPACE]){
        character.setSpeed(0);
        character.pauseAnimation();
        character.setCurrentCycle("down");
    }
}

    </script>
</head>
<body onload = "init()">
</body>
</html>
```

You need to take a few new steps to build an animation, but the results are completely worth the effort.

1. **Obtain an animation image.**

   You can either create an image yourself, or look at the excellent resources like OpenGameArt.org to find work that others have done. Of course, you have a responsibility to respect other's work, but there is some great work available in very permissive licenses today. Be sure the image is organized in rows and columns and that each sub-image is exactly the same size. You may have to mess with your image editor to ensure that the image is in the right format and that you know the size of each sub-image.

2. **Attach the animation image to your sprite.**

   You'll be attaching the entire image to your sprite, but just displaying a small part of it at any one time. This is easier than working with a bunch of images, and it's also more efficient.

3. **Create an animation object with the** loadAnimation() **method.**

   When you invoke the loadAnimation() method of an object, you're creating an animation tool that helps manage the animation. The first two parameters are the size of the entire image (width and height), and the second two parameters are the width and height of each sub-image. If you get these values wrong, the animation will appear to scroll. Keep playing until you get these values right:

```
character.loadAnimation(192, 128, 24, 32);
```

4. **Build the animation cycles.**

   Each row will be turned into an animation cycle. The default version (without any parameters) works fine in most situations. Look up the documentation for the more advanced usages of this tool:

```
character.generateAnimationCycles();
```

5. **Rename the cycles.**

   The animations created with the buildAnimationCycles() command have default names, but it's almost always better to attach your own, more meaningful names. Add an array with a name indicating what each row represents:

```
character.renameCycles(new Array("down", "up", "left",
        "right"));
```

6. **Set the animation speed.**

   The animation speed indicates how fast the animation will run. A value of 500 seems right for most applications, but you can adjust this value so the character's walk cycle looks like it's actually propelling the character:

```
character.setAnimationSpeed(500);
```

7. **Set which cycle you intend to display.**

   The setCurrentCycle() method allows you to choose the cycle with one of the names you indicated in the renameAnimationCycles() step:

```
character.setCurrentCycle("down");
```

8. **Use the** pauseAnimation() **command to pause the animation.**

   In my example, I want the character to begin standing still, looking toward the user. The pauseAnimation() command makes the animation temporarily stop.

9. **Use** playAnimation() **to begin the animation.**

   This method will continuously loop the current animation cycle.

As you can see, animation adds a huge amount of fun to gaming and opens up the whole realm of role-playing games to your repertoire.

Chapter 9

Going Mobile

Games are fun, but today everybody wants games that work on mobile devices. After all, a lot of us carry smartphones or tablets wherever we go. If people can play your game on a mobile device, you can reach a huge audience.

Here's some good news: The HTML5 games made in this book will already work pretty well on mobile devices. With a few new skills, you'll be well on your way to making great games for phones and tablets.

Using HTML5 as a Mobile Language

Mobile development is a specialized form of programming. In the past, it has required specialized tools and knowledge. However, HTML5 and the `simpleGame` library provide tools that apply the game-programming knowledge you have to mobile devices.

Don't you need a special language?

Up to now, most mobile development has been done in specialized programming languages: Objective-C for the iPad and iPhone devices, and a special form of Java for Android-based devices. You can still write games using these platforms, but it's a bit tricky:

- ✔ **The languages are complex.** Objective-C and Java are much more complex than the JavaScript you deal with in this book, so it takes a lot longer to be ready to make a game.

- ✔ **You need an emulator.** To test a game using these languages, you need some sort of emulator on your computer so you can see how your game will look on the devices.

- ✔ **You need a license.** At least on the Apple platforms, you have to purchase a license. (Not a problem on Android.)

- ✔ **The App Store takes a cut.** If you charge for your game, the App Store will take a percentage, just for being the App Store.

- ✔ **You'll need multiple versions.** You can't easily write a game for both the iPhone and the Android. Because they use entirely different languages, you'll have to rewrite your code if you want it to work on both device platforms.

- ✔ **Apple can reject you.** It's possible after all your hard work that your program will be rejected. There are multiple delivery options for Android apps, so this is really just a problem for IOS developers.

HTML5 is a great compromise

You probably know where I'm going next. HTML5 games are a great solution to many of these problems. Write your game on the web browser and a lot of these issues go away:

- ✔ **Write for a single platform.** For the most part, you'll write for the web browsers rather than a specific platform, so the same exact code will work on iPhone and Android.

- ✔ **Most testing can be done on a local machine.** Much of your testing can be done on a regular computer, simplifying the testing.

- ✔ **No App Store.** All you need for distributing your games is a web server (and I show you how to use one in section "Putting Your Game on a Server" in this chapter). There's no approval process, no chance of being rejected.

- ✔ **You already know most of what you need.** If you've been reading this book, you're almost there. This chapter will show you a few mobile-specific tricks that will take you the rest of the way to your own mobile games.

So what else do you need?

A few things make mobile game development special. First, the size of mobile devices is unpredictable. Tablets may have a screen the same size as a small desktop computer, but cell phones can have very different-sized screens.

Second, the input mechanisms are different. Traditional computers use the mouse and keyboard as primary input mechanisms, but mobile devices have different approaches to input. Some devices have keyboards and some do not. Even those with keyboards don't always treat them the same way as computer keyboards. Most mobile devices have a virtual keyboard, but this isn't really suitable for gaming. For mobile gaming, it's often best to build a virtual keyboard yourself with only the keys you need for a particular game. Of course, `simpleGame` makes this easy to do.

Mobile devices generally have a touch input, meaning the screen is receptive to finger touches and swipes. At first, this may seem a lot like a mouse, but it's not exactly the same thing. A touch screen doesn't really have anything like a mouse click event, because moving and clicking the mouse is the same thing on a touch interface. `SimpleGame` has a library that allows you to work with the touch interface as though it were a normal mouse in some situations. It also allows you to control your game with a simple virtual joystick.

Many mobile devices also support the accelerometer, which is a tool that detects motion in the device. You can use this feature to control elements in your game.

Note that the support for mobile interface elements is very experimental. It isn't officially supported in any major browser yet, but you'll find most things work in the latest mobile devices. All of the mobile features work on an iPad 2 (my main mobile device). I also tested on an Android phone with less success, but when I played around with a newer Android tablet at a phone store, I found all the examples worked.

Putting Your Game on a Server

If you've been following along in the book, you've built some really great games so far. These games work nicely on your own machine, but what if you want to show them to other people? If you want to show games to other folks, you'll probably want to put your games on a web server.

If you're going to test your game on mobile devices, you'll definitely need a web server, because that's how you'll get your game to the mobile device.

Although it's possible to code a game directly on a mobile device, the on-board editors are typically not very good, and mobile operating systems really don't encourage on-board editing. Building code without a real keyboard is a frustrating experience. For mobile gaming, it makes a lot of sense to do your coding on a regular computer and then put it on a web server. You can then test it with your mobile device. Some features I cover in this chapter (using an accelerometer or touch screen) cannot be tested on a standard computer, so you'll need some way to get the game on the web.

Of course, to put your game on a web server, you'll need access to (stay with me here) a web server. Fortunately, this is very easy to do. Just do a quick web search for *free web hosting,* and you'll find plenty of places to put your code online for free or for a very low cost. For current purposes, a free hosting plan should be fine. You won't need a large amount of server space, and you won't even need features like PHP and MySQL, though if these features come with your service, they can be a bonus. If you want to find out how to use these tools, please check out my book *HTML, XHTML, & CSS All-In-One For Dummies* for complete information on using these technologies.

If you want to have a special name associated with your site (like I use for my examples), you can purchase a domain name. Most servers will allow you to search for and purchase a domain name for about $10 a year. If you don't want to purchase a domain name, you can often get a subdomain (a domain name associated with the hosting provider) for free. If you're going to be a bit more serious, you should probably purchase a domain so people can find your site.

The biggest downside of a free service is usually its dependability. In order to offer server space for free, a provider will generally have dozens or hundreds of clients sharing the same physical machine. If one of these other clients does something irresponsible, like running a spambot or creating an out-of-control program, your server may go down temporarily. Typically, when you pay even a little bit for a server, you get much more reliability. The cheapest paid hosting services generally cost very little ($2 to $5 a month) and offer a bit more security than the completely free services.

Using a control panel

When you're using a remote server, most of the time, you'll be given access to a control panel. After you sign up for service, the provider will send you a link to a special control page, along with a username and password combination. Keep this information handy because it's critical to managing your web server.

You rarely manage a server directly. Instead, you'll generally use a web browser to control your server remotely. Most servers use a variation of a program called *cPanel*. Figure 9-1 shows cPanel running in one of my servers.

Figure 9-1:
cPanel
allows you
to control
your server
through
the web
browser.

Even if your server doesn't use cPanel, your server will almost always use something similar. Remote server software usually has the following functions:

- ✓ **Script installations:** Often you'll find tools for installing various scripts and tools, including content-management systems like Drupal and Joomla. Although these are very exciting options, they are beyond the scope of this book. Again, for more information on this type of application, check out my book *HTML, XHTML, & CSS All-In-One For Dummies.*

- ✓ **Site builders:** You'll often see some sort of tool for helping you to build a website. Although these can be convenient, you know how to build a basic page yourself, so they aren't necessary.

- ✓ **File-management tools:** There will be some way to manage the various files on your server. It will feel a lot like the file manager on your local computer. You can use this tool to upload files to your server, change the filenames on your server, create new directories, and so on. This will be one of your most important tools.

- ✓ **FTP support:** Most servers offer something called FTP or SFTP access. FTP stands for *File Transfer Protocol,* and SFTP is *Secure File Transfer Protocol.* You'll normally be given some kind of FTP logon information including a URL, a username, and a password. Your FTP account information is not necessarily the same as the information you use to log on to the control panel. FTP is a more efficient way to manage the remote files. See the later section "Using an FTP client" for details on how to use FTP to keep your site up to date.

✔ **Domain management:** Frequently, there will be one or more domain names attached to your account. You should see information in cPanel about these domains, including when the rental of the name will expire.

✔ **Much more:** There will often be many more options, which are not all absolutely necessary for current purposes. These features frequently include databases, error logs, and e-mail management.

Uploading a page with a control panel

Although you can often do basic HTML and JavaScript editing right on the server, it's usually safer and easier to do most of the work on your local machine. When you're ready to distribute your program to the world, you can use the cPanel application (or whatever variation your provider provides). Here's the process:

1. **Prepare your game on the client machine.**

   Be sure that everything is working pretty well on your local machine first. If possible, organize your application to be as self-contained as possible. Put all resources used by your game in the same directory, and have only the things you need in the directory.

2. **Consider using relative references.**

   Code all links to images or external files in your game as a local reference. (Don't use `http://`; instead, simply indicate a filename.) This way, if you move all the files together, the references will still work on the local server.

3. **Log on to the control panel.**

   Use the logon information provided by your service to log on to the control panel application using your normal web browser.

4. **Find the file-management tool.**

   There will be some sort of tool for file management. These tools are all a bit different, but they'll generally look something like Figure 9-2.

5. **Navigate to the web directory.**

   Most servers have a special directory that is exposed to the web. You may need to check your documentation to find out exactly where you are supposed to put your files. Often you will be asked to place files in a directory called `public_html`, `htdocs`, or `www`. This varies by server, so you'll need to check your documentation. If you put files in the wrong directory, they may not be visible.

6. Make a subdirectory for your game.

It's best to make a subdirectory containing all the files your game needs when you build the game on your own machine. You can then create a similar subdirectory on the server and copy all files to the server at once.

7. Upload all your files.

Remember, a game normally consists of several files — the HTML/ JavaScript code, the `simpleGame.js` library, your image files, and all other external CSS or JavaScript files. Be sure you copy *all* these files to the server, or things will not work correctly. There's usually some sort of upload command that allows you to browse your local file system and select a file to upload. Repeat this process for all your files. If you want to upload many files at once, look into the FTP instructions in the next section.

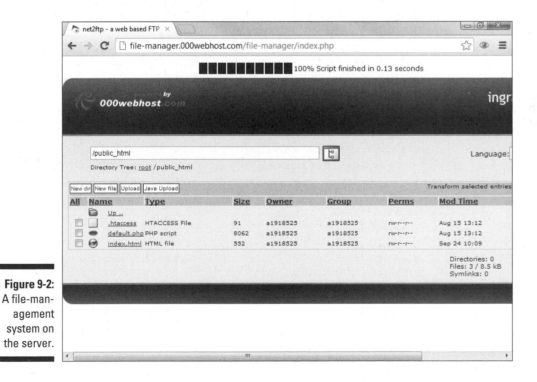

Figure 9-2:
A file-man-
agement
system on
the server.

8. Test on the desktop browser.

Use your desktop machine's browser to check that your server is working correctly. Your service provider will indicate the address of your main site. You'll probably want to build some kind of index page on your main site to point to each of your games. Check with your standard browser first to be sure that you know where your game is and what the URL is.

9. Test on the mobile device.

Use your device's browser to check the game. Some devices have multiple browsers, so you may want to check on more than one to ensure that the game is working correctly. Unfortunately, there's a great deal of variance in mobile browsers, so it's nearly impossible to determine if a game works on all. I tested primarily in Safari on an iPad 2 and Android Chrome.

Using an FTP client

Because you'll often be transferring a large number of files, it might be easier to use a special tool called an *FTP client.* As I mentioned earlier, FTP stands for *File Transfer Protocol,* and it's a mechanism used for more sophisticated file transfer problems. To use FTP, you'll need some sort of FTP client. I like FileZilla (shown in Figure 9-3) because it's free, easy to use, and it works exactly the same on all major operating systems.

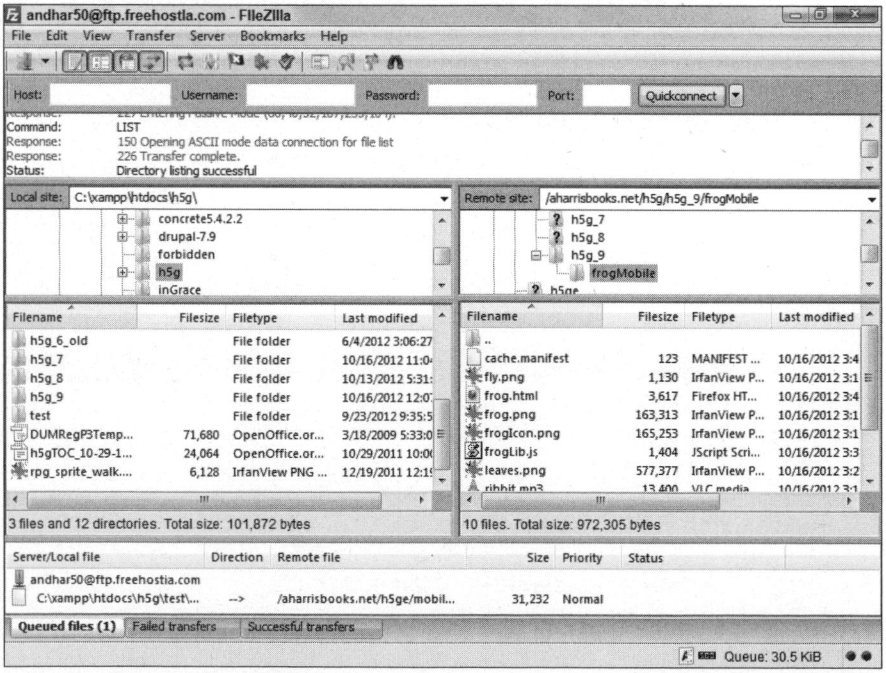

Figure 9-3: Using FileZilla to transfer files to my server.

FileZilla and other FTP programs all do pretty much the same thing. Here's how to use FileZilla:

1. **Download and install FileZilla.**

   You can download FileZilla for free at `http://download-filezilla-ftp-free.com`. (There is also a link at my main page: `www.aharrisbooks.net`.)

2. **Gather the logon information.**

   You'll need to get your FTP logon information from your service provider. Normally, this consists of a special address (like a URL, but it begins with `ftp://`), a username, and a password. These are not necessarily the same credentials used to log on to the server.

3. **Enter host information.**

   There's a place along the top of the editor to enter your logon information. Put the address (which usually begins with `ftp://`) in the `host` box, with your username and password in the other boxes. You can typically leave the `port` box blank because this information is normally determined automatically. (If in doubt, try port 21 or 22.)

4. **Connect to the FTP server.**

   Click the Connect button to make the connection. A flurry of obscure messages will fly through the top panel. In a few seconds (if all went well), you'll see a directory listing of the remote system in the right panel.

5. **Use the left panel to manage local files.** The left panel controls the local file system. Use this to find files on your local computer. It's a normal file-management system like My Computer or Finder.

6. **Use the right panel for remote files.**

   The right panel controls the remote server file system. It works exactly like the local system, except it allows you to manipulate files on the remote system. Use this system to move to the appropriate directory on the remote system. You can also create a new directory or rename files with the appropriate buttons on this screen.

7. **Drag files to transfer them.**

   To transfer files between machines, simply drag them. Drag from the local machine to the remote machine to upload files, or in the other direction to download them. You can move many files at a time in this manner.

8. **Watch for errors.**

   Most of the time, everything works great, but sometimes there is a problem. The bottom panel shows potential error messages. If there is an error, you may need to reload a file.

9. **Make a bookmark.**

You're likely to need this link again, so use the `Add bookmark` command on the `Bookmarks` menu to add a bookmark to this server. When you add a bookmark, you can also indicate which directories should be open on each machine, so you'll be ready to work as soon as you open the bookmark. You may also want to add this host in the Site Manager (found in the File menu) to keep track of the site for future connections.

Most remote servers run some variation of the Unix operating system. You may not be familiar with Unix, but it really works a lot like the systems you already know. However, it has one feature that may be new to you: file permissions. Most of the time, an FTP program will automatically get the file permissions right, but if the browser cannot see a file after you upload it to the server, try right-clicking that file in FileZilla and look at its properties. Most web files should have a permission set called `644` (which means you can read and write the file, everyone else can read it, and nobody can run it on the server). If it's set to something else, try changing it to `644`. Web directories should typically have `755` permission, which is almost always the default.

Making Your Game App-Ready

Of course, your games are really web pages, but you're going to make them work in a way that also makes them act like apps. You need to do a couple of things to make that happen. You can add an icon to your game so it appears on the desktop, you can modify the size so the game takes up the entire screen, and you can have your game stored offline so it is still available even when you don't have access to the Internet.

Managing the screen size

The first thing to consider is the screen size. This is an easy thing to change, but it can have big implications in your game. A game that works fine at one size can be much easier or harder at a different size. You can change the size and position of the game with the `Scene` object's `setSize()` and `setPos()` functions. Figure 9-4 shows a sample with a few screen sizes I've found useful.

It can be a bit tricky to determine the optimum screen size, but you can go to a site like `www.binvisions.com/articles/tablet-smartphone-resolutions-screen-size-list` to see a list of common screen resolutions.

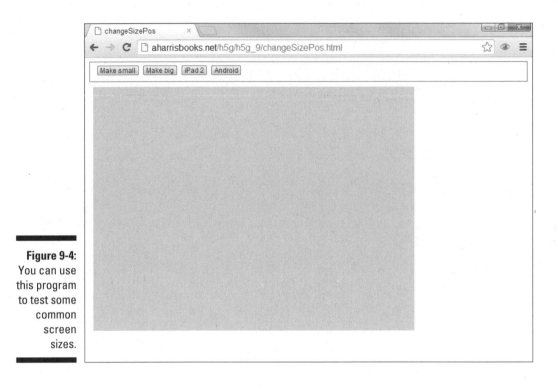

Figure 9-4:
You can use
this program
to test some
common
screen
sizes.

In general, you'll find 1024 x 768 and 800 x 600 to be the most commonly used screen sizes. With some experimentation, I've found that it makes sense to go a little smaller than these resolutions. Of course, if you have a particular device you want to program for, you can simply size your program directly for your device.

After you know the size you want, you can simply use the `Scene` object's `setSize()` method to change the screen to whichever size you prefer.

Remember that for many games, changing the screen size will actually change the gameplay. (For example, Pong is much more difficult on a larger screen than on a smaller one.) Also, most input will happen on the actual screen, so think about how large thumbs are, and try to design your game so the user's fingers don't obscure any onscreen action.

Making your game look like an app

There are a couple of wonderful tricks you can do for IOS users. You can design your game so the user can add an icon directly to the desktop. The user can then start the game like any other app. You can also make the browser hide the normal browser accoutrements so your game doesn't look like it's running in a browser!

It turns out that both these effects are quite easy to accomplish. Modern versions of IOS (the iPhone and iPad operating system) already have the capability to store any web page on the desktop. Just view the web page in Safari and click on the Share button. You'll find an option to save the web page to the desktop. You can instruct your users to do this, and they'll be able to launch your game like a normal app.

However, the default icon for a saved app is quite ugly. If you want a nice-looking icon, you can save a small image from your game as a .png file and put it in the same directory as your game. Then you can add this line to your page (in the header), and that image will appear on the desktop when the user saves your game:

```
<link rel="apple-touch-icon" href="plane.png" />
```

As an added bonus, the iPhone and the iPad will automatically adjust the image to look like an Apple icon, adding a glassy effect and rounded corners.

Figure 9-5 shows an icon I made for an app-ready variant of the frog game. (Refer to Chapter 7 for information on how to make the frog game.)

Figure 9-5:
An Apple icon for the frog game is in the upper-left corner.

Of course, this icon trick is an Apple-only mechanism. With most versions of Android, any bookmark you've designated with your main browser can be added to the desktop, but there is no custom icon option. The `apple-touch-icon` directive will simply be ignored if you're using some other OS.

Removing the Safari toolbar

Although your game looks good from the main screen, when the user activates the game, it's still obvious that the game is part of the web browser. You can easily hide the browser toolbar with another line in the header:

```
<meta name="apple-mobile-web-app-capable" content="yes" />
```

This code will not do anything different unless the game is called from the desktop. However, in that case, it hides the toolbar, making the game look and feel like a full-blown app. As an added bonus, this runs the game in a full-screen mode, giving you a little more room for gameplay.

Figure 9-6 illustrates how the modified frog game looks when run as an app.

Again, this is an Apple-specific solution. There isn't an easy way to achieve the same effect on the Android devices.

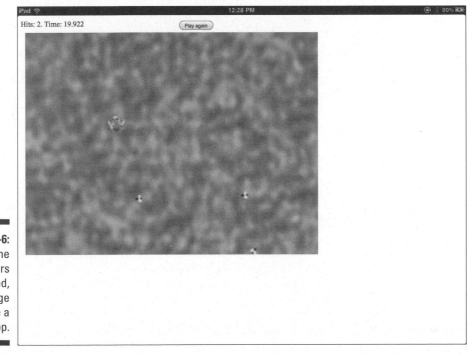

Figure 9-6: With the toolbars removed, this page looks like a normal app.

Storing your game offline

Now your game is looking a lot like an app, except it runs only when you're connected to the Internet. HTML5 has a wonderful feature that allows you to store an entire web page locally the first time it's run. Then, if the user tries to access the game and the system can't get online, the local copy of the game is run instead. In essence, the game is downloaded the first time it is played.

This is a relatively easy effect to achieve:

1. **Make your game stable.**

   Before you can use the offline storage mechanism, you'll want to make sure your game is close to release ready. At a minimum, you'll need to be sure you know all of the external files needed by the game.

2. **Build a** `cache.manifest` **file.**

   Look at the directory containing your game, and create a new text file called `cache.manifest`.

3. **Write the first line.**

   The first line of the `cache.manifest` file should contain only the text `CACHE MANIFEST` (all in capital letters).

4. **Make a list of every file in the directory.**

   Write the name of every file in the directory, one file per line. Be careful with your capitalization and spelling.

5. **Add the manifest attribute.**

   The `<html>` tag has a new attribute called `manifest`. Use this to describe to the server where the cache manifest can be found:

   ```
   <html lang = "en"
         manifest = "cache.manifest">
   ```

6. **Load the page normally.**

   You'll need to load the web page once in the normal way. If all is set up correctly, the browser will quietly make a copy of the file.

7. **Test offline.**

   The best way to test offline storage is to temporarily turn off wireless access on your machine and then try to access the file. If things worked out, you will be able to see your page as though you were still online.

8. **Check server settings.**

   If offline storage is not working, you may need to check with your server administration. The `text/manifest` MIME type needs to be configured on the server. You may have to ask your server administrator to set this option in the `.htaccess` file for your account:

   ```
   addtype text/cache-manifest .manifest
   ```

 Note that it can take the cache-manifest mechanism several hours to recognize changes, so when you make changes to your page, these changes aren't automatically updated to the local browser. That's why it's best to save offline archiving for near the end of your project development cycle.

Managing Alternate Input

The most obvious differences between mobile games and their desktop cousins are the different input mechanisms. Users of traditional computers primarily use the mouse and keyboard for input, and mobile devices often don't have either of these mechanisms. The touch screen of a mobile device is different than a mouse, and mobile devices also frequently allow tilt controls with a built-in device called an *accelerometer* (which, as I mention earlier in the chapter, is a tool that detects motion in the device).

If you want your games to work on mobile devices, you'll need some way to replace the keyboard and mouse with these mobile alternatives. The `simpleGame` toolkit has some nice features for doing exactly this. You can make buttons to emulate the keyboard, read the touch screen like a normal mouse, use a virtual joystick to emulate the arrow keys, and respond to motion.

Adding buttons

The keyboard is one of the easiest ways to get input in a standard browser, but most mobile devices do not have keyboards (even when they do, they're often not available to the gaming interface). The first problem is to figure out how to get user input when there's no keyboard. Fortunately, the `simple Game` library has a very handy feature called the `GameButton` for quickly adding a button to the screen. Figure 9-7 shows a very simple game with a single button.

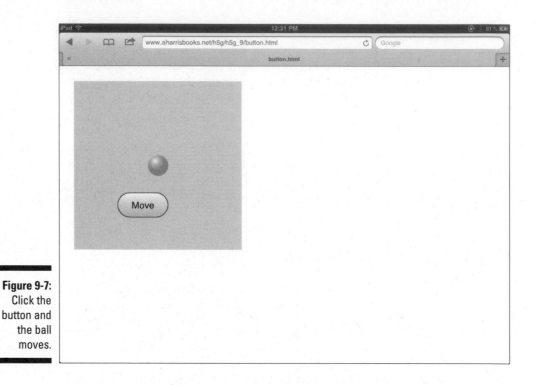

Figure 9-7:
Click the
button and
the ball
moves.

The GameButton custom button object begins with the features of a standard HTML button but then adds a few tricks to make it suitable for gaming. You can activate the button with a regular mouse or with the touch controls, making it ideal for games that can be played on both types of devices. The button.html page illustrates the button in action:

```html
<!DOCTYPE HTML>
<html lang="en-US">
<head>
    <meta charset="UTF-8">
    <title>button.html</title>
    <script type="text/javascript"
            src = "simpleGame.js"></script>
    <script type="text/javascript">
        var btnMove;
        var game;
        var ball;

        function init(){
            game = new Scene();
            game.setSize(200, 200);
            ball = new Sprite(game, "redBall.png", 25, 25);
            ball.setSpeed(0);
```

```
                     ball.setPosition(100,100);

                     btnMove = new GameButton("Move");
                     btnMove.setPos(70, 150);
                     btnMove.setSize(60, 30);
                     game.start();
                 } // end init

                 function update(){
                     game.clear();
                     checkButtons();
                     ball.update();
                 } // end update

                 function checkButtons(){
                     if (btnMove.isClicked()){
                         ball.setSpeed(3);
                     } else {
                         ball.setSpeed(0);
                     } // end if
                 } // end checkButtons
             </script>
        </head>
        <body onload = "init()">

        </body>
        </html>
```

As usual, the new and interesting elements are indicated in bold. Here's how you add a game button to a game:

1. **Create a variable for the button.**

   Like any other game element, you begin by creating a variable to refer to the button. I call mine btnMove because it's a button that moves things. (I'm full of surprises like that.)

2. **Build the** GameButton **object.**

   Build the GameButton object in the init() method. The single parameter indicates the button's caption.

3. **Set the button's size and position.**

   You'll want to think a bit about how your gameplay will work on mobile devices. Place your buttons where they can easily be reached by the player without blocking too much of the view. Note that you'll also want to make the buttons big enough to be pressed during the heat of the game. (Onscreen buttons are much better for tablet-based games, where there's a little more room than on tiny phone screens.)

4. **Check button status during** `update()`.

   Just as you normally check keyboard status during the `update()` function, you can also call a function to check your button status. Of course, you'll need to write this function.

5. **Read the button's** `isClicked()` **method.**

   If the button is currently being pressed, the value of `isClicked()` is true. If the button is not currently being pressed, `isClicked()` returns false. Use this method to determine the current state of each button and act accordingly.

6. **Treat a button much like the keyboard.**

   Because testing the buttons ultimately returns Boolean (true or false) values, checking for buttons usually feels a whole lot like checking for the keyboard.

7. **Consider adding buttons only when necessary.**

   If you want, you can design a game to display (and test) buttons only when a touch screen is available. The `Scene` object has a special variable called `touchable`. This variable is true if the library senses a touch screen, and false otherwise. You can use this variable to generate a custom interface that adapts to the playing environment.

Normally, you'll add several buttons to your interface, one to replace each key you expect the user to use (for example, arrows and the space bar). In this way, you can create a virtual keyboard on the screen. You may need to test the size and position of each key to get a comfortable gameplay experience.

Note that the caption of the button is ordinary HTML, so if you want to make your buttons based on images, you can simply add the appropriate `<img>` tag as a button caption.

Responding to the mouse

Because web browsers are very inconsistent in the way they report the mouse's position, mouse input in normal JavaScript is a bit tricky. The `simpleGame` library handles this by adding `getMouseX()` and `getMouseY()` methods to the `Scene` object. These methods are not always exactly correct, but they are close enough for most game programming.

Any time you want to read a normal mouse, just use the `Scene` object's `getMouseX()` and `getMouseY()` functions to determine the approximate mouse position.

Most of the time when you want the mouse position, it's because you're going to move an object where the mouse is or point an object toward the mouse.

Often, you'll want to hide the mouse cursor, so you can use the Scene object's hideCursor() method to hide the cursor. (Of course, you can retrieve the cursor with the showCursor() method.)

If you want to read a touch screen, there's one more simple step. The simpleGame library has a virtual joystick object called Joy. Create an instance of this class to turn on the touch screen reading features.

Note that the touch interface of mobile devices is not exactly like the mouse, so it needs a different interface. However, once you've created a Joy object, the getMouseX() and getMouseY() functions will make touch input act just like a normal mouse.

Figure 9-8 demonstrates touchMouse.html, which hides the normal mouse cursor and moves a ball wherever the mouse is currently pointing. This particular example works with both a traditional browser and a touch screen device.

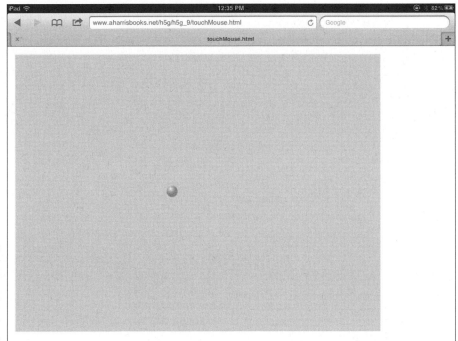

Figure 9-8:
The ball
follows
the mouse
pointer.

The `simpleGame` library dramatically simplifies the process of working with the mouse pointer by providing some easy method calls. Here's the code:

```html
<!DOCTYPE HTML>
<html lang="en-US">
<head>
    <meta charset="UTF-8">
    <title>touchMouse.html</title>
    <script type="text/javascript"
            src = "simpleGame.js"></script>
    <script type="text/javascript">
    var ball;
    var game;
    var joy;

    function init(){
        game = new Scene();
        ball = new Sprite(game, "redBall.png", 25, 25);
        ball.setSpeed(0);
        game.hideCursor();
        joy = new Joy();
        game.start();
    } // end init

    function update(){
        game.clear();
        followMouse();
        ball.update();
    } // end update

    function followMouse(){
        x = game.getMouseX();
        y = game.getMouseY();

        if (game.touchable){
          // move object a bit higher for touch screens
          y -= 100;
        } // end touch screen test
        ball.setPosition(x, y);
    }

    </script>
</head>
<body onload = "init()">
</body>
</html>
```

Getting a sprite to follow the mouse is just a matter of knowing what methods to call.

1. **Hide the mouse cursor.**

   The `Scene` object has a `hideCursor()` method. This is the easiest way to hide the normal mouse pointer. Normally, when you follow the mouse with an object, you mean for that object to act like the new mouse pointer, so you'll hide the normal arrow.

2. **Create a variable for the virtual joystick.**

   If you'll be working with a touchpad device, you'll need a variable to contain the virtual joystick object. I call mine `joy`. (If this game will be used only on desktop machines with normal mice, you won't need the joystick object.)

3. **Initialize the joystick.**

   Make an instance of the `Joy` object in the `init()` function. Just creating the joystick will tell the engine to expect touch input and map it to the normal mouse commands.

4. **Add a `followMouse()` function.**

   It's generally good to create a new function to handle input. The `followMouse()` function will tell the object to follow the mouse. Of course, if you're building an object that follows the mouse, you can make this a method of that object if you prefer. See Chapter 6 for more on building custom methods for your objects.

5. **Use `getMouseX()` and `getMouseY()` methods.**

   The `Scene` object has methods called `getMouseX()` and `getMouseY()`. Use these methods to get the X and Y coordinates of the mouse on the scene. Note that the coordinates are not always exact.

6. **Check to see if you have a touch screen.**

   The `Scene` object has a `touchable` property that is true if the browser has a touch screen. You don't normally want the object to be hidden by your finger, so often you'll want to offset an object when you're using a touch screen for input.

7. **Move the object higher than your finger.**

   In a touch screen environment, you normally want the sprite to still be visible, so you'll often offset the Y axis by some amount so it isn't obscured by the player's finger. Subtract some value from Y to get this effect.

Reading the Virtual Joystick

Many touch-based games use a virtual joystick mechanism. The user touches the screen to begin input, and then swipes to provide input. Swiping to the left is read just like moving a joystick to the left. The farther the user swipes, the larger the input value is. The `simpleGame` library has a virtual joystick object that makes it easy to implement a virtual joystick on your touch-based devices. Figure 9-9 shows `joy1.html`, which is a simple program illustrating joystick input.

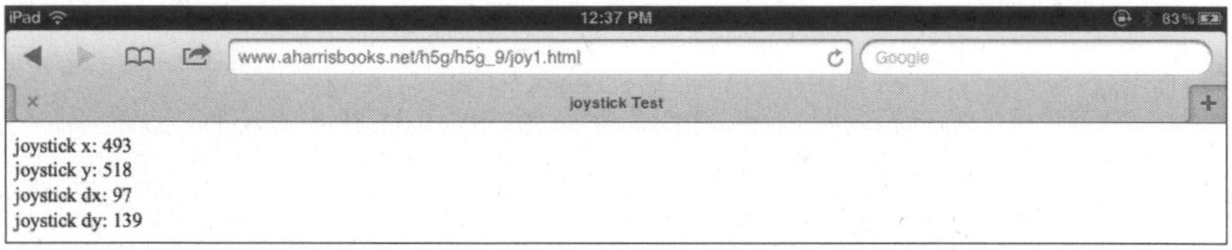

Figure 9-9:
This program reads inputs from a virtual joystick.

The virtual joystick works by returning numeric data. It's often easiest to understand how it works by looking at the numeric output before mapping it to a visual element.

```
<!DOCTYPE HTML>
<html lang="en-US">
<head>
    <meta charset="UTF-8">
    <title>joystick Test</title>
    <script type="text/javascript" src = "simpleGame.
        js"></script>
    <script type="text/javascript">

    var game;
    var output;
    var joystick;

    function init(){
        game = new Scene();
        output = document.getElementById("output");
        if (game.touchable){
            joystick = new Joy();
        } else {
            alert("This test requires a touch-based
        interface");
        }
        game.start();
    } // end init

    function update(){
        if (game.touchable){
            jx = joystick.getMouseX();
            jy = joystick.getMouseY();
```

```
                jdx = joystick.getDiffX();
                jdy = joystick.getDiffY();

                result = "joystick x: " + jx + "<br />";
                result += "joystick y: " + jy + "<br />";
                result += "joystick dx: " + jdx + "<br />";
                result += "joystick dy: " + jdy + "<br />";

                output.innerHTML = result;


            } else {
                alert("This example expects a touch
        screen");
            }
        } //  end update
    </script>
</head>
<body onload = "init()">
    <div id = "output">Nothing here yet</div>
</body>
</html>
```

The virtual joystick is quite easy to use:

1. **Create a variable for the joystick.**

   I will call mine `joystick`. Kind of catchy, I think.

2. **Create the joystick if possible.**

   Use the `game.touchable` property to determine if a touch interface is present. If not, send a message to the user. (Look ahead to the section "Using virtual arrow keys" for how to make a game that works for keyboard and touch interfaces.)

3. **Get the mouse position.**

   When the virtual `Joystick` object detects a touch on the screen, it triggers `mouseX` and `mouseY` values. Use the joystick's `getMouseX()` and `getMouseY()` methods to determine the X and Y positions of the touch. In this way, the touch interface acts much like the traditional mouse. (Note that `Scene.getMouseX()` and `Scene.getMouseY()` compensate for the scene's position in the browser, and the joystick versions refer to the actual position of the touch on the screen.)

4. **Get a `diffX` and `diffY` reading from the joystick.**

   Here's how a virtual joystick works: When the user touches the screen, the library tracks the coordinates of the initial touch. It then measures how far the user has swiped away from the original spot. The difference in X is called `diffX`, and the difference in Y is called `diffY`. Use the `getDiffX()` and `getDiffY()` methods of the virtual joystick object to determine how many pixels in X and Y the user has moved since touching the screen.

5. **Display the current values.**

For this first pass, it's important to understand what the joystick is displaying, so just take the values and print them to an onscreen output.

Controlling an object with the virtual joystick

Of course, the point of a virtual joystick is to move stuff around on the screen. Take a look at `joy2.html` as shown in Figure 9-10 to see how you can move a simple ball around the screen. As always, you really need to see this program in action. In fact, you need to run it on a touch-based device to really have fun with it.

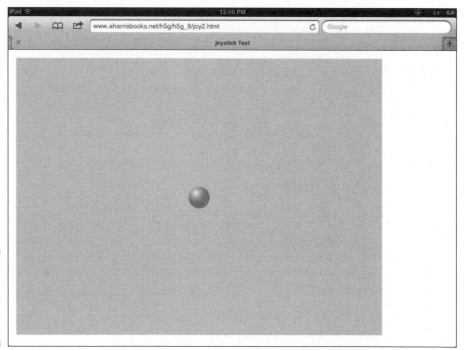

Figure 9-10: Now the virtual joystick moves the ball.

Here's the code:

```
<!DOCTYPE HTML>
<html lang="en-US">
<head>
    <meta charset="UTF-8">
    <title>joystick Test</title>
    <script type="text/javascript" src = "simpleGame.js"></script>
    <script type="text/javascript">

        var game;
        var ball;
        var joystick;

        function init(){
            game = new Scene();
            ball = new Sprite(game, "redBall.png", 50, 50);
            if (game.touchable){
                joystick = new Joy();
            } else {
                alert("This game requires a touch screen");
            } // end if
            ball.setSpeed(0);
            ball.setPosition(400, 300);
            game.start();
        } // end init

        function update(){
            game.clear();

            if (game.touchable){
              ball.setDX(joystick.getDiffX());
              ball.setDY(joystick.getDiffY());
            } // end touchable

            ball.update();

        } //  end update

    </script>
</head>
<body onload = "init()">
    <div id = "output"></div>
</body>
</html>
```

This example is even simpler than the previous one.

1. **Create a simple ball sprite.**

   For this example, a simple ball is used. Create it like any other basic sprite.

2. **Build a joystick object.**

   Make a virtual joystick object.

3. **Map the joystick's** diffX **and** diffY **to the ball's** dx **and** dy **values.**

   In this very simple mapping, I displace the ball by exactly as many pixels per frame as I moved my finger since the last touch. This gives extremely sensitive motion, so you might want to adjust the sensitivity by dividing the diffX and diffY by some scaling factor.

Driving with joy (sticks)

Now you can make an adaptable game that works with a regular keyboard or virtual joystick input. Take a look at joystickCar.html in Figure 9-11.

Figure 9-11:
Drive the car with a joystick!

This program reads the virtual joystick if one is available, or the keyboard if the game is running on a normal desktop machine.

```
<!DOCTYPE HTML>
<html lang="en-US">
<head>
    <meta charset="UTF-8">
    <title>joystickCar.html</title>
    <script type="text/javascript"
```

```
            src = "simpleGame.js">
</script>
<script type="text/javascript">

var game;
var car;
var joy;

function init(){
    game = new Scene();
    car = new Sprite(game, "car.png", 30, 20);

    if (game.touchable){
        joy = new Joy();
    } else {
        alert("Not a touch screen. Using keyboard");
    } // end if

    game.start();
} // end init

function checkKeys(){
    if (keysDown[K_UP]){
        car.changeSpeedBy(1);
    }
    if (keysDown[K_DOWN]){
        car.changeSpeedBy(-1);
    }
    if (keysDown[K_LEFT]){
        car.changeAngleBy(-5);
    }
    if (keysDown[K_RIGHT]){
        car.changeAngleBy(5);
    }
} // end checkKeys

function checkJoy(){
    dx = joy.getDiffX();
    dy = joy.getDiffY();
    car.setSpeed((dy * -1) / 5);
    car.changeAngleBy(dx / 10);
} // end checkJoy

function update(){
    game.clear();
    if (game.touchable){
        checkJoy();
    } else {
        checkKeys();
    } // end if
```

```
        car.update();
   } // end update
   </script>
</head>
<body onload = "init()">
</body>
</html>
```

The adaptable game is just like the car examples described in Chapter 5 but now it can alternately accept a virtual joystick input if played on a touch screen.

1. **Check to see if a touch interface is available.**

   As usual, use `Scene.touchable` to see if the user has a touch screen.

2. **Use the `checkJoy()` function if possible.**

   If the library sees a touch interface, use the `checkJoy()` function to follow joystick input.

   Otherwise, use the `checkKeys()` function for input.

   If there is no touch screen, use the keyboard for input instead. Check Chapter 5 if you need a refresher on how to read keyboard input.

3. **Change the car's angle with `diffX`.**

   When the user moves the joystick from side to side, the car will turn.

4. **Modify `diffX` to get an appropriate turning rate.**

   The default value of `diffX` will create a car that's difficult to control, so you may need to dampen the turning rate by dividing by some value. I divided by ten to get what seemed like the right performance.

5. **Change the car speed with `diffY`.**

   Use `diffY` as the basis for changing the car's speed. The car will move quickly if the user pulls the joystick up, and will back up if the user pulls the joystick down.

6. **Invert `diffY` by multiplying by –1.**

   Remember that computer screens are inverted, so if the user pulls the joystick up, there will be a negative `diffY` value. Compensate by multiplying `diffY` by negative 1.

7. **Adjust the sensitivity of `diffY`.**

   Probably the default rate will be too difficult for the user to control, so you'll generally want to divide by some value to get an easier speed control. I divided by five, but you'll need to experiment for your own games.

Using virtual arrow keys

I added one more convenience feature to the simpleGame library. There's a simple variation of the Joystick object that maps the virtual joystick into ordinary arrow keys. This variation works the same on both normal keyboard-based interfaces and touch-based machines.

I don't show a screen shot, because it looks like any other ball-based game.

```
<!DOCTYPE HTML>
<html lang="en-US">
<head>
    <meta charset="UTF-8">
    <title>virtualKeys</title>
    <script type="text/javascript"
            src = "simpleGame.js"></script>
    <script type="text/javascript">
    var game;
    var ball;
    //activate virtual arrow keys when joystick is present
    var virtKeys = true;

    function init(){
        game = new Scene();
        ball = new Sprite(game, "redBall.png", 30, 30);
        ball.setSpeed(0);

        var joy = Joy();

        game.start();
    } // end init

    function update(){
        game.clear();
        checkKeys();

        ball.update();
    } // end update

    function checkKeys(){
        ball.setDX(0);
        ball.setDY(0);

        if (keysDown[K_UP]){
            ball.setDY(-5);
        }
        if (keysDown[K_DOWN]){
            ball.setDY(5);
        }
        if (keysDown[K_LEFT]){
```

```
            ball.setDX(-5);
        }
        if (keysDown[K_RIGHT]){
            ball.setDX(5);
        }
    }

    </script>
</head>
<body onload = init()>


</body>
</html>
```

The most interesting part about this program is what *isn't* there. Although it does respond to the virtual joystick, there is no explicit joystick testing. Here's how it works:

1. **Turn on virtual keys.**

   In the main part of your code, create a variable called `virtKeys` and set it to `true`. The virtual joystick will look for this variable.

2. **Create a virtual joystick.**

   If the `virtKeys` variable is set to `true`, your joystick object will detect motion and automatically map it to arrow keys. For example, moving the virtual joystick up maps to the up arrow. Moving the joystick down maps to the down arrow, and left and right are likewise treated as key presses.

3. **Only check for the keyboard.**

   If you're using the `virtKeys` mechanism, there's no need to do a separate joystick check. Just check the keyboard, and if you're on a touch-based device, the joystick behavior is quietly transferred to the keyboard.

The virtual arrow-keys technique is great when you want a quick way to make a program that works for both a keyboard and a mobile device. You may need to experiment with buttons or some other input mechanism if you need additional input.

Tilting at windmills with the accelerometer

Mobile devices have another very intriguing input mechanism. You can control many mobile games by tilting the device. This works with a special on-board tool called the *accelerometer*, which tracks motion. The accelerometer actually measures rotation, and you can use it to get nice tilt controls in your game.

Reading the tilt

Figure 9-12 shows a game with tilt controls, but you can tilt the book all you want and you won't see anything interesting. You'll really need to look at this example on your mobile device.

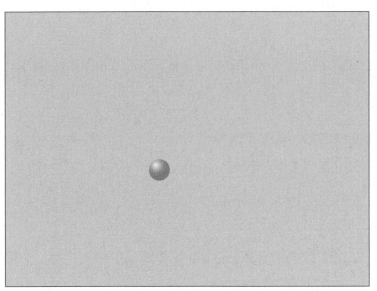

Figure 9-12:
Tilt the
screen to
move the
ball.

The simpleGame library has a special object called Accel that encapsulates the accelerometer. It works very much like the Joy object.

1. **Create an** Accel **object.**

   SimpleGame has an Accel object. Create this object to turn on accelerometer testing.

2. **Use methods to determine tilt.**

   The Accel object has special methods called getAX() and getAY() that indicate the rotation amount.

3. **Modify acceleration values.**

   The AX and AY values display the amount of rotation around the X and Y axis, respectively. The values range from –9 to 9. Generally, you'll need to modify the tilt values to get exactly the behavior you want. This usually involves a few simple math calculations.

Here's the code for `accel.html`:

```html
<!DOCTYPE HTML>
<html lang="en-US">
<head>
    <meta charset="UTF-8">
    <title>accel.html</title>
    <script type="text/javascript"
            src = "simpleGame.js"></script>
    <script type="text/javascript">
    var game;
    var ball;
    var accel

    function init(){
        game = new Scene();
        ball = new Sprite(game, "redBall.png", 50, 50);
        accel = new Accel();

        game.start();
    } // end init

    function update(){
        game.clear();

        newDX = accel.getAY();
        newDY = accel.getAX();

        newDX *= -5;
        newDY *= -5;

        ball.setDX(newDX);
        ball.setDY(newDY);

        ball.update();

    }

    </script>
</head>
<body onload = "init()">

</body>
</html>
```

The accelerometer is easy to use:

1. **Make a variable to hold the accelerometer object.**

   I normally call my variable `accel`.

2. **Use `accel.getAX()` to get rotation around X.**

   The `getAX()` method returns the percentage of tilt around the X axis. The X axis goes from side to side on the screen, so rotation around X is normally tied to motion along the Y axis!

3. **Use `acccel.getAY()` to determine rotation around Y.**

   Likewise, the `getAY()` method describes the percentage of tilt along the (vertical) Y axis. Normally, you'll use `getAY()` to control horizontal motion.

4. **Don't be concerned about the Z axis.**

   You can also read rotation along the Z axis (which goes from the center of the screen to your nose), but this is generally not helpful.

5. **Assume (for now) that the neutral position is lying perfectly flat on a table.**

   You'll get zero values for `getAX()` and `getAY()` when the device is lying completely still on a perfectly flat table. Look ahead to the next section "Calibrating the accelerometer" for advice on setting another position to be the default.

6. **Experiment with scaling factors.**

   You'll generally have to multiply the `getAX()` and `getAY()` results by some amount to get the behavior you want. I multiplied both by negative five to get appropriate values for `dy` and `dx`. You'll need to experiment to get exactly the behavior you want.

Calibrating the accelerometer

By default, the accelerometer assumes the neutral position is perfectly horizontal — that is, the device is lying flat on a table. However, these are mobile devices, and gamers will often want to have the neutral position be somewhere else. When I'm sitting up, I may prefer to have the device at a horizontal position. If I'm playing a game while lying on the couch, I'd prefer a more vertical neutral position. It's pretty easy to add a calibration mechanism to your game so it is more comfortable for the user. Figure 9-13 shows such a feature in place.

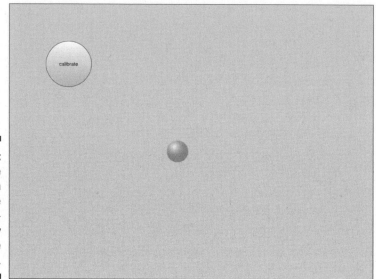

Figure 9-13:
Now the
user can
reset the
acceler-
ometer by
clicking the
button.

You know the drill. You've got to play with this on a device with tilt controls. The basic technique for calibrating tilt controls is to keep track of an offset value for AX and AY. When the user chooses to recalibrate, the offset values are changed to make a new neutral position. Here's the relevant code:

```
<!DOCTYPE HTML>
<html lang="en-US">
<head>
    <meta charset="UTF-8">
    <title>accel.html</title>
    <script type="text/javascript"
            src = "simpleGame.js"></script>
    <script type="text/javascript">
    var game;
    var ball;
    var accel;
    var btnCalibrate;
    var offsetAX = 0;
    var offsetAY = 0;

    function init(){
        game = new Scene();
        ball = new Sprite(game, "redBall.png", 50, 50);
        accel = new Accel();
        btnCalibrate = new GameButton("calibrate");
        btnCalibrate.setSize(100, 100);
        btnCalibrate.setPosition(100, 100);
```

```
            game.start();
    } // end init


    function checkButton(){
        if (btnCalibrate.isClicked()){
            offsetAY = accel.getAY();
            offsetAX = accel.getAX();
        }
    }


    function update(){
        game.clear();

        checkButton();

        newDX = accel.getAY() - offsetAY;
        newDY = accel.getAX() - offsetAX;

        newDX *= -5;
        newDY *= -5;

        ball.setDX(newDX);
        ball.setDY(newDY);

        ball.update();

    }

    </script>
</head>
<body onload = "init()">

</body>
</html>
```

Somehow you need to trigger the calibration. For this example, you add a basic calibration button. Here's how it works:

1. **Add** offsetAX **and** offsetAY **variables.**

   These two variables indicate how much the device's neutral position is different than the standard flat-on-the-table attitude. Begin the variables at value zero.

2. **Add a calibrate button.**

   For this example, I allow the user to recalibrate by clicking a button. See the earlier section "Adding buttons" if you need a refresher on how to add buttons to your game.

3. **Check for a button press.**

   As normally, I create a function to read any button presses.

4. **If the button is pressed, get new offset values.**

   When the button is active, find the current AX and AY values by requesting them from the Accel object.

5. **Subtract offsets from ax and ay on every frame.**

   Before any other calculations, subtract the offsetAX from AX and offsetAY from AY. This will effectively set the new neutral position to however the device was set the last time the button was clicked.

Although a calibrate button is very easy to implement, sometimes the calibration is done automatically. If you prefer, just determine offsetAX and offsetAY during the init() function, and the attitude of the device during the init() function becomes the default attitude. This doesn't allow the user to reset the calibration, but it does prevent cluttering the screen with a rarely used button.

Chapter 10

Documenting simpleGame

• •

In This Chapter

▶ How `simpleGame` is organized

▶ Main characteristics of the `Scene` class

▶ Using the `Sprite` class

▶ Working with the `Timer` and `Sound` objects

▶ Using the virtual joystick for mobile input

▶ Working with the accelerometer on mobile devices

▶ Creating virtual buttons

▶ Reading the keyboard

▶ Modifying the game engine

• •

*T*he `simpleGame` library streamlines HTML5 game development. It's a powerful tool, and there are many details. This chapter simply walks through every single object and method in the library and explains how everything works in detail.

Overview of SimpleGame

The `simpleGame.js` library was designed with a few key features in mind:

✓ **Ease of learning:** Perhaps the most important design goal was to create a library that is easy to learn and use. The library has a relatively small number of objects, and it strives to use straightforward language whenever possible.

✓ **Hiding complexity:** Game programming often requires a great deal of complexity. HTML5 game development can be especially tricky. Many of the concepts needed in a game engine (collision detection, sound effects, vector projection) involve complex math and programming, which is hidden from the game developer when possible.

✓ **Platform-agnostic:** The library was designed to work as well as possible on many platforms. It works on most modern browsers as well as mobile devices.

✓ **Mobile-friendly:** The library aims to support not only traditional desktop web browsers but also mobile devices like cell phones and tablets.

✓ **Reasonably powerful:** On a modern computer, the library can perform about as well as many other web and mobile gaming platforms, including Flash.

✓ **Object-oriented:** The library uses objects throughout, with a consistent scheme. All the main features are supported by an appropriate object, which has properties and methods that allow you to manipulate the object.

✓ **Free and open source:** The `simpleGame.js` library is available for anyone to use for free. You can also modify the library and add your own features.

The Scene Object

The central object of the `simpleGame` library is the `Scene`. When you create a `Scene` object, two primary things happen: The `Scene` creates a `canvas` tag to hold all the visual aspects of the game, and it begins a timing loop that causes a function called `update()` to run 20 times per second.

You create the `Scene` object variable as a global variable so it is available to all functions. You'll normally initialize `Scene` as the first line of your `init()` function. The `Scene` constructor requires no parameters. The `Scene` object is first described in Chapter 5, with more features described throughout the book.

Primary properties of the Scene object

The `Scene` object has a number of interesting properties you can read directly:

✓ `touchable`: The `touchable` property returns `true` when the browser detects a touch screen and `false` when there is no touch screen. This is an ideal way to determine if the game is currently being run on a mobile device. You should never change this property directly. Just use it to determine if the current device has a touch interface (usually with an `if` statement).

✔ `canvas`: The `canvas` property provides a reference to the canvas element produced by the scene. You can directly modify the canvas element (changing its size, for example), but it's much better to use the various methods provided for this purpose.

✔ `height`, `width`: These two properties show the current height and width of the game area. Use the `setSize()` method to assign new values to height and width.

✔ `top`, `left`: These two properties are used to describe the current position of the playing area's top-left corner. Use the `setPosition()` method to change the position of the game surface.

Important methods of the Scene class

Like most objects, the `Scene` object is controlled with methods, which are used to manage the scene and change its behavior and appearance.

✔ `start()`: The `start()` method is used to begin the game. Normally, you'll call the `start()` method at the end of the page's `init()` function, triggering the beginning of the game. The `start()` method adds the canvas to the page and begins the timing loop, which causes `update()` to be called 20 times per second. See Chapter 5 for more information on initializing a scene.

✔ `clear()`: This method clears the canvas, drawing the background color (use `setBackground()` to change the background color). Typically, you'll call `clear()` at the beginning of the `update()` function. Failing to clear the scene can lead to trails of sprites drawn on the playing surface. Chapter 5 describes how to use the `clear()` method.

✔ `stop()`: The `stop()` function is used to end the game. The timing loop is no longer called, so the screen pauses. If you want to clear the screen, call clear() before stopping the game. If you want to reset the game, the easiest way is to reload the page: `document.location.href = ""`. You can find out more about stopping and restarting the game in Chapter 7.

✔ `setSize(width, height)`: This method changes the size to the given width and height (measured in pixels). It may be necessary to adjust the size to make your game work well on mobile devices. This function is illustrated in Chapter 9.

✔ `setPos(left, top)`: This method changes the position of the game surface to the given values.

✔ `setSizePos(width, height, left, top)`: This is a utility function that allows you to change the size and the position at the same time.

✔ setBG(color): This method changes the background color of the playing area. You can use any of the normal CSS color values (named colors or hex values). The game canvas is repainted to the indicated color every time the scene's clear() method is activated.

✔ hideCursor(): This method allows you to hide the mouse cursor. It is especially useful when the game uses mouse or touch screen information as an input.

✔ showCursor(): The showCursor() method makes the ordinary mouse cursor visible again after being hidden by hideCursor(). The cursor methods are detailed in Chapter 9.

✔ getMouseX(), getMouseY(): These two methods are used to return the position of the mouse on the game canvas. Note that these methods (unlike the joystick variations of the same methods) compensate for the position of the canvas. Mouse and joystick techniques are fully discussed in Chapter 9.

✔ hide(): Hides the game canvas. This is useful when you want to use the game's timing loop but you don't necessarily want to show the canvas. (I used this for a few examples throughout the book when the canvas itself wasn't needed.)

✔ show(): Displays the game canvas after it has been hidden by hide().

The Sprite Class

Scenes provide the background of a game, but the other key element in simpleGame is the Sprite class. Nearly every game element is based on the sprite, so understanding what the sprite can do is the key to writing games in simpleGame. The Sprite class is first introduced in Chapter 5, and it is further described throughout the book.

The Sprite class is quite large, so the various properties and methods are broken into several different categories.

The sprite constructor has a number of important parameters:

```
mySprite = new Sprite(scene, imageFile, width, height)
```

You need to create each sprite as a global variable, and the sprites should all be initialized in the init() method. You must indicate all the required parameters when creating a sprite:

✔ scene: Sprites are always associated with a given Scene. Generally, you'll create a Scene first and then create sprites attached to that scene.

✔ `imageFile`: This is the filename of the image the sprite will be based on. Typically, this will be a smaller image in a web-friendly format (`.gif`, `.jpg`, or `.png`). The `.svg` format is also allowed by most browsers. Usually, you'll want to design your sprites so they face east by default. This will cause the direction properties to work as expected.

✔ `width`, `height`: These are the width and height of the sprite.

Main properties of the sprite

The sprite has a number of properties. You can read values from these properties, but it's normally best not to change them directly. Instead, use the appropriate method to change the behavior or appearance of a sprite. Basic sprite methods are described in Chapter 5, but you'll see more advanced techniques used throughout the book, especially in Chapter 8.

✔ `canvas`: The `canvas` element upon which the sprite is drawn.

✔ `width`, `height`: The width and height of the sprite. Important not only for the visual display of the element but also in collision detection.

✔ `cWidth`, `cHeight`: Size of the canvas containing the element. This information can be useful when you make a custom boundary action. See the `checkBounds()` method for more information.

✔ `x`, `y`: Position of the sprite. Do not change these values directly, but use one of the many sprite motion mechanisms. However, you can use these properties to discover the current position of the sprite.

✔ `dx`, `dy`: Motion of the sprite. Do not change these values directly, but you can use these properties to determine how quickly the sprite is moving vertically (`dy`) or horizontally (`dx`).

✔ `speed`: You can use this property to view the speed of the sprite, but do not change it directly. Instead, use one of the speed methods described later.

Appearance methods of the Sprite

Use these methods to change the appearance of the `Sprite` element:

✔ `changeImage(imgFile)`: Changes the image to the image file. The file should be in a web-safe format, and should not be larger than the intended display size.

✔ `setImage(fileName)`: Another name for `changeImage()`. Works exactly like `changeImage()`.

✔ update(): This method draws the sprite on the screen. Typically, you will update each sprite at the end of the main program's update() function. Sprites that are updated first appear at the bottom of the screen, so if you want a sprite to appear above another sprite, update it later.

✔ hide(): Hides the sprite. The sprite will still calculate speed and position, but it will not be displayed on the screen, and it will not collide with other sprites.

✔ show(): This function displays a sprite that was hidden with the hide() method.

✔ report(): This is a utility method that displays the current position, dx, dy, speed, and angle to the debugging console. It is intended only for debugging purposes, but can be quite handy when you're trying to discover what a sprite is supposed to be doing.

Movement methods of the sprite

One of the most important jobs of the Sprite object is to move around the screen in interesting ways. At its very essence, position is stored as an (x, y) coordinate pair. You can directly set the position of the sprite, but there are many convenience methods that give you better control of sprite motion. The basic motion format is a motion vector (dx, dy). You can set these values directly with appropriate methods, but sprites also have speed and angle attributes that can give much more interesting behavior. In fact, a sprite has two different angle measurements, the imageAngle and the moveAngle. The imageAngle determines which direction the sprite is facing, and the move-Angle determines the direction of motion. If you simply change the angle, you're changing both the image and movement angles at once. All angles in simpleGame are measured in degrees using normal navigation formatting, with 0 degrees pointing up and 90 degrees pointing to the right.

✔ setPosition(x, y): Immediately changes the position of the sprite to the give X and Y coordinates.

✔ setX(newX), setY(newY): Allow you to change X and Y to some new value.

✔ setDX(newDX), setDY(newDY): Change motion in X or Y axis. If you set the dx value to 5, for example, the sprite will move five pixels to the right every frame until the dx value is changed again. The angle and speed settings of the sprite will be affected by changes in dx and dy. (This is why you must always use functions to change dx and dy — if you change the properties directly, the speed and angle will no longer be accurate.) The sprite will continue moving at the indicated speed and direction until DX or DY is changed again directly or indirectly.

✔ `changeXby(newDX)`, `changeYby(newDY)`: Immediately change the X or Y value by the indicated amount, but do not change DX or DY. After this method is called, the sprite will continue to move according to its DX and DY values.

✔ `setSpeed(speed)`: Sets the speed to the indicated value. Speed is determined in pixels per frame. You can set speed to a positive or negative value. The speed will change immediately with this method. If you want a more realistic change in speed, use `changeSpeedBy()` or `addVector()`.

✔ `getSpeed()`: Returns the current speed based on the current settings of `dx` and `dy`.

✔ `changeSpeedBy(diff)`: Changes the speed by the `diff` amount. A positive value will cause the sprite to speed up in the `moveAngle` direction, and a negative value will slow the sprite down. It is possible to attain negative speeds, which will cause the sprite to move backward. You may want to assign top and bottom speeds to keep your sprite from moving so quickly that it is difficult to control.

✔ `setImgAngle(degrees)`: Changes the angle at which the sprite is drawn. *Does not* affect the motion angle. Use this mechanism to rotate a sprite without changing its direction of travel. Immediately sets the image angle to the indicated angle. The `degrees` value should be an integer between 0 and 360, but larger and smaller values will be accepted and adapted to appropriate values. This method immediately turns to the indicated angle. Use `changeImgAngleBy()` for animated rotation.

✔ `changeImgAngleBy(degrees)`: Changes the image angle by the indicated degree measurement. Use a positive value to rotate the sprite clockwise and a negative number to rotate counterclockwise.

✔ `getImgAngle()`: Returns the sprite's current image angle in degrees.

✔ `setMoveAngle(degrees)`: Immediately sets the sprite's motion angle to the indicated angle. Does not affect visual rotation of the image, so this can be used when you want to decouple the direction a sprite is pointing and the angle at which it travels. (This technique is frequently used for skidding behavior, for example.)

✔ `changeMoveAngleBy(degrees)`: Changes the movement angle by the indicated amount. You use it to modify the motion angle over time.

✔ `getMoveAngle()`: Returns the sprite's current motion angle in degrees.

✔ `setAngle(degrees)`: A utility function that sets both the image and motion angle. You use it when the sprite will be traveling in the same direction it's pointing (as in most simple driving games without skidding).

✔ `changeAngleBy(degrees)`: Changes both the motion and image angle at the same time. Used to turn the sprite gradually.

✔ turnBy(degrees): Another name for changeAngleBy().

✔ addVector(degrees, thrust): A very powerful method that adds a motion vector to the current sprite. The function applies a vector in the direction indicated by degrees and with the force indicated by thrust. Skillful use of this method can lead to many interesting physics-based behaviors. See Chapter 8 for a complete examination of this flexible method, which is used for gravity, skidding, and orbits, among other things.

Boundary methods of the sprite

With all this movement, it isn't surprising that sprites sometimes leave the confines of the game canvas. Most boundary-handling behavior is automatic, but you can either change the default boundary-checking mechanism, or you can add your own. Note that each sprite has a different boundary-checking behavior, so you can have more than one boundary mechanism in the same game. (Bullets frequently die when they leave a screen, whereas spacecraft may wrap around, for example.)

✔ setBoundAction(action): Determines what the sprite will do when it hits a screen boundary. The action value can be one of the following:

- WRAP: The sprite will keep the same speed and angle, but will appear on the opposite of the side it left. So if a sprite leaves the left side of the screen, it will appear on the right, but the speed and direction of travel will remain the same. WRAP is the default bound action.

- BOUNCE: The sprite will stay in the same spot, but its direction will be reversed. If it bounces off the top or bottom of the canvas, the dy value is inverted. If it bounces off the left or right of the canvas, the dx value is inverted.

- STOP: The sprite's speed will be set to zero, and the sprite will stay at the spot where it left the screen. It may appear only partially onscreen. If you want a stopped sprite to move again, you'll need to change its direction, position, or boundary action.

- DIE: The sprite will stop moving and will be hidden. It's not removed from memory, but it will no longer be displayed, nor will it register collisions.

- CONTINUE: The sprite will continue to travel beyond the visible canvas. Use this option only when there's some way of getting the sprite back (as in an orbit demonstration or when the off-screen coordinates are displayed, such as in an air-traffic control simulation). If the boundAction is set to some value the game engine does not recognize, CONTINUE will be set.

✔ `checkBounds()`: The `checkBounds()` function automatically uses the indicated bound action. If you need a custom bound action (for example, you want to wrap off the top and bottom but bounce off the sides), you can create your own `checkBounds()` method. However, you're then completely responsible for ensuring that your method handles all the possible boundary conditions. Never call `checkBounds()` directly (it's already called at the appropriate moment), but overwrite it if you need some sort of fancy boundary-checking behavior.

Collision methods of the sprite

The sprite has two main ways to check collisions. There is a standard `collidesWith()` method that checks for bounding-rectangle collisions. In addition, you can use the `distanceTo()` and `angleTo()` methods to get a better sense of the proximity of two sprites. Chapter 6 describes collision-detection in some detail.

✔ `collidesWith(sprite)`: Returns `true` if this sprite's bounding rectangle is currently overlapping the given sprite's bounding rectangle. Note that this is a very fast collision routine, but it's not pixel-perfect. In particular, long, thin sprites will have very different collision behaviors if they're diagonal, vertical, or horizontal. If you need more uniform collision mechanism, use the `distanceTo()` method instead. If either sprite is invisible, a collision will not be registered.

✔ `distanceTo(sprite)`: Returns the distance (in pixels) between this sprite and the target sprite. Useful for boundary-circle checking. If the distance between two sprites is less than some threshold, count it as a collision. Unlike the standard `collidesWith()` mechanism, the distance-based collision technique works the same regardless of the sprites' orientations. This method works whether the sprites are visible or not.

✔ `angleTo(sprite)`: Returns the angle (in degrees) from the current sprite to the given sprite. Use this method to have a guided missile that always points to a target or to apply a gravity vector between a planet and a spacecraft. This method works whether the sprites are visible or not.

Animation methods of the sprite

The `simpleGame` library has limited support for sprite sheet animations. See Chapter 8 for a description of this technique. The following methods assist with animations:

- ✔ `loadAnimation(width, height, cellWidth, cellHeight)`: Indicates that the image associated with the sprite is actually a sprite sheet. The first two parameters indicate the size of the overall sprite sheet, and the second two values indicate the width and height of a single cell within the sheet.

- ✔ `generateAnimationCycles()`: Generates a series of animation cycles. Default behavior presumes each row is a new state and each column is an animation within that state. Typically, rows indicate directions and columns indicate cells within the animation.

- ✔ `renameCycles(cycleNameArray)`: This method allows you to set string names to each of the cycles. These usually indicate directions or behaviors.

- ✔ `setAnimationSpeed(speed)`: This method indicates how quickly the animation will cycle. Setting a higher value will slow down the animation.

- ✔ `setCurrentCycle(cycleName)`: Changes the animation cycle to the one indicated by the cycle name. They're normally used to change animation state.

- ✔ `PlayAnimation()`: Begins (and repeats) the currently indicated animation.

- ✔ `PauseAnimation()`: Pauses the animation until it is restarted with a `playAnimation()` command.

Utility Classes

In addition to the main two classes, the `simpleGame` library includes a number of helpful utility classes. Use these classes to add features to your game, from sound effects to mobile device interface schemes.

The Sound object

The `Sound` class encapsulates the HTML5 audio object and makes it very easy to build sound effects. When you build a sound object, you'll actually be creating an HTML5 audio object that isn't displayed but that can be played with JavaScript code. Note that the sound object has the same limitations as HTML5 sound elements. Most importantly, no single audio format is guaranteed to play on every browser. For best results, create each sound effect twice (once in `.mp3` and once in `.ogg` format) and create a `Sound` object for each. Use of the `Sound` object is described in Chapter 6.

✔ `sndElement = new Sound(src)`: Creates a new `Sound` object. Generally, you'll want to store the sound in a global variable. The `src` attribute indicates the filename of the sound. For maximum effectiveness, create two objects for each sound effect (one in `.mp3` and one in `.ogg`).

✔ `play()`: Plays the sound effect encapsulated by the sound.

✔ `showControls()`: Shows the HTML5 control panel (a Play button and a simple scrubber) for the sound effect. By default, controls are turned off. This option was added as a workaround for an issue with iPhone and iPad browsers.

Note that the iPhone and iPad operating systems have a well-known problem playing back sound effects from JavaScript. IOS (the iPhone, iPad, and iPod operating system) refuses to preload a sound and will load the sound effect only after direct user feedback. In practice, this means you cannot load a sound in the background. However, there is a loophole. Use the `Sound` object's `showControls()` method to make the HTML5 audio control panel appear for each sound. The user can then manually load each sound by playing it once. When the sound is in memory, it will play within the game with no problems. Each time the page is reloaded, you will need to reload the sounds.

See Chapter 6 for complete details on how to use the sound object.

The Timer object

The `Timer` is a simple object designed to give you an easy way to work with elapsed time. It has two methods, and they are both quite straightforward:

✔ `reset()`: This command resets the timer. Use it whenever you want to begin counting some amount of time.

✔ `getElapsedTime()`: This method returns the number of seconds since the timer was started or reset.

If you look at the source code, you'll find another method, `getCurrentTime()`, but this is used only internally and isn't likely to be useful as it is. (It returns the current time in a format that's useful for calculations, but it's not human-readable.)

The `Timer` is explained in Chapter 6.

The virtual joystick

One of the most interesting features of the `simpleGame` library is its support for mobile devices. Because these devices often don't have keyboards, they rely on alternative input methods. The virtual joystick object is used to manage touch screen input.

✔ `joystickName = new Joy()`: Creates a virtual joystick object. Normally, it's best to do this after checking for the touchable interface through the `scene.touchable` property. However, if you create a virtual joystick and the browser cannot support it, the joystick commands will simply be ignored.

✔ `getMouseX()`, `getMouseY()`: These methods return the X and Y position of the touch. If a virtual joystick is turned on, the scene's `getMouseX()` and `getMouseY()` methods will reflect the mouse's position. Note that with a real mouse, there is always a value for `mouseX` and `mouseY`. With a touch interface, there isn't a meaningful value for `mouseX` and `mouseY` unless the user is currently touching the screen. Chapter 9 details the use of the touch screen and mouse.

✔ `getDiffX()`, `getDiffY()`: Return a value indicating how much the user has moved the mouse in X or Y since initially touching the screen. This is the foundation of the virtual joystick. See Chapter 9 for details on using the virtual joystick object.

✔ `virtKeys`: This is an ordinary variable. If you create a variable called `virtKeys` and set it to true *before you create a virtual joystick*, the joystick will automatically act like arrow keys. This is an easy way to build a multi-platform game. Use the arrow keys as the primary input interface, but add the virtual arrow key interface so mobile users can replace the keys with a virtual joystick. See Chapter 9 for more detail on using the virtual joystick in this way.

The virtual accelerometer

In addition to touch input, mobile devices also include support for motion-detection with a built-in accelerometer. The accelerometer measures rotation around all three axes, but X and Y turn out to be most useful.

✔ `AccelName = new Accel()`: Builds a new accelerometer object called `accelName`. If the device does not support an accelerometer, nothing will happen (so you'll want to include some other input type, such as the keyboard or buttons).

- ✔ getAX(): Gets acceleration around the X axis. Note that the X axis is side-to-side, so acceleration around this axis will often map to changes in Y.

- ✔ getAY(): Gets the acceleration around the Y axis, which is vertical. Normally, you'll map acceleration around Y to changes in an object's x or dx values.

- ✔ GetAZ(): Technically, this reads acceleration around the Z axis, which runs from the center of the screen to the user's nose. In reality, this is rarely used because these rotations will usually also trigger an acceleration around Y.

- ✔ getRotX(), getRotY(), getRotZ(): These utility functions indicate the amount of rotation around each of the axes since the last frame. They're provided as a service, but normally the getAX() and getAY() functions are sufficient for handling most rotation situations.

See Chapter 9 for more information on how to use the accelerometer for motion-sensing.

The game button

The game button provides a convenient button that can be used in both desktop and mobile games. It's essentially a standard HTML button, but it's optimized for game programming, especially on mobile devices as an alternative to keyboard input.

- ✔ buttonName = new GameButton(label): Creates a new button. The label text will become the text of the button.

- ✔ setPosition(x, y): Sets the position of the button to the indicated screen coordinates. The button can be placed on the playing surface or anywhere else on the screen.

- ✔ setSize(width, height): Sets the width and height of the button to the indicated values. Remember that buttons may be easier to press if they're larger.

- ✔ isClicked(): Returns a true value if the button is currently pressed or false if the button is not currently pressed. Use this method to easily check the state of the button.

Note that the label can be any valid HTML text, including plain text or an image (using the standard <img> tag). You can also use CSS to style your labels (use the standard button style) to make them semitransparent if you prefer. You can find complete discussion of the GameButton class in Chapter 9.

Keyboard array

The keyboard is a primary input mechanism for the `simpleGame` engine, so it's designed to be easy to use. As soon as the `Scene` is initialized, a special array called `keysDown` is created. There is an entry in this array for each of the main keys on the keyboard. Check the status of a key by using the keyboard constant as the index. The keyboard constants all begin with a capital "K," followed by an underscore and the letter name (for example, the A key is `K_A`, and B is `K_B`). In addition to the letter and number keys, the following keyboard constants are defined:

- ✔ K_UP
- ✔ K_DOWN
- ✔ K_LEFT
- ✔ K_RIGHT
- ✔ K_SPACE
- ✔ K_ESC
- ✔ K_PGUP
- ✔ K_PGDOWN
- ✔ K_HOME
- ✔ K_END

Note that these keys are defined for a standard U.S. keyboard, and some behavior may be different on different keyboards.

This system (unlike standard JavaScript keyboard techniques) allows for multiple keys to be pressed at one time.

Chapter 5 describes how to read the keyboard.

Making the Game Engine Your Own

The `simpleGame` library is already pretty feature-packed. But there's always room for improvement. If you're interested (and willing to dig around a little bit), you can poke around the code yourself to see how it works. If you want to add your own features, you can do so. A few adventuresome developers are already working on improvements to the library including support for tile-based worlds and enhanced animation features.

By all means feel free to experiment. If you add something really great, let me know, and I'll add it to the next version of `simpleGame`!

Part IV
The Part of Tens

The 5th Wave   By Rich Tennant

"Other than this little glitch with the landscape view, my app works great on a smartphone."

In this part . . .

This part contains some of the most fun stuff in the book. If you want to learn more about how simpleGame works, find great places to get free artwork, or see how a particular type of game is written, this is the part for you.

Chapter 11 is a list of game asset resources. There are many exceptional tools and resources for building the graphics and sound effects you'll need for your game. I provide links and descriptions for my favorites.

Chapter 12 is the geekiest chapter in the book. In this chapter, I go under the hood of the game engine and explain how many of the key features work. Read here to discover how the canvas element is used throughout the game engine, how the animation loop really works, and how the library handles sound effects and the keyboard. As I explain how angle measurements, vector projection, and transformations are used everyday by game programmers, you see why mathematics is so critical for game programmers.

Chapter 13 is just fun. I use the ideas presented throughout the book to build ten different game starters. Each game illustrates a different genre and introduces a practical concept or two. I provide the beginning code for a platform-jumping game, a whack-a-mole game, tile-based-worlds, a simple RPG combat system, a basic tic-tac-toe AI, and much more. I deliberately left the games unfinished so that you can take them as starting points and build something amazing on your own.

Chapter 11

Ten Great Game Asset Resources

*T*his book teaches all about game development, but to make a game, you'll need various tools — especially graphics and sound effects. In this chapter, I describe ten really great tools for making games (and I snuck in one extra tool for your consideration). Some are software, some are websites, and all are awesome.

Dia Diagramming Tool

Game development requires planning and documentation. Many times you'll want to have some sort of tool to help you plan your game, whether you're thinking about how the user goes from state to state in an adventure game or you're designing a screen diagram for your top-down racer. In any case, you'll probably want some kind of diagramming tool.

Dia is a very popular free tool, available at `http://projects.gnome.org/dia`.

Dia is a *vector* editor, which means it's particularly good at diagrams. You can place elements and then move them around, and you can draw lines and arrows between elements. When you move the elements, any lines drawn between them are automatically moved. Most of the diagrams in this book (including the state diagram in Chapter 1, the Word Story diagram in Chapter 2, and the frog game diagram in Chapter 7) were created in Dia.

You can see Dia being used in Figure 11-1.

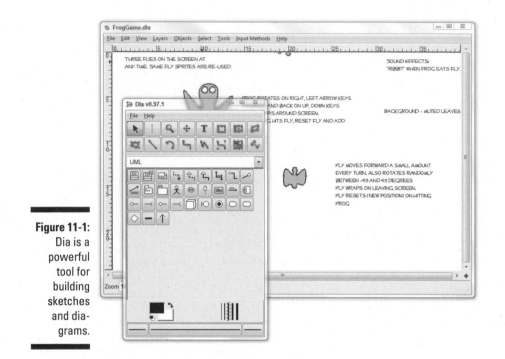

Figure 11-1:
Dia is a
powerful
tool for
building
sketches
and dia-
grams.

Dia is available as a free download for every major operating system.

GIMP — A Powerful Image Editor

Perhaps the most important tool for a game developer (apart from the pro-gramming language and game engine) is a solid graphical editor. My favorite graphical tool by far is GIMP.

GIMP (Gnu Image Manipulation Program) is available for all major operating systems for free at www.gimp.org. The software is quite similar to Adobe Photoshop and other high-end image editors. Figure 11-2 shows one of the images in the book being edited with GIMP.

GIMP supports all the main features of any high-end raster graphics editor, including the following:

✔ **Standard painting tools:** Any paint program should have things like pencils, paintbrushes, airbrushes, and erasers. GIMP includes these and other tools for cloning (copying part of an image to another part), an ink pen simulator, and a powerful fill tool with patterns and gradients.

✔ **Selection tools:** As you begin working on complex images, you'll probably want to select and modify specific parts of your image. GIMP has many ways to select elements, including standard lasso, circle, and rectangular selections. It also supports more sophisticated selection techniques like color selection, "magic" selection, Bézier paths, and a powerful foreground selection tool.

✔ **Modification tools:** You can use GIMP to modify parts of an image. Standard transformations like rotation, translation, and scale are available, as well as a perspective tool, and tools to smudge, blur, and heal.

✔ **Layer support:** Image manipulation can get complex, so some sort of organization technique can be really helpful. Layers are used to separate parts of your image so you can edit elements in isolation. Each layer can have transparency built in so you can see the underlying layers.

A program as powerful as GIMP can be somewhat overwhelming, so you may need some help. I have a free bonus chapter from a previous Wiley book (*Game Programming — The L Line*) explaining how to build gaming graphics in GIMP. You can check out that tutorial online at www.aharrisbooks.net/pythonGame/Appendix_D.pdf.

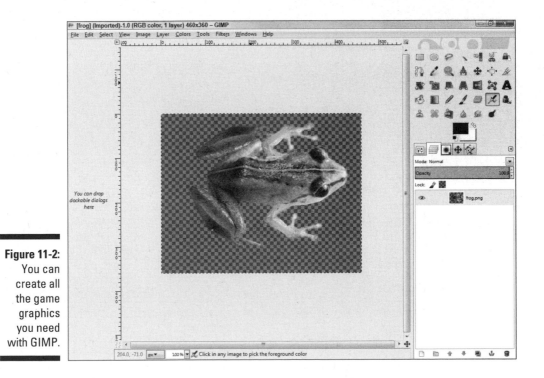

Figure 11-2:
You can create all the game graphics you need with GIMP.

Ari's SpriteLib

While GIMP is extremely powerful, it can be quite difficult to build a great sprite image. Fortunately, there are some very nice online sprite images you can use for free in your own games. One of my favorites is called Ari's SpriteLib, available at www.widgetworx.com/widgetworx/portfolio/spritelib.html.

The SpriteLib is a library of excellent custom images. You can use the images freely in your games. It contains nice images for a tank game, some wonderful 2D aircraft, some spacecraft, aliens, and other wonderful characters.

There's a great chance you'll be able to find something you can use in this wonderful library.

Figure 11-3 shows one of the sprite sheets available in Ari's SpriteLib.

Figure 11-3: These images are perfect for incorporating into a game.

Reiner's Tilesets

If you're looking for more images you can incorporate into your games, take a look at Reiner's tilesets at www.reinerstilesets.de. Reiner is a game developer and artist who has released hundreds of incredible free graphics over the years. Most of his 2D graphics come in a ZIP file containing dozens of individual images. You may want to use a tool like GIMP (described earlier in this chapter) to put the selected sprites into a single sprite sheet. See Chapter 8 for information on how to work with sprite sheets.

Reiner's library contains hundreds of high-quality images. Most of them were created with 3D modeling packages and then rendered into 2D graphics, so they provide the illusion of 3D.

You'll find many interesting graphics in this set, including terrific RPG and fantasy models, as well as a number of very nice vehicle and other projects.

Figure 11-4 shows a page from Reiner's online archive.

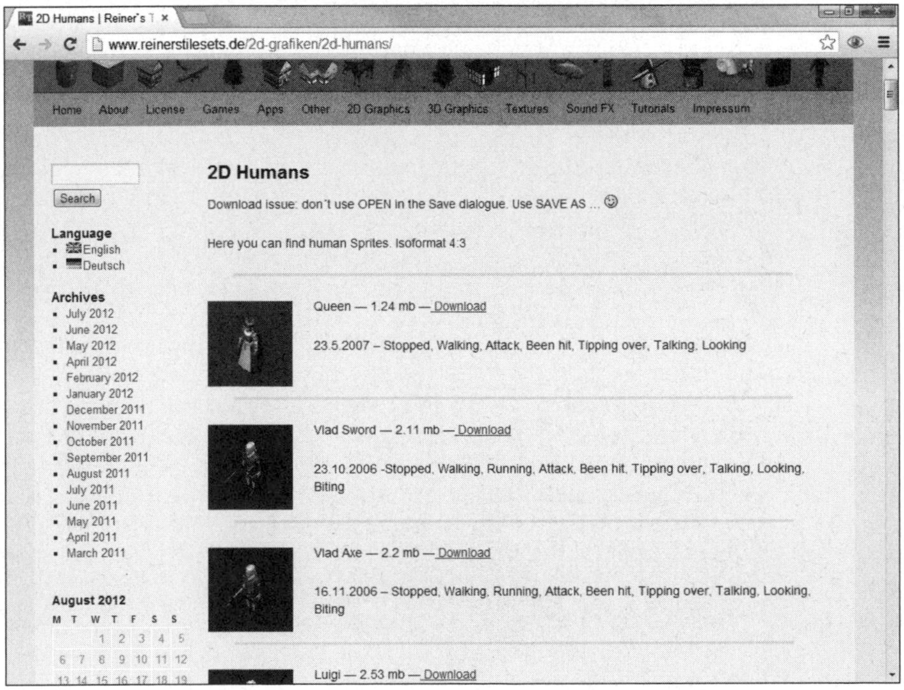

Figure 11-4:
Reiner's tilesets include hundreds of quality game images.

OpenGameArt

OpenGameArt.org is a website, but more than that, it's a community of game artists and developers. Many of them put really wonderful game art online for others to share. This is a great site to visit once in a while. You'll find a huge number of really super game-art projects there. I've been especially impressed by the character sprite sheets and the tilesets that are available on this site. Note that not everything posted on this site is available for reuse. You may need to write to an artist to ask for permission to use an asset.

One of the most interesting things on this site is a resource called the *Liberated Pixel Cup (LPC)*. This was a contest that encouraged artists to build open game-art resources, and then challenged programmers to put those resources together to build fun games. The contest focused on RPG characters with a common theme and style. This means you can probably use multiple characters together with some success. You can find a complete list of resources and the completed games for the LPC at

```
http://lpc.opengameart.org
```

Many of the images on the OpenGameArt site are stored in the .xcf format, which is the default image format for GIMP, mentioned earlier in this chapter.

One of my favorite resources to come out of the LPC is called the Universal-LPC sprite sheet. This is a massive GIMP file that incorporates all the various character art that has been contributed to the site. Each element is on a separate layer, so you can mix and match to build your own character. The universal sprite sheet is available here:

```
https://github.com/makrohn/Universal-LPC-spritesheet
```

Note you'll need to click on the "ZIP" button to download the sprite sheet.

You'll also find some really great sound effects on the OpenGameArt site. As with the images, you may need to track down the developer to get permission to use the sounds. Often, you'll see numerous sound effects in a single file, and you'll need a tool like Audacity to edit the sounds and put them in the format you need for your game (see section "Audacity – Useful for Sound Effects," later in this chapter).

Blender

Among the hottest trends in gaming today are the so-called 2.5D games. Essentially, you use a 3D modeler to build your various elements, but then you put them together in a 2D game engine.

I actually used this technique for some of the images shown in this book. Figure 11-5 shows one of these images (the hovercar from Chapter 13) being built in Blender, an especially powerful 3D modeling package available for free on all major operating systems. You can download Blender at www. blender.org.

3D modeling packages can be intimidating and expensive. It can take some time to learn how to build a good-looking model, but the results can be well worth it.

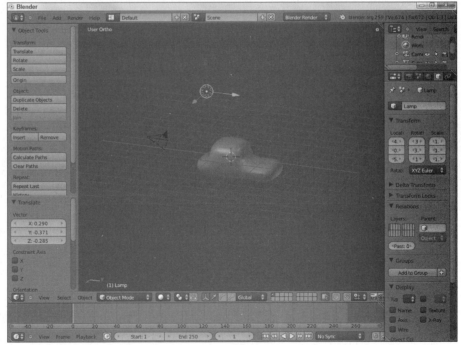

Figure 11-5:
You can use Blender to build your own game images.

If you want more help with Blender, a nice video tutorial is available at `www.blendtuts.com/2010/06/blender-25-interface.html`. This will give you the basics of using Blender, but you'll definitely need to spend some time to discover everything Blender has to offer.

Note that Blender contains its own game engine. It's a very powerful and useful tool for building 3D games. Maybe one day somebody will write a book about it . . .

Audacity — Useful for Sound Effects

If images are the key to games, audio effects are the next most important asset for a great game. Elsewhere in this chapter, I provide links for many nice audio resources, but you'll still need to have access to an audio editor. Audacity is a very powerful free audio tool, available at `http://audacity.sourceforge.net`. It incorporates a number of essential audio-editing features:

- **Recording capabilities:** Often the easiest way to get a sound effect is to simply record it yourself. Audacity is an easy way to record audio files with a standard microphone.

- **Audio editing:** You'll frequently need to modify an audio file in some way — eliminating empty space, combining sound effects, adjusting the volume, or changing the sampling rate. Audacity supports all these operations.

- **Special effects:** You can apply many interesting special effects to your sound effects, including playing sounds backward, removing hiss, changing the pitch, and adding echoes.

- **Support for many formats:** For HTML5 gaming, you're generally best off saving each file in both `.ogg` and `.mp3` formats. Audacity allows you to export a sound effect in either format. (*Note:* Some versions may require you to download a separate file for MP3 export, but this is a straightforward process. Just follow the instructions available here: `http://manual.audacityteam.org/o/man/faq_installation_and_plug_ins.html#lame`.)

I edited every audio file used in this book with Audacity. Figure 11-6 shows the main user interface.

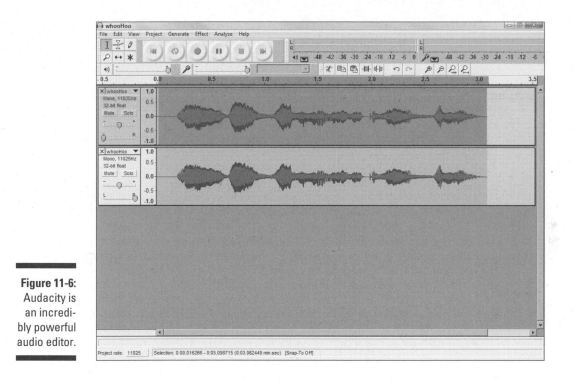

Figure 11-6:
Audacity is
an incredi-
bly powerful
audio editor.

Freesound.org

Freesound.org, at `www.freesound.org`, is an online audio effects database. The database has a great search function that allows you to search for a sound effect by keyword. You can also limit the search by license. You can isolate only those files that have (for example) a very liberal creative commons license.

I was able to find 17 goat sounds (and a llama — I didn't know they made any sounds) on this site, so the next time I need to make a goat game, I'll be ready to roll.

SoundJay.com

SoundJay is another terrific free resource for sound effects. This is a library of well-organized sound effects in many categories. All of the sounds are available for free and without requiring any royalties.

You can begin browsing SoundJay at `www.soundjay.com`.

The sound effects come in `.wav` and `.mp3` formats, so you'll probably also want to make an `.ogg` version with Audacity (described earlier in this chapter).

BFXR Incredible Eight-Bit Sound Effects

Some consider the 8-bit era of the '80s to be the classic gaming era. Even if you don't remember them the first time through, the sound effects from the early days of gaming are enjoying a comeback.

BFXR is an incredible program that allows you to create your own amazing old-school sound effects. It is a simple digital synthesizer, as shown in Figure 11-7.

When you visit the BFXR website at www.bfxr.net, you'll see a somewhat dizzying display of buttons and sliders, but you really don't have to understand everything to have a lot of fun. Grab some headphones if you value your relationships with others in your home, and start pressing some buttons. You can generate a random sound effect by clicking the Randomize button. The other buttons (laser, explosion, hurt, and so on) are also random, but have presets that make the random sound more likely to fit the specific category. Each time you click a button, you get a new random sound effect.

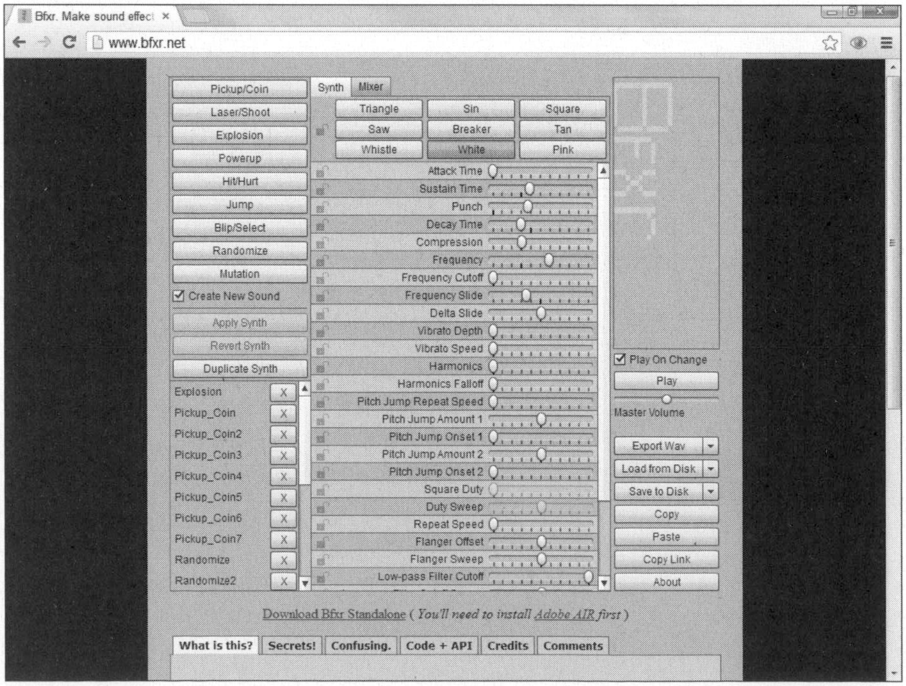

Figure 11-7:
BFXR is a great tool for creating your own sound effects.

Every sound you generate is stored in a list, so you can compare the sounds and listen to them again. When you find a sound you like, you can modify it by playing with the various sliders. Even if you don't understand exactly what you're doing, you can often make very interesting sound effects with some experimentation.

You can save your sounds in two formats. The Save to Disk button saves the file in a native format so you can reload in BFXR and continue playing. When a sound is ready for final use, click the Export Wav button to generate a .wav file. You'll probably want to use Audacity to convert the file to the .ogg and .mp3 formats preferred by simpleGame.

InkScape

GIMP uses a popular graphics technique called "raster graphics." This is consistent with the way graphics are stored and displayed in the computer hardware. There is another way to think about graphics called "vector graphics." The vector technique is attractive for gaming because it's a bit more flexible and allows for arbitrary scaling and rotation without data loss.

Until very recently, web browsers did not natively support vector graphics (which is one reason Flash was so popular among designers and developers). This is changing with HTML5.

Inkscape is a very powerful vector graphics tool that allows you to easily build images using the vector techniques. You can download Inkscape for free from inkscape.org.

The simpleGame engine allows sprites to be stored in Inscape's standard SVG format. You can also export an image to the more standard png format.

You can find a huge number of open and freely available SVG files at openclipart.org.

These files can be edited right in the browser, or you can download them and edit them with Inkscape.

I have a simple character file you can modify if you wish, available at www.aharrisbooks.net/h5g/basicChar.svg.

Chapter 12

Ten Concepts Behind simpleGame

The simpleGame library is designed to be easy to use. Like most code libraries, it simplifies sometimes complex code. You can use simple Game just fine without understanding how it works, but at some point, you'll need to know how the various technologies work. In this chapter, I show some of the key concepts used to create the simpleGame engine.

Many of the ideas are code, but some are really math concepts. If you've ever asked your math teacher when you would use math, game programming is at least one answer. A game programmer really needs to have a solid grasp of math, at least some algebra, geometry, and trigonometry. It's even better to have some knowledge of linear algebra, statistics, and calculus. (On my campus, game programming students typically get a math minor.) It's fine if you don't understand all the math right now, but be sure to look over these ideas to see how things work.

Feel free to look over the code of simpleGame to see how everything fits together. Throughout this chapter, I provide somewhat simplified versions of the code used in simpleGame, but of course you're welcome to look over the actual library. A link is available at my website: www.aharrisbooks.net. In fact, you can even make changes in the library if you wish, but you should probably begin by ensuring that you understand how things work.

Some ideas mentioned here use more advanced concepts in programming and mathematics than I expect for the reader of an introductory book, but looking over these ideas gives you an ideal preview of things you can learn as your studies continue.

Using the Canvas Tag

The `simpleGame` engine's `Scene` object uses one of the most exciting new features of HTML5 — *the canvas tag*. This exciting tag allows you to draw images and other elements directly on a portion of the browser.

Looking at a canvas

Figure 12-1 shows a basic page displaying a canvas with two rectangles and an image.

```
<!DOCTYPE HTML>
<html lang = "en">
<head>
  <title></title>
  <meta charset = "UTF-8" />
  <style type = "text/css">
  </style>
  <script type = "text/javascript">

  function draw(){
    var canvas = document.getElementById("surface");
    var imgBall = new Image();
    imgBall.src = "redBall.png";

    if (canvas.getContext){
      var con = canvas.getContext('2d');
      con.fillStyle = "rgb(255, 255, 0)";
      con.fillRect(40, 140, 150, 50);
      con.drawImage(imgBall, 100, 100, 50, 50);


    } // end if
  } // end draw

  </script>
</head>

<body onload = "draw()">
  <h1>Basic Canvas Demo</h1>

  <canvas id = "surface"
          width = "200"
          height = "200">
    <p>Your browser does not support the canvas tag...</p>
  </canvas>
</body>
</html>
```

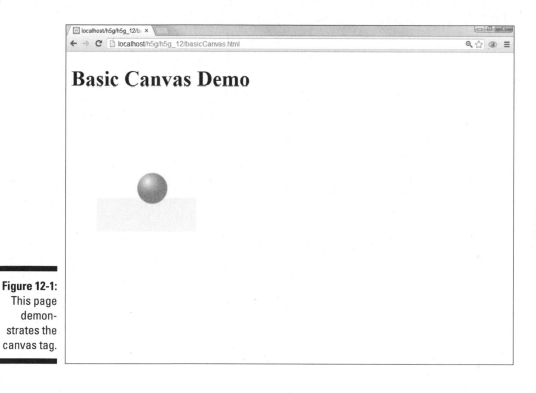

Basic canvas drawing

The canvas tag is an HTML tag, but it's mainly used as a placeholder in HTML. The canvas tag has a *context* attribute, which allows the programmer to draw graphics directly on the page. Here's how this example works:

1. **Add a canvas tag to the HTML.**

   Normally, you'll create a canvas tag in the HTML, but the simpleGame library automatically adds a canvas tag and appends it to the end of the page body.

2. **Create a function for drawing.**

   In this example, the canvas is drawn in a function called when the page initially loads. In simpleGame, the drawing function will be called 20 times per second.

3. **Get a drawing context.**

   The canvas tag supports a 2D drawing context (yes, 3D is coming, but it's not yet widely supported). Use the getContext() method to make a reference to the drawing context.

4. **Create a JavaScript** `Image` **Object.**

   `Sprite` objects in the `simpleGame` library are based on JavaScript images. Begin by creating an `Image` object in JavaScript.

5. **Set the image's source attribute.**

   To link a file to the `Image` object, set the `src` property of the `Image` object to an image file in the same directory as your program. This will associate an image with your document, but the image will not be drawn on the page; instead, it's stored in memory to be used in code.

6. **Set the fill style.**

   You can draw filled and open drawings with the canvas tag. The `fillStyle` can be set to colors as well as patterns and gradients.

7. **Create rectangles.**

   You can draw an open rectangle with the `strokeRect()` method and a solid rectangle with the `fillRect()` method. In the `simpleGame` library, the `Scene` object's `clear()` method simply draws a filled rectangle in the scene's background color.

8. **Draw the image in the canvas.**

   Use the `drawImage()` method to draw an image inside a canvas. There are many variations of this method, but the one used in `simpleGame` specifies the image's position and size.

Of course, there's a great deal more to the canvas tag than this simple demo. I show a few other features in the section "Transformations in Canvas," later in this chapter. For much more information, please see my book *HTML5 Quick Reference For Dummies*. I have an entire chapter on the canvas tag and its various features in that book. You can view all the examples for that book (and indeed all my books) at my website: www.aharrisbooks.net.

Creating an Animation Loop

If the canvas defines the space in a game, an animation loop defines time. Most JavaScript games use a mechanism called `setInterval()` to cause repeated behavior. This function takes two parameters: a function name and a delay value.

Here's some code that simply counts ten times a second:

```
<!DOCTYPE HTML>
<html lang="en-US">
<head>
```

```
    <meta charset="UTF-8">
    <title>counting.html</title>
    <script type="text/javascript">
    var counter = 0;
    var output;

    function init(){
        output = document.getElementById("output");
        setInterval(count, 100);
    }

    function count(){
        counter++;
        output.innerHTML = counter;
    }
    </script>
</head>
<body onload = "init()">
    <div id = "output">
        nothing here yet
    </div>
</body>
</html>
```

The process is straightforward, and you can use it any time you want something to happen at regular intervals:

1. **Create a function that will be repeated.**

   In this simplistic example, the function `count()` will be called ten times per second.

2. **In your initialization code, call `setInterval()`.**

   This will set up the repeated call to the function.

3. **Indicate the function that will repeat.**

   The first parameter is the name of the function that will be repeated. Note that because you're treating the function as a variable, you *do not* include parentheses with the function name.

4. **Indicate the delay.**

   The second parameter is a delay value in milliseconds (a millisecond is 1/1000th of a second). This example runs at a delay of 100 milliseconds, which is 10 frames per second. The `simpleGame` library runs at 20 frames per second.

In `simpleGame`, when you create a `Scene` class, in addition to setting up a canvas, you're also, via the `Scene` class, creating an interval that repeatedly calls the `update()` method of your game. This is why you need to have an `update()` method.

Angles in the Outfield

The `simpleGame` engine allows you to work with all angles in degrees according to the normal navigational system (0 degrees is straight up; angles increase clockwise). Mathematicians use an entirely different system. Figure 12-2 illustrates the difference.

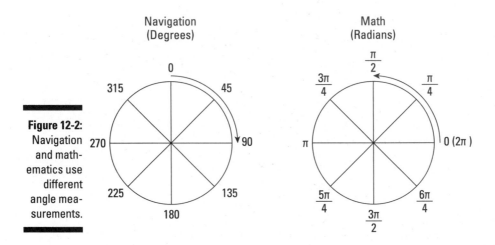

Figure 12-2: Navigation and mathematics use different angle measurements.

Degrees are a perfectly fine (if made up) unit of measurement, but when it comes to mathematical manipulations, they get messy. Mathematicians use another unit called *radians*. The best way to describe a radian is with a true story. When we were dating, my wife had an elderly Doberman. The dog was frequently tied to a post with a cable in the backyard. Over the years, the dog inscribed a perfect circle around that post in the backyard. One day I came over and found that the cable had broken loose at the post, but the dog was still walking around in the circle, dragging the cable behind her. The angle inscribed by the cable in the circular groove was exactly one radian! I was immediately thrilled by this unintentional canine math moment. My wife continues to humor my frequent geekiness episodes. We have a puppy now, and I'm working on teaching him trigonometry.

Radians are most easily expressed as a ratio of pi. pi (π) is defined as the ratio between the circumference and the diameter of a circle. Almost all angle calculations in radians use pi as a starting point.

If you want to convert from degrees to radians, you typically use this formula:

```
radians = (degrees * pi) / 180
```

If you want to go the other direction, the formula is similar:

```
degrees = (radians * 180) / pi
```

JavaScript has a prebuilt constant for pi called `Math.pi`.

The `simpleGame` library takes care of all this for you. I designed the library so you can enter angle measurements in degrees, but these measurements are quietly converted to radians for all the internal math. When you ask for an angle (with the `Sprite` object's `getMoveAngle()` method, for example), you'll get a measurement in degrees, even though the angle is actually stored in radians.

Angle measurements get a little trickier in computing math because radians increase counterclockwise whereas degrees increase clockwise. Also, in most coordinate systems, Y increases upward, but in computer graphics, Y increases downward. The `simpleGame` library quietly handles these issues for you. Feel free to look over the code to see how I handled these details with a little bit of math.

Transformations in Canvas

The `Sprite` class has the capability to move and rotate, but these features are not built into normal JavaScript. I used the transformation features of the canvas tag to get this behavior.

Transformations are math operations that can be applied to any drawing or image to change the appearance. There are three major transformations:

- **translation:** Moves a particular amount in X and Y.
- **rotation:** Rotates around a particular point.
- **scale:** Changes the size of the drawing in X and Y.

The canvas element allows all these operations on any type of drawing. However, the way the canvas element does this gets a little closer to math than you may have gotten before. Transformations in the canvas element can be hard to understand until you understand a little about how they really work.

Coordinates inside coordinates . . .

In math, you don't really transform *objects*. Instead, you modify the *coordinate system* and draw your image in the newly transformed coordinate system. It's common in a vector-drawing application to have several hidden coordinate systems working at once. That's important, because it's the way canvas transformations work. Essentially, when you want to perform transformations on an object, you do the following:

1. **Announce the beginning of a temporary coordinate system.**

   The main image already has its own coordinate system that won't change. Before you can transform anything, you need to build a new coordinate system to hold those changes. The (poorly named) `save()` command indicates the beginning of a new coordinate system definition.

2. **Move the center with** `translate()`.

   The origin (0, 0) starts in the upper-left corner of the canvas by default. Normally, you'll build your transformed objects on the (new) origin and move the origin to place the object. If you translate (50, 50) and then draw an image at (0, 0), the image will be drawn at the origin of the temporary coordinate system, which will be at (50, 50) in the main canvas.

3. **Rotate the coordinate system with** `rotate()`.

   The `rotate()` command rotates the new coordinate system around its origin. The rotation parameter is a degree in radians.

4. **Scale the coordinate system in X and Y.**

   You can also alter the new coordinate system by applying X and Y scale values. This allows you to create stretched and squashed images.

5. **Create elements in the new coordinate system.**

   After you've applied all the transformations you want, you can use all the ordinary canvas drawing techniques. However, these drawings will be drawn in the virtual coordinate system you just made, not in the canvas's main coordinate system.

6. **Close the temporary coordinate system.**

   Generally, you'll want to apply different transformations to different parts of your canvas. When you're finished with a particular transformation, use the `restore()` command to close out the new coordinate system. All subsequent drawing commands will use the default coordinate system of the canvas object.

Transforming an image

It can be hard to understand how mathematical transformations work because they seem so simple on the surface. Build a program to see how this all fits together. Pay attention to how I create a temporary coordinate system.

```html
<!DOCTYPE HTML>
<html lang = "en">
<head>
  <title>transform.html</title>
  <meta charset = "UTF-8" />
  <script type = "text/javascript">

  function draw(){
    var drawing = document.getElementById("drawing");
    var con = drawing.getContext("2d");
    var car = new Image();
    car.src = "car.png";
    con.save();
    con.translate(100, 100);
    con.rotate(Math.PI / 4);
    con.scale(3.0, 1.5);
    con.drawImage(car, -25, -25, 50, 50);
    con.restore();

    //draw a rectangle using the ordinary
    //coordinate system
    con.strokeStyle = "red";
    con.lineWidth = 5;
    con.strokeRect(0, 0, 200, 200);

  } // end draw

  </script>
</head>

<body onload = "draw()">
  <h1>Transformations</h1>

  <canvas id = "drawing"
          height = "200"
          width = "200">
    <p>Canvas not supported</p>
  </canvas>

</body>
</html>
```

The transformation looks like Figure 12-3.

Transformations

Figure 12-3:
This image
has been
translated,
scaled, and
rotated.

This program does the normal canvas setup and then creates a transformation that translates the image to the center of the canvas, rotates the image, and changes the image's size:

1. **Create a page with a canvas.**

   Normally, `simpleGame` will create the canvas for you, but in this case, I'm making a canvas element by hand.

2. **Do all the normal setup stuff.**

   This involves the regular housekeeping: getting access to the canvas and its context and creating the image.

3. **Begin a new coordinate system.**

   The `save()` command doesn't really save anything. It indicates the beginning of a new coordinate system. Any drawing commands that occur between this `save()` statement and the matching `restore()` will follow transformation functions.

4. **Translate the new system.**

   Move the coordinate system to (100, 100), which is the center of the canvas.

5. **Rotate the new system.**

   Rotate the image by pi / 4 radians, which is 45 percent.

6. **Scale the new system.**

   Multiply the X values by 3 and the Y values by 1.5.

7. **Draw an image.**

   Because this image is drawn inside a save() / restore() block, it's drawn with the transformations intact. Note that I offset the actual drawImage() command by half the original image's width and height. I do this in the game engine so the x and y properties of the sprite refer to the center of the sprite, rather than the top-left corner.

8. **End the subsystem with** restore().

   The restore() command closes up the temporary coordinate system so all subsequent commands will refer to the parent coordinate system. (If Tim Berners-Lee is reading this: Call me. I'll help you come up with better names for things next time . . .)

9. **Draw a red rectangle in the default system.**

   The red stroked rectangle is drawn outside the normal coordinate system, so it's not scaled or rotated.

The main design of the Sprite object is an image surrounded by a transformation. When you create a sprite, it builds the image object, and it defines a transformation with translation, rotation, and scale. As you manipulate the position, angle, and speed of the sprite, you're really simply changing the values sent to the transform. I offset the image so the (x, y) properties of the sprite specify the center of the sprite. That way, sprites rotate around their center, which gives a more natural appearance.

Vector Projection

The Sprite object stores the sprite's position as x and y, and motion is stored as dx (difference in x) and dy (difference in y). The computer uses dx and dy to determine how to move a sprite on each frame, but often it's much easier to think in speed and direction. Wouldn't it be great if you could figure out the appropriate dx and dy values for any speed and direction? Fortunately, the ancient Greeks came up with a system for solving exactly this kind of problem. Once you understand this technique, called *vector projection*, you'll be able to calculate the dx and dy values for any angle, any speed.

Examining the problem

It's easiest to think about a sprite's motion in terms of its speed and direction. These two characteristics taken together are called the sprite's *motion vector*. A vector is simply a mathematical construct that has a direction and a magnitude. If you want to move a sprite at a certain speed in a certain direction, you need a way to translate the motion vector into dx and dy values so that you know exactly how much to add to x and y during the current frame. (dx and dy are sometimes known as the vector *components*).

The distance the sprite should travel in a frame is also the speed of that sprite (in pixels-per-frame). Sometimes it's easier to think of this value as a speed, and sometimes it's easier to think of it as a distance. It's really both. Mathematicians sometimes sidestep this issue by simply calling the length r (for radius, like in a circle). You'll see yet another name for this length (hypotenuse) when you bring in trigonometry. This all seems confusing, but it's actually one of the nice things about math. There's often a number of ways to look at a problem, and the different names for things can help you see how a particular kind of problem-solving can help. In math books, you'll usually see the length/speed marked as r, so that's what I use.

The angle is a bit more straightforward, as it just indicates the angle. Mathematicians typically use lowercase Greek symbols for angles. The symbol theta (θ) is commonly used for a generic angle. Again, because that's what you're likely to see in a math book, I use the same thing here.

Take a look at Figure 12-4 to see some notation commonly used in this kind of problem.

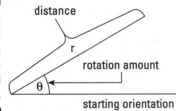

Figure 12-4:
Speed and direction are commonly called *r* and *theta*.

distance

r

rotation amount

θ

starting orientation

For the sake of argument, assume that you want to make a sprite travel at a speed called r, in a direction called theta. The symbol θ as it appears on the diagram is pronounced "theta." It is a letter in the Greek alphabet.

It's important to notice that the rotation amount is measured from the x axis. In fact, this is one reason mathematicians use this particular kind of angle measurement.

Building a triangle

Given any r and theta values, you can easily make a triangle by drawing horizontal and vertical lines as in Figure 12-5.

Figure 12-5:
Draw horizontal and vertical lines (dashed) to make a triangle.

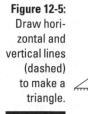

Once you've created the triangle, it's easy to see how dx and dy are related to r and theta. The length of the horizontal line shows exactly how far you have to move in the x axis to get from the beginning to the end of the line. The length of this horizontal line will be the value for dx. The vertical line indicates how far you have to travel in the y axis to get from the beginning to the end of the line, so the length of the vertical line is dy.

Would you like sides with that?

Now comes the clever part: The Greeks noticed that every right triangle preserves certain ratios. For example, if theta is 30 degrees, the ratio between the lengths of dx and r will remain the same, no matter how long they are. If you have access to these ratios and you know one angle and one side length of a right triangle, you can figure out all the other angles and side lengths.

Figure 12-6 shows the notation used to think about triangles in this way.

Figure 12-6:
The sides of the triangles have different names in trigonometry.

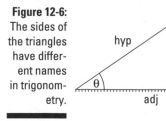

It's easier to think about the triangle if you give the sides some new names:

- ✔ **The hypotenuse** is the longest side, opposite the right angle. This side is also the length the sprite will move.
- ✔ **The adjacent side** is the side touching the angle in question. For this problem, the adjacent side is also dx.
- ✔ **The opposite side** is the side opposite theta. For vector projection problems, the opposite side is dy.

Math teachers sometimes refer to the mythical term SOHCAHTOA as a mnemonic device for remembering how the various ratios work. Here's what it means:

- ✔ **SOH:** The length of the opposite side divided by the length of the hypotenuse is called the *sine* of theta. This is abbreviated sin(theta) = opp/hyp or *SOH*.
- ✔ **CAH:** The length of the adjacent side divided by the length of the hypotenuse is called the *cosine* of theta. This is abbreviated cos(theta) = adj/hyp or *CAH*.
- ✔ **TOA:** The opposite side length divided by the adjacent side length is called the *tangent* of theta. The tangent relationship is sometimes stated tan(theta) = opp/adj or *TOA*.

Solving for dx and dy

After you have all this notation in place, it's actually not that difficult to solve for dx. Figure 12-7 shows the formula.

$$\sin \theta = \frac{opp}{hyp} = \frac{dy}{r}$$

$$dy = r * (\sin \theta)$$

Figure 12-7:
Here's how to solve for dx and dy.

$$\cos \theta = \frac{opp}{adj} = \frac{dx}{r}$$

$$dx = r * (\cos \theta)$$

It's not nearly as frightening as it looks. Here's what's going on:

1. **Determine the trigonometry function you need.**

   Cosine of theta is the opposite side divided by the adjacent side (COH = opposite over adjacent.) This will be handy for figuring out the value of dx.

2. **Translate to vector terms.**

   Translate the formula into terms that work for the actual problem: `cos(theta) = dx / r`.

3. **Solve for dx.**

   With a little algebra, you can transpose the problem so it solves for dx: `dx = r * cos(theta)`. Given any length (*r*) and angle (*theta*), you can use this formula to determine dx.

4. **Repeat for dy.**

   The process is almost the same for dy, except the sin function turns out to be more useful.

Converting components back to vectors

It's also possible to go in the other direction. For example, you might know two points and want to know the angle and direction between them. To calculate the angle, return to SOHCAHTOA. If you divide the opposite side (dy) by the adjacent side (dx), you'll get the tangent of theta. Using the arctangent function (usually abbreviated `atan`), you can get the angle between dx and dy in radians. This can then be converted to degrees. Likewise, you can use the famous Pythagorean theorem to determine the distance between any two points. Figure 12-8 illustrates the formulas used to determine the angle and distance between any two points.

Figure 12-8:
Given any two points, you can mathematically determine the angle and distance between them.

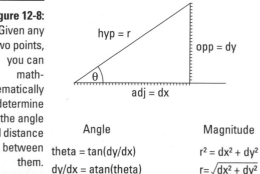

Angle

$theta = tan(dy/dx)$

$dy/dx = atan(theta)$

Magnitude

$r^2 = dx^2 + dy^2$

$r = \sqrt{dx^2 + dy^2}$

Using the Sound Object

The Sound object simply encapsulates an HTML5 audio element. The actual code from simpleGame.js is straightforward enough:

```
function Sound(src){
  //sound effect class
  //builds a sound effect based on a url
  //may need both ogg and mp3.
  this.snd = document.createElement("audio");
  this.snd.src = src;
  //preload sounds if possible (won't work on IOS)
  this.snd.setAttribute("preload", "auto");
  //hide controls for now
  this.snd.setAttribute("controls", "none");
  this.snd.style.display = "none";
  //attach to document so controls will show when needed
  document.body.appendChild(this.snd);

  this.play = function(){
    this.snd.play();
  } // end play function

  this.showControls = function(){
    //generally not needed.
    //crude hack for IOS
    this.snd.setAttribute("controls", "controls");
    this.snd.style.display = "block";
  } // end showControls

} // end sound class def
```

The sound element actually acts in a way similar to the sprite: It creates an object around a standard HTML element and adds a few new features to it. Here's how I designed this object:

1. **Build the sound as an object.**

   The sound element is actually an object. This allows me to customize the sound and add new methods to it. Check Chapter 6 for more information on building custom objects.

2. **Create an audio element.**

   The document.createElement() command allows you to build any sort of HTML element you might want. In this case, the snd attribute is an audio element.

3. **Set the** src **attribute.**

   When the programmer creates an instance of the Sound class, she is expected to send a src parameter. This is used to specify the actual sound file that will be played.

4. **Try to preload the sounds.**

   The audio element has a preload property. If it is set to auto, the sound will load before being played the first time. Unfortunately, this feature does not work in the IOS system.

5. **Turn off the controls.**

   A standard audio HTML element contains a control panel with volume, a play button, and a scrub bar. In a game, you typically do not want these features, so I set the controls attribute to none. I also modify the CSS to hide the element.

6. **Add the sound to the document.**

   If you want a created element to appear on the web page (as I sometimes will with the Sound class), you use the body.appendChild() method to attach the element to the visual display.

7. **Create a** play() **method.**

   The play() method is quite simple. It simply plays the sound.

8. **Add** showControls **as a workaround for IOS.**

   As mentioned, Apple's mobile devices do not support audio preloading, so if you want to play sounds on one of these devices, you need to make the controls visible. This is easy to do with the showControls() method.

Reading the Keyboard

The keyboard is a primary input technology, especially for desktop machines. The standard way to read the keyboard is to set up special functions called *event-handlers*. JavaScript has a number of predefined event-handlers you can implement. The keyDemo.html program illustrates a couple of keyboard handlers in action.

```
<!DOCTYPE HTML>
<html lang="en-US">
<head>
    <meta charset="UTF-8">
    <title>keyDemo.html</title>
```

```
<script type="text/javascript">

var keysDown = new Array(256);
var output;

function init(){
  output = document.getElementById("output");
  initKeys();
  document.onkeydown = updateKeys;
  document.onkeyup = clearKeys;
} // end init

updateKeys = function(e){
  //set current key
  currentKey = e.keyCode;
  keysDown[e.keyCode] = true;
  output.innerHTML = "current key: " + currentKey;

}

clearKeys = function(e){
  currentKey = null;
  keysDown[e.keyCode] = false;
  output.innerHTML = "current key: None";
}

initKeys = function(){
  //initialize keys array to all false
  for (keyNum = 0; keyNum < 256; keyNum++){
    keysDown[keyNum] = false;
  } // end for
} // end initKeys

//keyboard constants
K_A = 65; K_B = 66; K_C = 67; K_D = 68; K_E = 69; K_F = 70; K_G = 71;
K_H = 72; K_I = 73; K_J = 74; K_K = 75; K_L = 76; K_M = 77; K_N = 78;
K_O = 79; K_P = 80; K_Q = 81; K_R = 82; K_S = 83; K_T = 84; K_U = 85;
K_V = 86; K_W = 87; K_X = 88; K_Y = 89; K_Z = 90;
K_LEFT = 37; K_RIGHT = 39; K_UP = 38;K_DOWN = 40; K_SPACE = 32;
K_ESC = 27; K_PGUP = 33; K_PGDOWN = 34; K_HOME = 36; K_END = 35;
K_0 = 48; K_1 = 49; K_2 = 50; K_3 = 51; K_4 = 52; K_5 = 53;
K_6 = 54; K_7 = 55; K_8 = 56; K_9 = 57;
</script>
</head>
<body onload = "init()">
  <div id = "output">
      Press a key to see its code
  </div>
</body>
</html>
```

Managing basic keyboard input

This particular example demonstrates basic keyboard-checking as well as the more sophisticated technique used in simpleGame. Here's how the basic version works:

1. **Assign a function to** onkeydown.

   The document.onkeydown attribute is a special property. If you assign a function to this property, that function will be automatically called each time the operating system recognizes a key press. In this example, I assign the function updateKeys.

2. **Create the function, including an event parameter.**

   The updateKeys() function will automatically be given an event object (normally called e).

3. **Determine which key was pressed.**

   The e.keyCode property returns a numeric code indicating which key was pressed. In the keyDemo program (as well as simpleGame), the currentKey variable holds this numeric value.

4. **Compare the key to one of the keyboard constants.**

   It's hard to remember which keys are associated with which numeric values, so keyDemo and simpleGame provide a list of keyboard constants. They're easy to remember: K_A is the A key, and K_SPACE is the space bar. Of course, you can add other keys if there's some key you want to use that isn't available.

Responding to multiple key presses

The currentKey mechanism is simple to use, but it turns out to be less than ideal for gaming situations. Frequently, the player will have multiple keys pressed at once. For this reason, simpleGame uses a more sophisticated technique.

1. **Create an array called** keysDown.

   This array is a global variable with 256 values. Each element of the array will be a Boolean (true or false) value, indicating whether the associated key is currently pressed or not.

2. **Initialize the** keysDown **array.**

   The default value for each element of keysDown should be false (as presumably no keys are pressed during initialization). This is done in a function with a simple loop.

3. **When a key press is recognized, set the corresponding Boolean.**

   In addition to setting the `currentKey` variable, set the corresponding value in the `keysDown` array to true.

4. **Make a second event handler for key up conditions.**

   When the document senses a key being released, a second event-handler sets the appropriate member of `keysDown` to false.

Managing the Touch Interface

The touch interface is a new feature of HTML5 specifically aimed at mobile browsers. At first glance, it may seem that touch screens act just like the mouse, but this is not the case. A mouse always has a position, and it has multiple buttons that can be pressed. A touch screen device registers a position only when it's touched, so there is no hover state. Also, many devices allow more than one finger on the screen at a time, so there's a possibility of multiple positions. Finally, touch screens are frequently read as gestures, so it becomes important to determine (for example) the length of a swipe. The `controller.html` page illustrated in Figure 12-9 shows how to read a touch interface. It describes a number of touch techniques that are integrated into `simpleGame`.

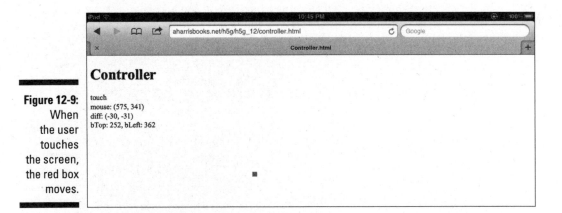

Figure 12-9: When the user touches the screen, the red box moves.

Of course, to get the full effect of this program, you need to view it on a mobile device with a touch interface.

Look over the code to see some of the techniques used to manage touch interfaces.

```
<!DOCTYPE HTML>
<html lang="en-US">
<head>
<meta charset="UTF-8">
  <title>Controller.html</title>
  <script type="text/javascript">
  var touchable;
  var output;
  var box;
  var result = "No touch";
  var touches = [];
  var startX, startY;
  var mouseX, mousey
  var diffX = 0;
  var diffY = 0;
  var bTop = 0;
  var bLeft = 0;
  var SENSITIVITY = 50;
//smaller numbers = more sensitive

function init(){
    touchable = 'createTouch' in document;
    output = document.getElementById("output");
    box = document.getElementById("box");
    if (touchable){
      document.addEventListener('touchstart', onTouchStart, false);
      document.addEventListener('touchmove', onTouchMove, false);
      document.addEventListener('touchend', onTouchEnd, false);

    } // end if
    setInterval(update, 10);
  } // end init

  function onTouchStart(event){
    result = "touch";
    touches = event.touches;
    mouseX = touches[0].screenX;
    mouseY = touches[0].screenY;
    startX = mouseX;
    startY = mouseY;
  } // end onTouchStart

  function onTouchMove(event){
    event.preventDefault();
    touches = event.touches;
    mouseX = touches[0].screenX;
    mouseY = touches[0].screenY;
    diffX = mouseX - startX;
    diffY = mouseY - startY;
  } // end onTouchMove
```

```
function onTouchEnd(event){
  result = "no touch";
  touches = event.touches;
  diffX = 0;
  diffY = 0;
} // end onTouchEnd

function update(){
  output.innerHTML = result + "<br />";
  output.innerHTML += "mouse: (" + mouseX + ", " + mouseY + ") <br />";
  output.innerHTML += "diff: (" + diffX + ", " + diffY + ") <br />";

  //move box according to controller
  bTop += parseInt(diffY/SENSITIVITY);
  bLeft += parseInt(diffX /SENSITIVITY);

  output.innerHTML += "bTop: " + bTop + ", bLeft: " + bLeft;

  box.style.top = bTop + "px";
  box.style.left = bLeft + "px";

} // end update

</script>
<style type="text/css">
  #scene {
    width: 100px;
    height: 100px;
    color: white;
    background-color: black;
  }

  #box {
    width: 10px;
    height: 10px;
    background-color: red;
  }

  /* remove special touch styles */
  * {
    -webkit-touch-callout: none;
    -webkit-text-size-adjust: none;
    -webkit-tap-highlight-color: rgba(0, 0, 0, 0);
    -webkit-user-select: none;
  }
</style>
</head>
<body onload = "init()">
  <h1>Controller</h1>

  <div id = "box"
```

```
        style = "position: absolute; left:0px; top: 0px;">
  </div>

  <div id = "output">
    No touch
  </div>

</body>
</html>
```

Handling touch data and events

As in most interesting problems, the data is really the key. Here is the data you need to keep track of for this problem:

- ✔ **mouseX and mouseY:** At its simplest, a touch interface acts somewhat like a mouse. These variables keep track of where the touch is happening on the screen.

- ✔ **diffX and diffY:** It's common to treat a touch interface as a virtual joystick. This is accomplished by storing the initial X and Y position of a touch and then comparing those initial values to motion. So, if you touch and slide left, the diffX will register a negative value.

- ✔ **startX and startY:** These variables store the initial position of a touch and are used to calculate diffX and diffY.

- ✔ **touches[]:** Many devices support *multi-touch*, which means you can touch the screen with more than one finger at a time. The touch mechanism supports this feature by storing all touches as an array of touch objects. The simpleGame library focuses on one touch, which is touches[0].

- ✔ **SENSITIVITY:** This variable is actually treated as a constant. The diffX and diffY values that come from the virtual joystick are too sensitive for real use, so they are divided by a sensitivity constant to give more useful inputs. You can change this value to get a more or less sensitive virtual joystick.

The touch mechanism relies heavily on custom events to do its magic. Here's how it works:

1. **Determine if touch is supported.**

   If the document object has a createTouch method, the device has touch support. This mechanism is used throughout simpleGame to determine if the device supports touch input.

2. **Add event listeners.**

   When the user touches the screen, three possible events are triggered: `touchStart`, `touchMove`, and `touchEnd`. In the `init()` function, you can assign functions to each of these events.

3. **When a touch starts, register the starting positions.**

   Record the current position as `mouseX` and `mouseY`. Also, copy these values to `startX` and `startY` so subsequent movement can be used as the basis of the virtual joystick.

4. **When the touch moves, register the difference.**

   When the user moves a finger after the initial press, the `onTouch-Move()` function will activate. This function records `mouseX` and `mouseY`, and also determines the difference between these current values and the `startX` and `startY` variables.

5. **When the touch ends, reset the joystick.**

   The `diffX` and `diffY` variables act like a joystick, so when the touch is finished, these values should be reset to zero.

6. **Disable default touch behavior.**

   Mobile websites already have default behavior for touches (scrolling and resizing the screen). If you're using the touch interface as a virtual mouse or joystick, you'll want to turn off this default behavior. This is done both through the `event.preventDefault()` method and a few specialty CSS attributes.

Note that this example is a bit simplistic, and the actual behavior in `simpleGame` is a more sophisticated example of the same principles.

Collision Detection

Collision detection is a major part of game programming because most interesting things in games occur after a collision between sprites. JavaScript does not have a built-in collision routine, so I added one.

Enabling bounding-box collisions

Here's the basic code for collisions from `simpleGame.js`:

```
this.collidesWith = function(sprite){
    // a method of the sprite object
    //check for collision with another sprite
```

```
    //collisions only activated when both sprites are visible
    collision = false;
    if (this.visible){
      if (sprite.visible){
          //dcfinc borders
          myLeft = this.x;
          myRight = this.x + this.width;
          myTop = this.y;
          myBottom = this.y + this.height;
          otherLeft = sprite.x;
          otherRight = sprite.x + sprite.width;
          otherTop = sprite.y;
          otherBottom = sprite.y + sprite.height;

          //assume collision
          collision = true;

          //determine non-colliding states
          if ((myBottom < otherTop) ||
              (myTop > otherBottom) ||
              (myRight < otherLeft) ||
              (myLeft > otherRight)) {
                collision = false;
          } // end if

      } // end 'other visible' if
    } // end 'I'm visible' if

    return collision;
} // end collidesWith
```

The `simpleGame` library uses a very standard type of collision detection called *bounding rectangle detection*. Essentially, this works by ignoring the actual pixels of the sprites, but looking instead at the rectangular shapes containing the sprites. This leads to a very fast and efficient (if somewhat inaccurate and inconsistent) collision routine.

The collision routine not only checks for whether two objects are colliding, but it also ignores collisions if either of the sprites is invisible:

1. **Set the initial collision value to false.**

   The `collision` variable is a Boolean indicating whether the two objects are considered overlapping or not. Initially, the value for collisions is set to false.

2. **Ensure that both sprites are visible.**

   In the `simpleGame` engine, sprites have a `visible` property. If this is set to `true`, the sprite is displayed on the screen and registers collisions. Before checking for collisions, ensure that both sprites are visible with a pair of nested `if` statements.

3. **Determine boundary variables.**

   The coding is easier to follow if you begin by creating variables to represent the top, bottom, and sides of each sprite.

4. **Set `collision` to `true`.**

   It's easier to find conditions that prove two rectangles do not collide, so begin by assuming they're colliding.

5. **Test for noncolliding states.**

   If one sprite's bottom is smaller than the other one's top, the sprites do not collide. Check the other three conditions that would prevent a collision. If any of these are true, the sprites are not colliding, so set `collision` to `false`. Note that the `||` operator stands for the Boolean operation `or`. I'm not typically a big fan of Boolean logic in `if` statements (at least for beginning programmers), but the logic is pretty straightforward in this case.

6. **Return the collision state.**

   The function returns the value of the `collision` variable. If the sprites are found to be colliding, the function returns the value `true`. Otherwise, the function will return the value `false`.

Calculating the distance between sprites

The `distanceTo()` method of the `Sprite` object provides an alternative collision mechanism. This technique doesn't actually check for collisions. Instead, it returns the distance (in pixels) between the centers of the two sprites. You can then check this against some threshold value to determine whether the sprites have collided.

```
this.distanceTo = function(sprite){
    // method of the Sprite object
    //get centers of sprites
    myX = this.x;
    myY = this.y;
    otherX = sprite.x;
    otherY = sprite.y;
    diffX = myX - otherX;
    diffY = myY - otherY;
    dist = Math.sqrt((diffX * diffX) + (diffY * diffY));
    return dist;
} // end distanceTo
```

Distance is calculated by the old, faithful Pythagorean theorem:

1. **Find the differences in** X **and** Y.

   This will determine the sides of a right triangle, which can be used to determine the distance between the objects.

2. **Use the Pythagorean theorem.**

   Remember that A squared plus B squared equals C squared, so if `diffX` is A, `diffY` is B, and distance is C, you can add the squares of `diffX` and `diffY` and then take the square root of the sums to determine the distance.

Using the distance for collisions is about as fast as a bounding-box collision, but has two additional advantages: The collision sensitivity can be adjusted (by picking a larger or smaller threshold), and the distance required for a collision is independent of the image's size or rotation. See Chapter 6 for a discussion on how to use both techniques in `simpleGame`.

Boundary Checking

Once sprites begin moving, there is always the possibility they'll leave the screen. Typically, game developers respond in one of five ways: wrap, bounce, stop, die, or continue. The `simpleGame` library has a boundary-checking routine that allows you to easily specify which of these default behaviors to use. The sprite's `boundAction` property indicates which action should be used. You can use the boundary-checker to do the following:

1. **Determine the borders.**

   The borders are determined by the canvas width. To make things easier, I assigned variables called `topBorder`, `bottomBorder`, `leftBorder`, and `rightBorder`.

2. **Check to see if the user is off a border.**

   I then made another series of variables that contain Boolean values indicating whether the sprite is off one of the borders: `offRight`, `offLeft`, `offTop`, and `offBottom`. Use basic if statements to determine if the sprite is off the screen in one of these ways.

3. **Determine the boundary action.**

   Use a simple `if` statement to determine which boundary action is currently set for the sprite.

4. **If the** boundAction **is** WRAP:

   Change the x or y variable to the opposite side, but leave the dx and dy values alone.

5. **If the** boundAction **is** BOUNCE:

   Invert dy if the sprite bounced off the top or bottom, and dx if the sprite bounced off the left or right. It's not necessary to change x or y directly.

6. **If the** boundAction **is** STOP:

   Simply set the speed to zero regardless of which boundary was exited.

7. **If the** boundAction **is** DIE:

   Set the speed to zero and invoke the sprite's hide() method. This will cause the sprite to disappear and no longer be considered in collision calculations.

8. **Any other** boundAction **is considered** CONTINUE.

   No action is necessary here because the sprite will continue moving even though it's not visible. If this is the desired effect, you should somehow indicate to the user where the sprite is, or provide some way for the sprite to return.

Here is part of the code for the collision-checking routine:

```
offRight = false;
offLeft = false;
offTop = false;
offBottom = false;

if (this.x > rightBorder){
  offRight = true;
}

if (this.x < leftBorder){
  offLeft = true;
}

if (this.y > bottomBorder){
  offBottom = true;
}

if (this.y < 0){
  offTop = true;
}

if (this.boundAction == WRAP){
  if (offRight){
      this.x = leftBorder;
```

```
      } // end if

      if (offBottom){
         this.y = topBorder;
      } // end if

      if (offLeft){
         this.x = rightBorder;
      } // end if

      if (offTop){
         this.y = bottomBorder;
      }
   } else if (this.boundAction == BOUNCE){
      if (offTop || offBottom){
         this.dy *= -1;
         this.calcSpeedAngle();
         this.imgAngle = this.moveAngle;
      }

      if (offLeft || offRight){
         this.dx *= -1;
         this.calcSpeedAngle();
         this.imgAngle = this.moveAngle;
      }

   } else if (this.boundAction == STOP){
      if (offLeft || offRight || offTop || offBottom){
         this.setSpeed(0);
      }
   } else if (this.boundAction == DIE){
      if (offLeft || offRight || offTop || offBottom){
        this.hide();
        this.setSpeed(0);
      }

   } else {
     //keep on going forever
   }
} // end checkbounds
```

If you want to change a sprite's boundary action in simpleGame, you can use the setBoundAction() method to do so.

Note that a few situations may require different behaviors. For example, you may want to wrap around the sides but stop at the top or bottom. If you need a more specific behavior, just build a new checkBounds() method for your sprite. However, you'll need to check all boundaries because your new checkBounds() will completely overwrite the one built into simpleGame.

Chapter 13

Ten Game Starters

In This Chapter

▶ Learning to build various game types

▶ Storing high scores on the browser

▶ Building tile-based worlds

▶ Creating simple artificial intelligence algorithms

▶ Writing a lot of games!

*F*or the final chapter, take a look at a number of different games that can be built with the skills learned throughout the book. Each of the games featured below is a "starter" game. I illustrate some key ideas and sometimes introduce a new concept or two. None of the games is completely finished: I deliberately left the graphics simplistic, and left out many details like audio, scorekeeping, and multiplayer functionality.

For each program, I illustrate the basic type of game I'm trying to produce, point out a few key technologies or ideas, and give you some suggestions on how to build your own game from this starting package.

Note that I'm not printing out every code listing in this chapter. Instead, I encourage you to play around with each game on my website, (www.aharris books.net) look at the code yourself, download it, and modify it as much as you wish.

I reproduce code snippets that illustrate a particular idea from a code example when that makes sense.

In this chapter, I also am including GIMP images in .xcf format so you can see my original images and change them as you wish.

Lunar Lander

This is one of the oldest game types. The basic idea is to replicate landing on a planet without an atmosphere. The Apollo astronauts had a limited amount of fuel to slow a rapidly moving spacecraft and bring it to the surface safely. This game, shown in Figure 13-1, is a variation of that theme.

The essence of a lunar-lander game is the interplay between thrust and gravity. The game relies heavily on the addVector() method described throughout Chapter 8. Gravity imparts a small downward thrust every frame, which can be counteracted by thrust from the arrow keys.

The game features four different lander images (to provide feedback that the user is applying thrust), which are simply swapped with the setImage() method as needed.

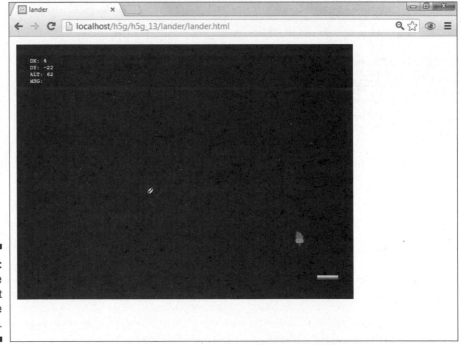

Figure 13-1:
Land the
spacecraft
on the
platform.

The eagle has landed

The most interesting part of this game is the landing routine. The ordinary collision routine is not specific enough to handle this type of collision, as the landing will be considered a safe landing only if a number of conditions are true. The cleanest way to check for multiple conditions is in a deeply nested `if` structure, like the following:

```
tLander.checkLanding = function(){
  if (this.falling){
    if (this.y > 525){
      if (this.x < platform.x + 10){
        if (this.x > platform.x - 10){
          if (this.dx < .2){
            if (this.dx > -.2){
              if (this.dy < 2){
                this.setSpeed(0);
                this.falling = false;
                message = "Nice Landing!";
              } else {
                message = "too much vertical speed";
              } // end if
            } else {
              message = "too fast to left";
            } // end if
          } else {
            message = "too fast to right";
          } // end if
        } // end 'x too big' if
      } // end 'x too small' if
    } // end 'y not big enough' if
  } // end 'are we falling?' if
} // end checkLanding
```

When you're checking for several conditions at once, it's best to create a separate `if` statement for each. Place each `if` statement inside the next, so the most deeply nested part of the code represents success.

1. **Determine if you're falling.**

   I created a Boolean variable called `falling` that describes whether the spacecraft is falling or landed. If `falling` is true, the gravity force is turned off. It only makes sense to check for a landing state if you're currently falling.

2. **Check the Y value.**

   Because the platform is placed at a Y value of 550, the lander will appear to be landed when its Y value is larger than 525. I'm really only concerned with the bottom of the lander touching the top of the platform. Note that this check happens inside the `falling` check. If any condition fails, it is not necessary to check the others.

3. **Check the X value.**

   I want the center of the lander to be within ten pixels of the center of the platform, so use a pair of nested `if` statements to check the X locations.

4. **Check horizontal speed.**

   For a safe landing, the craft must have a `dx` value between -0.2 and 0.2. (This is somewhat arbitrary, but upon testing, it feels about right.) This is best checked with a pair of nested `if` statements.

5. **Check vertical speed.**

   If everything else is working well, check to see that the craft is not falling too rapidly. Use the `dy` property to determine how quickly the spacecraft is falling.

6. **Provide feedback with `else` clauses.**

   A deeply nested structure like this shows you the real value of proper indentation and commenting. Provide feedback in the various `else` clauses to explain why the landing was considered a failure. (Notice I didn't provide feedback when the lander is too far from the platform because this state happens during most of the gameplay.)

Producing a text console

Another interesting part of the code is the mechanism for displaying text data to the user. The easiest way to do this is through a simple HTML `div`. Use CSS to place the `div` exactly where you want it to be. While I rarely use absolute positioning in normal web development, it makes sense in the context of creating a label for a game. Note that you might need to set the `z-index` property to a high value to ensure it appears above the canvas, or it may not be visible to the user. Here's the CSS that makes my label look like output on the screen:

```
#stats {
    position: absolute;
    font-family: monospace;
    left: 50px;
    top: 50px;
    z-index: 999;
    color: white;
}
```

Enhancing the game

This is just a starting point for the game. Many other interesting features could be added:

- ✓ **Fuel:** Add a fuel variable that is decremented each time the user applies thrust. Vertical thrust should use more fuel than horizontal adjustments. If the fuel level gets below zero, ignore further thrust inputs. This mechanism puts a realistic complication into the game.

- ✓ **Powerups:** Add some other features the user can earn: bonus fuel, less intense gravity, a wider platform.

- ✓ **Multiple landings:** Maybe move the landing pad after a successful landing, or have the user carry an object to a second platform.

- ✓ **Obstacles:** Put space junk or buildings in the way that will crash the player on contact.

- ✓ **Change the theme:** The same mechanics can easily be used for a helicopter or hot air balloon game.

Mail Pilot

This is an example of a scrolling racer game. This type of game has long been a staple of the video game universe because there can be so many interesting variations. In this particular iteration, you're a pilot flying a plane over an island archipelago. Your job is to fly over the islands and avoid the clouds. The game features user control of the airplane's X position and an endlessly scrolling world.

Figure 13-2 shows this game in action.

The approach to this game is quite similar to all games in the book:

- ✓ **Identify the key variables:** In this game, the main variables are the airplane, the islands, and the clouds. All are implemented sprite objects.

- ✓ **Create each object in isolation:** As I did with the frog game first introduced in Chapter 7, identify what each object should do and implement those basic features.

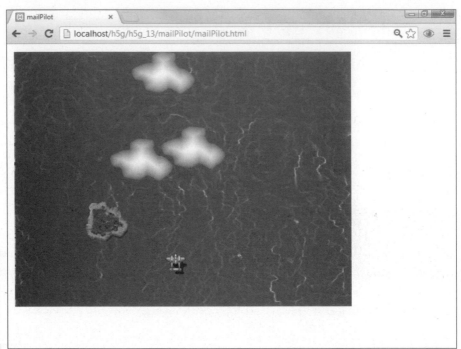

✔ **Build a single element; then convert it to an array:** The `clouds` object is really an array. It's very common to have arrays of objects. The key is to build a single element first that does what you want and then convert that object to an array. Typically, when you do so, you'll build two custom functions. The first function creates the array and uses a `for` loop to initialize each object in the array. The second function also has a `for` loop that steps through each object, invoking any of its event functions and updating each object on the screen.

✔ **Manage interactions:** Most of the interesting things that happen in an arcade game occur when objects collide, so collision routines are an important part of game development.

Building an "endless" background

One interesting feature of this game is the endless tiled background. The user avatar doesn't move forward at all. Instead, the illusion of motion comes from having a background that moves down perpetually, making it look like the plane is moving up.

Of course, it's impossible to create a truly endless background, but you can do a couple of tricks to produce a believable illusion:

1. **Build a sprite for the background.**

   The easiest way to get the moving background behavior is to simply make the background a very large sprite.

2. **Create an image larger than the scene.**

   As this particular graphic is meant to tile vertically, I make it the width of the scene (800px) but much taller than the scene (1440px tall for a 600px tall scene). Larger sizes lead to less-obvious repetition but will be more resource-intensive. If you want horizontal scrolling, make your image larger on the X axis than the scene.

3. **Duplicate the top and the bottom.**

   The key to an "endless" scrolling effect is to have the top and bottom (or left and right of a horizontal image) identical to each other. Use the copy and paste tool of your graphics package with the Clone and Smudge tools to get this effect.

4. **Overwrite the** checkBounds **function.**

   The background sprite will need custom boundary behavior, so over-write the sprite's checkBounds method.

5. **Check to be sure the background never leaves the screen.**

   In the Mail Pilot example, the sprite starts far above the scene and moves downward. With some testing (and the console.log() command), I was able to determine that my background begins to leave the scene at a Y value of 720. Use an if statement to check for when that happens.

6. **Move the background so the identical section is showing.**

   The top and bottom of my ocean gif are the same, so when the ocean is about to leave the scene, the user is seeing the top of the large ocean gif. Change the Y value so the user is now seeing the identical bottom of the same .GIF, and keep it moving. You may need to use console.log() and some testing to get it to work exactly like you want.

Here's the code for the checkBounds() method so you can see it in action. Note that you'll have to change the specific values to match your image size.

```
tOcean.checkBounds = function(){
   //seamless ocean gif repeats
   if (this.y > 720){
       this.setPosition(400, -120)
   } // end if
} // end checkBounds
```

Improving the top-down racer

This type of game is very popular because it's easy to write and can be modified in a number of simple ways to get many different types of games. Here are a few suggestions:

- **Add a scoring mechanism.** The most obvious improvement is to add some sort of scoring system. Award points for touching the islands and take away life for touching clouds.

- **Build up the difficulty level.** Consider adding more clouds, changing the size of the various elements, or changing the speed.

- **Add powerups.** Powerups are simple sprites that provide some sort of benefit or disadvantage when they're activated (usually by shooting or running over the powerup). The options are nearly limitless but here are a few starter ideas: Temporarily allow vertical as well as horizontal motion, change the speed, and make the plane larger or smaller.

- **Change the motion.** Right now, the plane moves only on the horizontal axis. Allowing motion on the vertical axis as well will dramatically change the gameplay.

- **Add weapons.** Add bullets for an interesting twist. If you want a lot of bullets, you'll need to create an array.

- **Switch to horizontal scrolling.** You can switch to horizontal scrolling quite easily. You can also allow scrolling in either axis, but you'll have to really think through the boundary-checking aspects.

The Marble-Rolling Game

This game is designed specifically for mobile devices with an accelerometer (although it works on a desktop). The idea is to tip the device to move a ball into the blue goal without hitting any of the blocks. Every time the user achieves the goal, the game is redrawn with an additional block, making the game harder and harder. The game is shown in Figure 13-3.

Managing dual input

Perhaps the most interesting part of this game is its novel input mechanism. It feels very natural to tilt the screen for ball motion. Check Chapter 9 for details on using the accelerometer to get tilt input. The essential plan is this:

1. **Create an** `Accel` **object.**

   Turn on the accelerometer by creating an instance of the `Accel` object.

2. **Build a** `checkAccel()` **method.**

   I added a method to the `Ball` object that checks the accelerometer.

3. **Get the accelerometer rotation.**

   Use the `getAX()` and `getAY()` methods to find the amount of rotation around these axes.

4. **Convert rotation to** `dx` **and** `dy` **values.**

   Use the mechanisms described in Chapter 9 to convert rotation to appropriate motion values.

5. **Add an optional keyboard input.**

   It's much easier to debug a program on a desktop than on a mobile device, so often I'll add an alternate input option so I can test as much of the program as possible before moving to the mobile platform. Use the `Scene` class's `touchable` property to determine whether you're using a mobile device. This approach also makes the game playable for a wider array of users.

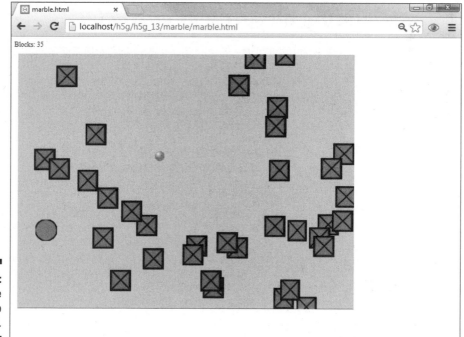

Figure 13-3:
Tilt the device to roll the ball.

Here's the code (in the main `update()` function) for checking which type of input is available:

```
//get input from accelerometer or keyboard
if (game.touchable){
    ball.checkAccel();
} else {
    ball.checkKeys();
}
```

And here's the `checkAccel()` method of the `Ball` object:

```
tBall.checkAccel = function(){
    //use the accelerometer to get input
    newDX = accel.getAY();
    newDY = accel.getAX();

    newDX *= -5;
    newDY *= -5;

    ball.setDX(newDX);
    ball.setDY(newDY);
} // end checkAccel
```

Building an array of obstacles

Another interesting feature of this game is the ever-increasing level of difficulty. Getting the difficulty level of a game correct is very challenging. You want the game to be beatable, but beating the game needs to feel like an accomplishment. One way to achieve this goal is to begin with a very easy level of difficulty and then ramp up until the game becomes more difficult.

For the marble game, I use an array of blocks as the obstacle. When the game begins, there are only ten blocks on the screen, so it's quite easy to get to the target without hitting any blocks. Each time the player reaches the target, the game scene is redrawn with one more block.

The blocks and the goal are drawn at random positions on the screen. However, you need to be careful not to create an impossible situation. The `Block` object's `reset()` method tries to place a block at a random position on the screen. However, if the block collides with the goal, the game will be difficult to win. Likewise, if the block collides with the ball's current position, the player will immediately lose. If either of these conditions occurs, the block is redrawn until a legal position is available.

I allowed blocks to overlap each other freely, but you could add this constraint as well. Here's the block resetting routine:

```
tBlock.reset = function(){
    //don't let me overlap the goal or ball
    keepGoing = true;
    while(keepGoing){
        newX = Math.random() * this.cWidth;
        newY = Math.random() * this.cHeight;

        this.setPosition(newX, newY);
        keepGoing = false;
        if (this.collidesWith(goal)){
            keepGoing = true;
        } // end if
        if (this.distanceTo(ball)< 150){
            keepGoing = true;
        } // end if
    } // end while loop
} // end reset
```

Improving the marble game

The marble game is quite playable as it is, but any game can be improved. Here are a few suggestions:

- ✓ **Add a time limit.** Require the user to reach the target at a specified time.

- ✓ **Add new kinds of barriers.** Barriers of different sizes will change the gameplay.

- ✓ **Change the ball's boundary action.** In my version of the game, the ball wraps around the screen. This adds an additional tactical element to the game, but you may prefer to stop at the border.

- ✓ **Add powerups.** You can always add special elements that temporarily change gameplay. Maybe consider making the ball invincible for a few seconds, or inverting gravity (multiply dx and dy both by -1). You could also temporarily change the size of the ball or have a powerup that resets the current level.

- ✓ **Create moving blocks.** The game entirely changes if the blocks also move. You'll probably want them to move very slowly in a random direction because this feature could make the game much harder.

- ✓ **Make cosmetic improvements.** Of course, you can always add sound effects, a high score mechanism, and improved graphics.

Whack-a-Mole

The whack-a-mole genre re-creates a classic physical arcade game. In the original game, you have a series of holes and a big hammer. As a mole pops out of a hole, the user smacks it with a hammer, and it goes back into the hole. This game is easy to re-create for both mobile and traditional desktops, and it can be frantic fun. Figure 13-4 shows this game in action.

My version creates a number of moles in random positions. Each mole has two states: up and down. The mole starts in the down state. A mole in the down state has a random chance of popping up in any frame. A mole that is currently up stays up for a limited time. If the user clicks a mole in the UP state, the mole drops and the player earns a point. If the mole stays up past a time limit, the mole drops, and the player loses a life.

Building a mole in a hole game

The main concept of this game is the mole. It's a simple `Sprite` object with two states. Everything the mole does is really about changing states.

The mole has a few properties that separate it from a normal sprite:

- `state`: The most important property of the mole is `state`. This can be either UP or DOWN. Various game behaviors cause the state to change.

- UP and DOWN: These values are treated like constants, and they are used to indicate the two possible states of the mole.

- `imgUp` and `imgDown`: These are the images representing the two states. Obviously, I created ridiculously simplistic images for the states. Note that both state images should be the same size, or the sprite will appear to jump around the screen when it changes state.

- `popupPerc`: This property indicates the likelihood a mole that's currently down will pop up. The initial value is 1 percent. Remember this value will be checked 20 times per frame, so at 1 percent, a down mole will pop up (on average) every 5 seconds. Modify this value to change the game difficulty (larger numbers will cause moles to pop up more frequently).

- `popupLength`: This property indicates how long a mole will stay visible once it has popped up. The default value is 3 seconds, but you can adjust this to make the moles disappear more quickly or stay visible longer.

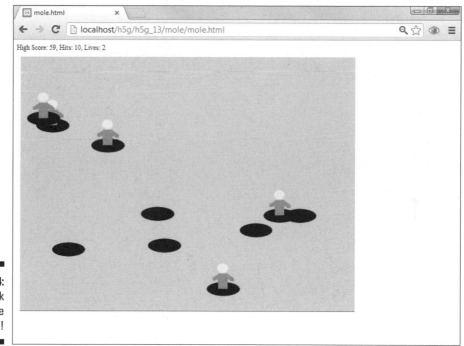

Figure 13-4:
Whack
those
moles!

Here are the main methods of the mole object:

- ✓ setState(state): Sets the state to the specified state value. States are stored as constants (UP and DOWN). When the state is changed, the mole's state property is modified, and the mole's image is modified to reflect the current state. If the state is set to UP, a timer begins, which will be used to track how long the mole is visible.

- ✓ CheckClick(): Checks to see if the mole is currently clicked. If the mole is currently UP, hide the mole and increment the score.

- ✓ CheckTime(): The behavior of this function depends on the mole's status. If the mole is currently down, randomly determine if it should pop up. If the mole is up, check to see if the popupLength has been exceeded. If so, lose a life and consider ending the game.

The checkTime code is the most interesting code in the mole game, so here is that method:

```
tMole.checkTime = function(){
    //if down, consider popping up
    if (this.state == DOWN){
        randVal = Math.random();
        if (randVal < this.popupPerc){
```

```
                    this.setState(UP);
            } // end if
        } else {
            //if up, check to see how long we've been up
            time = this.timer.getElapsedTime();
            if (time > this.popupLength){
                this.setState(DOWN);
                //lose a life
                lives--;
                if (lives < 0){
                    saveHighScore();
                    alert("You lose");
                    document.location.href = "";
                } // end if
            } // end if
        } // end if
    } // end checkTime
```

Other features of the mole game

Once a single mole has been created and is acting correctly, it's easy to build a lot of them. As usual, I created an array to handle a large number of objects of the same type. Modify the NUM_MOLES constant to change the number of moles in the game.

Also note that I added a virtual joystick if the scene registers a touch object. This will cause the touch screen to act just like a virtual mouse, and will allow the game to be played on a touch device. (It turns out to be a really great game for touch screens, but you should avoid using a real hammer.)

One more interesting feature is the high score mechanism. The computer keeps track of the high score on that particular machine. The high score mechanism uses a relatively new feature called *localStorage*. It's similar to the well-known cookie mechanism, but safer, more powerful, and a lot easier to use.

The getHighScore() function loads the current high score. If there isn't yet a high score, it will be set to zero.

```
function getHighScore(){
    //get the high score on this machine using localStorage
    highScore = parseInt(localStorage.getItem("moleHighScore"));
    console.log("highScore: ", highScore);
    if (highScore == "null"
        || highScore == null
        || isNaN(highScore)){
        highScore = 0;
    } // end if
} // end getHighScore
```

The `saveHighScore()` function is called when the game ends. It checks to see if the current high score has been exceeded. If so, the new high score is saved.

```
function saveHighScore(){
    if (hits > highScore){
        alert("New high score!");
        localStorage.setItem("moleHighScore", hits);
    } // end if
} // end saveHighScore
```

Even if the user leaves the page or turns off the browser, the high score will be maintained.

The `localStorage` mechanism only keeps track of the current browser. It cannot be used to check global high scores. This requires server-side programming, which is beyond the scope of this book.

Improving the mole game

As always, you can improve this game many ways.

- ✓ **Improve graphics and sound.** The default graphics are pathetically weak, and this game has no sound effects to speak of. These are easy ways to improve the program.

- ✓ **Change the screen size.** This game is highly dependent on screen size. A larger screen can be much more difficult than a smaller screen.

- ✓ **Modify the number of moles.** This is an easy way to change the difficulty level. More moles will be more difficult, unless they begin to overlap.

- ✓ **Prevent overlapping moles.** As a default, the placement of each mole is completely random, so they can overlap. Use the techniques described in the marble game earlier in this chapter to prevent a mole from spawning on top of another hole.

- ✓ **Make a more orderly setup.** I actually like the randomness of this game, but the traditional version uses an orderly grid for the moles. Line up the moles so they are in a more organized pattern on the screen.

- ✓ **Change mole settings.** The `popupRate` and `popupTime` properties give you a great way to modify the behavior of each mole. You might adjust these values over time to make the game speed up.

- ✓ **Move the holes.** Consider moving the mole after it has gone down. This adds variety to the game.

Jump and Run on Platforms

The platform "jump and run" genre has long been a staple arcade genre for good reason. It provides a nice interactive experience and is relatively easy to modify for many different kinds of games.

The essential element of a platform game is — well — platforms. The action usually happens with a side view and a player character that responds to gravity. Normally, the player will jump around on platforms and fight enemies by shooting, jumping, or melee combat.

My prototype shows the essential features. It includes a player character that can jump and land on platforms. I've also included draggable platforms so you can edit the scene and see how the character interacts with various platform configurations.

You can see my example in Figure 13-5.

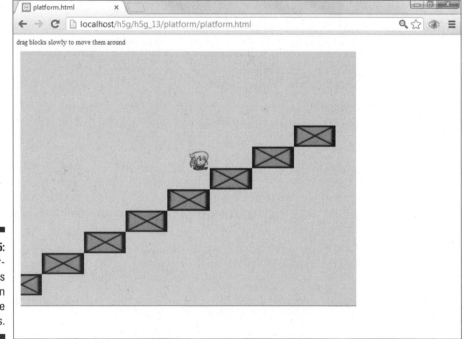

Figure 13-5:
The character jumps around on the platforms.

Jumping and landing

The key to a side-scrolling game is the jumping and landing mechanic. As with the lunar lander described earlier in this chapter, use a `falling` property to track whether the character should respond to gravity or not. Here's the code from the `checkKeys()` method that reads the up arrow and makes the character jump.

```
if (keysDown[K_UP]){

    if (this.falling == false){
        this.setImage("characterUp.png");
        this.y -= 5;
        this.falling = true;
        this.addVector(0, 15);
    } // end if
}else {
    checkFalling();
}// end if
```

The `checkFalling()` function checks each of the blocks. If the character is not touching any of the blocks, set falling to `true`. This will make the character fall once it moves off of a block.

Coming in for a landing

The interaction between the character and the blocks is important because you want the character to stop moving *before* it hits a block. This requires a technique called *predictive collision detection*, which sounds a lot more complicated than it is. Here's the mechanism:

1. **Move the element as normal.**

   Do the calculations to move the object (in this case the character) as normal. Note that the character isn't drawn yet, but new x and y values have been determined by adding `dx` and `dy`.

2. **Check for a collision.**

   Check to see if the character has collided with anything (in this case, each block in the array of blocks).

3. **If a collision occurs, back up the character.**

   You're checking for a collision, but you don't want the character to overlap with the block. Instead, you're interested in knowing whether the current motion vector would cause a collision.

4. **Subtract** dx **from** x, dy **from** y.

   A collision has been detected, so detract that collision by subtracting the motion vector. This results in the sprite being where it started before the collision was detected.

5. **Set the sprite's speed to zero.**

   Set the sprite's speed to zero so the next frame doesn't cause the sprite to crash into the block again.

The easiest way to get the predictive behavior is to add a backup() method to the Sprite object, which can be called on any type of collision:

```
tCharacter.backup = function(){
    //I'm overlapping something I shouldn't share
space with
    //back up to where I was before the collision
was detected
    X = this.x - this.dx;
    Y = this.y - this.dy;
    this.setPosition(X, Y);
} // end backup
```

Making draggable blocks

This game features another very interesting feature: Each block can be dragged to a new position so you can experiment with other block placements. Making any sprite draggable is relatively easy. Simply check to see if the block currently is being clicked. If so, set its position equal to the mouse position:

```
tBlock.checkDrag = function(){
    //allow the block to be draggable
    if (this.isClicked()){
        this.setPosition(scene.getMouseX(), scene.
getMouseY());
    } // end if

} // end checkDrag
```

Improving the platform game

The platform game is open to many kinds of enhancements:

- ✔ **Use multiple levels.** The default blocks are easy to build and work with, but they aren't very interesting. Experiment with different block shapes and positions to build interesting levels. You can store the block positions in arrays to make new levels, and simply reuse the blocks.

- ✔ **Consider a tile-based approach.** The platform example uses an arbitrary block placement scheme, but you can also use a tile-based approach. Look at the tile-based world described later in this chapter, in the "Miles and Miles of Tiles and Tiles" section, and convert it to a side-scrolling mechanism.

- ✔ **Add goals and enemies.** An obvious improvement to this game would be to include some goal to reach with some obstacle in the way. Consider how you might implement enemy characters. Will they move? Will they shoot? Also consider adding powerups to improve jumping speed, add a ranged weapon, or whatever else you can imagine.

- ✔ **Add more firepower.** Add a weapon to the character so it can shoot. In side scrollers, the weapon normally fires horizontally, but you can play around to get the behavior you want.

- ✔ **Improve the physics.** The dynamics of this game work pretty well, but you can improve them with a bit more tweaking. Follow the general outline of the existing program, but see if you can make it work exactly like what you want.

Pong — the Granddaddy of Them All

No game development book would be complete without a mention of the famous Pong game. While this wasn't technically the first video game, it was the first to attract popular attention, and it's by far one of the more influential games ever made. Figure 13-6 shows my take on this classic game.

Pong is a relatively easy game to write, but it does have a couple of features that can be surprising. It can be a bit tricky to get the ball-paddle collision to work correctly, and coming up with an interesting computer player can be challenging. Read on to see how it's done.

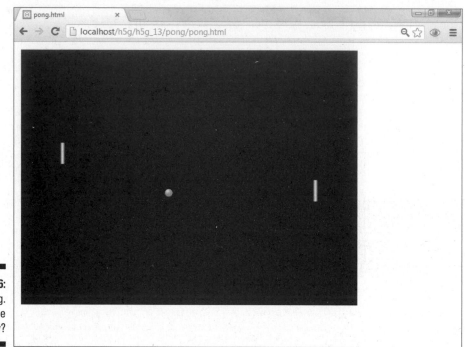

Figure 13-6:
It's pong.
What else
can I say?

Building the player paddle

The paddle object is quite straightforward, but there are actually two paddles with different behaviors. In my version of the game, the left paddle is
controlled by the player, and the right paddle is controlled by a computer AI.
I built a single paddle object that can serve as either a player or an AI paddle.
(This will simplify converting the game to a multiplayer game.) The player
paddle just follows the mouse:

```
tPaddle.followMouse = function(){
    //follows mouse for player control
    this.setImgAngle(90);
    this.setPosition(this.x, scene.getMouseY());
} // end followMouse method
```

Adding artificial stupidity

It's actually very easy to build an Artificial Intelligence (AI) for the opponent.
Simply set the paddle's Y value equal to the ball's Y value. However, this will

be boring, because the opponent will never miss, and will always hit the ball squarely in the middle of the paddle, making it easy to return. A perfect AI is no fun at all. What you need is to give the AI paddle some kind of attention issues (but we still love it).

The AI shouldn't directly follow the ball. Instead, it should check to see whether the ball is above or below it, and respond accordingly.

I added two variables to control the AI paddle's motion. The BRAINS constant is a percentage. If BRAINS is set to .5, the paddle will check for ball location only half the time. For an easier game, set the BRAINS value low. The other primary value is V_SPEED, or the vertical speed of the paddle. This indicates how quickly the paddle will move toward the ball. A higher value will create a more powerful AI player. Find the right combination of these two values to get the AI behavior you want. Here's the code for the autoMove() method:

```
tPaddle.autoMove = function(){
    //automatically moves
    this.setImgAngle(90);

    //don't move on every turn
    if (Math.random() < BRAINS){
        if (this.y > ball.y){
            this.setMoveAngle(0);
        } else {
            this.setMoveAngle(180);
        } // end if

        this.setSpeed(V_SPEED);
    } // end if
} // end autoMove
```

Building a ball to bounce off boundaries

While the ball is a seemingly simplistic sprite, it does have some interesting behavior. The ball has a unique boundary-checking scheme. It bounces off the top and bottom of the screen, but if it leaves the sides, it wraps (and one player or the other scores).

If you don't have a boundary scheme that fits one of the standard patterns, you can simply overwrite the checkBounds() method to do whatever you want. (Note that you don't need to explicitly call checkBounds(). It is automatically called by the sprite's update() method. Your custom version of checkBounds simply replaces the built-in version. Here's my variant:

```
tBall.checkBounds = function(){
    //overwrite checkbounds function to give
    //custom behavior

    //bounce off of top and bottom
    if (this.y < 0){
        this.setDY(this.dy * -1);
    }
    if (this.y > scene.height){
        this.setDY(this.dy * -1);
    }

    //wrap off of sides
    if(this.x < 0){
        this.setPosition(scene.width - 150,
this.y);
        //computer scores
    } // end if
    if (this.x > scene.width){
        this.setPosition(150, this.y);
        //player scores
    } // end if
} // end checkBounds
```

If the ball hits the top or bottom of the screen, invert dy to make it bounce. If it hits the left or right of the screen, move it to the other side (in front of the paddle, so it doesn't bounce off of the back of the paddle).

When the ball leaves the screen at the sides, somebody will score, so I left myself a comment indicating where the scorekeeping (and eventually end-of-game conditions) will go.

Putting some spin on the ball

In traditional versions of Pong, the ball can be controlled by choosing where on the paddle to hit the ball. If you hit the ball near the top of the paddle, the ball will move upward. If you hit the ball near the center of the paddle, it will fly across the screen horizontally, and if you hit near the bottom, the ball will move downward. A little bit of math gives you this behavior. (And you told your algebra teacher you'd never need this.)

```
tBall.checkBounce = function(paddle){
    //responds to a collision with the given
    paddle
    //Max and min dy
    MAX = 10
    if (this.collidesWith(paddle)){
        this.setDX(this.dx * -1);
```

```
            dy = this.y - paddle.y;
            dy = ((dy / paddle.height) * 2);

            dy *= MAX;
            this.setDY(dy);
        } // end if
    } // end checkBounce
```

The dx value is easy to calculate because you simply invert dx to move in the other direction. The dy value is calculated by determining the difference between the ball's y position and that of the paddle:

1. **Determine a maximum** dy.

   This value determines the highest level of deflection you'll allow. If the MAX value is set to 10, the ball's dy value will be -10 at the top of the paddle, 0 at the middle, and 10 at the bottom of the paddle.

2. **Invert** dx.

   If the ball is moving left, multiply the dx value by -1 to make it go right. If it's going right, the same operation (multiplying by -1) will make it go left. Any paddle collision inverts the ball's dx.

3. **Find the raw difference in** y **values.**

   Calculate how far apart the y value of the paddle and the ball are.

4. **Normalize this value.**

   If you divide the raw dy value by the height of the paddle, you'll get a range between -.5 and .5. Multiply that value by 2 to get a -1 to 1 range.

5. **Multiply the normalized** dy **by** MAX.

   Multiplying the normalized dy value by the MAX value will give a dy value between −MAX and MAX.

Improving the Pong game

While this Pong game has the basic behavior down, it's far from ready for actual play. Here are a few things to consider adding:

- ✔ **Add aesthetic appeal.** As usual, my game is functional but not very pretty. You can do a lot to make it look better, from customizing the paddles to adding ball animations and sound effects.

- ✔ **Add scorekeeping.** Without a scorekeeping mechanism, the game is kind of pointless. Add the ability to track user and computer scores. Also add some way to determine the end of the game.

✔ **Add powerups.** Add some spice to the game by having new variations: Change the size of each paddle, invert the control of the player paddle, change the ball speed, make the ball occasionally invisible, or invert the ball-paddle collision algorithm for starters.

✔ **Tune up the AI.** The AI I present here is functional, but it can be improved. For one thing, it gets pretty jittery when the ball is traveling in a flat trajectory. See if you can figure out a way to smooth out this behavior.

I'm a Fighter, Not a Lover — RPGs

The role-playing game (RPG) is one of the most enduring forms of gameplay. While role-playing games can work in many different ways, the general setup follows a familiar pattern. The user engages as a character with a set of basic characteristics. The player then collects objects and defeats enemies to eventually improve her performance, which leads to more difficult monsters.

The simple variation shown in Figure 13-7 illustrates a basic yet very flexible combat mechanic: The user controls a spear-wielding hero facing a dastardly orc.

This game features a number of important ideas: an animated character, a base class, and a simple combat system.

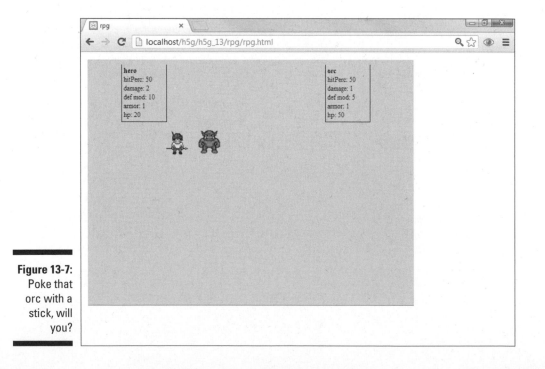

Figure 13-7:
Poke that orc with a stick, will you?

Building the base Character class

From a data point of view, monsters and heroes are actually very similar to each other. (I'll leave debate about the meaning of this point to philosophers.) Begin by building a generic Character class that supports all the common characteristics, and you can then easily modify this class to build all the heroes and monsters you can imagine. The keys to any character class are the statistics used in combat and leveling. You can handle this a number of ways, but my game uses a simplified combat form familiar to tabletop role-players:

- **Name:** While this may be obvious, the name is useful for reporting what is happening.

- hp: Hit points. This is the amount of damage a character can take. If you have a lot of hit points, you can take a lot of damage.

- hitPerc: This is the percentage of likelihood that a particular attack will hit. If the hitPerc is 50, attacks will land half the time. Higher values lead to more successful attacks.

- damage: The damage modifier indicates how much damage will be done upon a successful hit. This value indicates how many six-sided dice will be rolled. (Using dice gives a more believable damage value than a straight random value. For example, rolling two six-sided dice will produce the values five through nine much more frequently than 2 or 12.)

- defMod: This value is a defensive modifier. It's used to simulate dexterity and the ability to dodge an attack. The defense modifier is used to make an opponent less likely to land a blow.

- armor: Once an attack has landed, the armor value will absorb some of the damage. The larger the armor value, the harder it is to hurt the character.

The Character class holds all these values in properties, and it also contains two functions. The showStatus() function returns a string containing all the stats for the character. The fight() function manages a round of combat.

Here's the code for the fight() method:

```
tChar.fight = function(enemy){
    //assumes enemy is also based on Char
    hitPerc = (this.hitPerc - enemy.defMod) / 100;
    if (Math.random() < hitPerc){

        damage = 0;
        for (i = 0; i < this.damage; i++){
            damage += parseInt(Math.random() * 6);
        } // end for

        damage -= enemy.armor;
```

```
            enemy.hp -= damage;

            if (enemy.hp <= 0){
                alert(enemy.name + " is dead!")
                document.location.href = "";
            } // end 'enemy dead' if
        } // end "hit" if

    } // end fight
```

Here's how the `fight()` method works:

1. **Accept another character as a parameter.**

   The `fight()` method expects an enemy class, which should also be a character (or something based on the `Character` class).

2. **Determine the hit percentage.**

   Subtract the enemy's defense modifier from the attacker's `hitPerc`. This will give a value between 0 and 100. Divide this value by 100 to get a 0-1 float.

3. **Roll a random number.**

   The `Math.random()` function returns a value between 0 and 1. Compare this to the calculated `hitPerc` to find out if there has been a hit.

4. **Roll the dice.**

   Roll one six-sided die for each damage point, and add this value to a running total to determine how much damage is caused by this hit.

5. **Compensate for enemy armor.**

   Subtract the armor value from the damage amount.

6. **Subtract damage from the enemy `hp`.**

   Apply damage by subtracting it from `hp`.

7. **Check to see if the enemy is dead.**

   If the `hp` goes below 0, the enemy is dead.

The combat model is designed to be simple and flexible. All the various pickups or level improvements can be boiled down to modifying these characteristics. For example, if your character picks up a shield, simply add a value to the `armor` modifier. A stronger weapon may involve a better `toHit` percentage and/or more damage. As your character gets stronger, he gets more `hp`. Likewise, all the monsters are pretty much the same, but they'll have different values. For example, you can make a small creature that's difficult to hit with a small `hp`, small damage, and a large defense modifier. A large slow monster might have a lot of `hp` but a small defensive modifier.

The `Character` class is interesting, but it isn't really meant to be used on its own. Instead, it's designed to be a base for more specific characters. It has the minimal features you'd expect of any character, but then you can extend it (like you extend the sprite) to add more specific behavior.

One does not simply build an orc . . .

The `Orc` class is a simple extension of the `Character` class. In my example, the orc does very little, but I could easily extend it to move, drop treasures, or whatever. However, this version is quite straightforward. All I do is extend the `Character` class, setting specific values for the various parameters.

```
function Orc(){
    tOrc = new Character("orc", "orc.png");

    //orc is bigger than default but with weaker weapons
    tOrc.hitPerc = 50; // perc likelihood of hitting opponent
    tOrc.damage = 1;    // damage(d6) done on a successful hit
    tOrc.defMod = 5;    // subtract from opponent's hitPerc
    tOrc.armor = 1      // subtract from opponent's damage
    tOrc.hp = 50;       // amount of damage I can sustain

    tOrc.setSpeed(0);

    tOrc.setPosition(300, 200);

    return tOrc;
} // end orc
```

We need a hero

The hero is another extension of the `Character` class, but (as befits a hero) it has a bit more enhancement. The hero uses a sprite sheet animation like those described in Chapter 8. I produced the images from the marvelous resources at `openGameArt.org`. In particular, I used a wonderful GIMP file that allows you to build custom characters by turning on and off various layers in GIMP. I then simplified those images to create only what I needed to build my `Hero` class. See Chapter 11 for more information on the sprite sheet and `openGameArt.org`.

The `Hero` class is much like the default `Character` (in fact, it uses all the default combat values, so I don't change those at all). The main addition is the animation code. Here is a portion of that code:

```
function Hero(){
    tHero = new Character("hero", "hero.png");

    tHero.loadAnimation(512, 256, 64, 64);
    tHero.generateAnimationCycles();
    tHero.renameCycles(new Array("up", "left", "down",
        "right"));
    tHero.setAnimationSpeed(500);

    //leave all stats at their default values

    tHero.pause = function(){
        this.setSpeed(0);
        this.setCurrentCycle("down");
        this.pauseAnimation();
    }// end

    tHero.checkKeys = function(){
        if (keysDown[K_LEFT]){
            this.setSpeed(1);
            this.playAnimation();
            this.setMoveAngle(270);
            this.setCurrentCycle("left");
        }
```

I obviously left out some of the other keyboard-checking code, but you can see this program is a variation of the animation described in Chapter 8. The hero uses a *predictive collision* model to prevent walking into the orc. If a collision is noted, the hero simply backs up to the original spot before updating itself:

```
tHero.checkCollision = function(){
    //predictive collision detection

    if (this.collidesWith(orc)){
        //back up and pause
        this.x -= this.dx;
        this.y -= this.dy;
        this.pause();
        fight();
    }

} // end checkCollision
```

If the hero collides with the orc, the `fight()` mechanism begins. This is actually quite simple:

```
function fight(){
    hero.fight(orc);
    orc.fight(hero);

    heroStatus.innerHTML = hero.showStats();
    orcStatus.innerHTML = orc.showStats();
} // end fight function
```

The fight() function has the hero attack the orc, and then the orc attacks the hero. After the round, each character's statistics are displayed in the appropriate output.

Improving the role-playing game

This game simply begs for improvements. There are many ways to take this particular example further:

- ✔ **Add more monsters.** You can build an entire range of monsters. Note that each monster could simply be an image and the combat statistics. It's relatively easy to build a data structure that stores an entire array of ever-more challenging monsters to fight.

- ✔ **Add an inventory.** Allow the user to pick up various items. Each of the items will simply change a variable or two: making the player stronger, giving her more damage, or better defense against attack, for example.

- ✔ **Include a dungeon.** This game doesn't have a lot of atmosphere so far. Use some background graphics to add atmosphere. You can always use an array of blocks for barriers as you've seen in other examples in this chapter.

- ✔ **Add a tile-based dungeon.** Of course, tile-based worlds and RPG combat are natural companions. Look at the tile-based example later in this chapter for information on building a tile-based world to hold your monsters and treasures.

Tanks — and You're Welcome!

I've long enjoyed the artillery genre. This type of game gives you some sort of launch mechanism with semi-realistic physics, and has you launch projectiles (avians with anger issues or otherwise) at some sort of target. My take begins as a single-player game against a drone tank, but you can easily extend it to a two-player game or give the opponent more intelligence. Figure 13-8 shows the tank game in action.

Figure 13-8:
I'm shooting
at the evil
enemy tank.

Tanks, turrets, and shells

The most interesting thing about a tank-style game is the relationship between the tank, its turret, and the bullets it fires. In my game, the tank is controlled by the A and D keys, and the turret's angle is controlled by W and S (I use these keys to reserve the arrow keys for a two-player game if you ever want to do so).

The tank is a sprite, but the tank image (at least the player-controlled tank) doesn't include a turret. The turret is a separate sprite intended to be linked to the tank and rotated on its own. When the player moves the tank, the turret moves with it. When the user rotates the turret, the turret rotates, but the tank doesn't. The bullet is a third sprite, which appears when the user fires the tank. The bullet's initial position is determined by the tank's position, and the bullet's initial motion angle is determined by the turret's angle.

The turret sprite is the same size as the tank. Design the turret so it revolves around its center point (which, in the simplest case, will also be the center of the tank). Most of the turret sprite will be transparent so the tank can show through. (Check the raw images on my website if you're confused.)

Here's the code for the tank:

```
function UserTank(){
    tTank = new Sprite(game, "greenTank.png", 50, 25);
    tTank.setSpeed(0);
    tTank.setPosition(100, 550);

    tTank.turret = new Sprite(game, "turret.png", 50,
        25);
    tTank.bullet = new Bullet(tTank);

    tTank.checkKeys = function(){
        if (keysDown[K_A]){
            this.changeXby(-2);
        }

        if (keysDown[K_D]){
            this.changeXby(2);
        }

        //always move turret with me.
        this.turret.setPosition(this.x, this.y);

        //rotate turret

        if (keysDown[K_W]){
            this.turret.changeImgAngleBy(-5);
            if (this.turret.getImgAngle() < 0){
                this.turret.setImgAngle(0);
            } // end if
        }

        if (keysDown[K_S]){
            this.turret.changeImgAngleBy(5);
            if (this.turret.getImgAngle() > 90){
                this.turret.setImgAngle(90);
            }
        }

        if (keysDown[K_SPACE]){
            this.bullet.fire();
        }

        this.turret.update();
        this.bullet.checkGravity();
        this.bullet.update();

    } // end checkKeys

    return tTank;
} // end tank
```

The tank design is mildly complicated by having a dependent turret sprite, and a bullet sprite. Here's how to build this mish-mash of armored sprite goodness:

1. **Build the tank sprite first.**

   As with most examples in `simpleGame`, begin by building a temporary sprite for the tank (called `tTank`).

2. **Build a turret sprite.**

   The turret is a second sprite. It is a property of the tank, as well as a sprite in its own right. The turret is fairly simple, so it can be a stock sprite. It does not need to be a complete subclass.

3. **Build a bullet sprite.**

   Each tank has a sprite and a bullet. The bullet will need some specific behaviors (boundary-checking, collision, and gravity), so it will be a sub-class of the `Sprite` object. Look at the next section for information on building the bullet. For now, just know that the tank will need a bullet. Note that the bullet will need to know which tank it belongs to, so I send the current tank as a parameter.

4. **Read the keyboard.**

   The tank is currently set to use the WASD keys for input. (I did this to enable a two-player game later.)

5. **Move the tank left and right.**

   The left and right controls move the tank sprite itself. Move the turret so its center is always the same as the tank's center. This causes the turret to always move with the tank.

6. **Rotate the turret.**

   The up and down controls cause the turret to rotate. Set minimum and maximum values to keep the turret within a reasonable range of angles.

7. **Fire the bullet.**

   On the fire command (space bar by default), invoke the bullet's `fire()` method. (Of course, you'll need to write that in the `Bullet` class.)

8. **Update the turret.**

   Up to now, all `update()` calls have happened in the main `update()` function. However, the main game doesn't really need to update the turret. Because the turret is part of the tank, updating the tank should update the turret. Because the `checkKeys()` method will happen every frame, I update the turret to ensure that it draws correctly.

9. **Move the bullet.**

    If a bullet is active, use the `checkGravity()` method to track its current course while taking gravitational pull into account. If there is no bullet currently active, this line will be ignored.

10. **Update the bullet.**

    Again, the bullet feels like part of the tank, so it should be updated automatically.

Building a bullet

Okay, military purists, I know it's a shell, but for now, let's just call it a bullet. It's an arcade game, after all.

The bullet class will be fired by a tank. The bullet is a surprisingly sophisticated class, as it needs a `fire()` method (which will fire the bullet based on the tank and turret's current situation) and a `checkGravity()` method (which plots the bullet's trajectory in space).

Here's the `Bullet` class code:

```
function Bullet(owner){
    //owner is the tank owning this bullet

    tBullet = new Sprite(game, "bullet.png", 5, 5);

    tBullet.owner = owner;
    tBullet.hide();
    tBullet.setBoundAction(DIE);

    tBullet.fire = function(){
        //begin at center of my tank
        //pointing in tank turret's direction
        this.setPosition(this.owner.x, this.owner.y);
        this.setMoveAngle(this.owner.turret.getImgAngle());
        this.setSpeed(20);
        this.show();
    } // end fire

    tBullet.checkGravity = function(){
        this.addVector(180, 1);
    } // end checkGravity

    return tBullet;
} // end bullet
```

Here's the life story of a bullet in my game:

1. **Specify the owner tank.**

   When this game has multiple tanks firing at each other (which it clearly needs), there should be a lot of bullets flying around. Each bullet will need to know which tank it belongs to so it can fire from the right position in the right direction.

2. **Hide.**

   The `Bullet` object is created at the very beginning of the game, but it spends most of its life hidden away unseen. One of the first things you do is hide the bullet so it will be visible only after it's fired.

3. **Set boundary action to `DIE`.**

   Bullets typically die when they reach the end of the screen. The sprite is not removed from memory. It simply isn't displayed on the screen and doesn't respond to collisions. Setting the boundary action to `DIE` will cause the desired behavior.

4. **Fire from the owning tank's position.**

   When the bullet is fired, place it at the owning tank's position.

5. **Set the movement angle to the owning tank's turret angle.**

   The turret's main job is to indicate which angle is used as the bullet's starting trajectory.

6. **Provide a large movement speed.**

   Bullets should move quickly, so set an initial velocity of 20 pixels per frame. (You can add another control to allow the user to modify the initial velocity if you wish.)

7. **Reveal the bullet.**

   Invoke the bullet's `show()` method to make the bullet appear on the screen.

8. **Check for gravity.**

   All this function does is compensate for gravitational pull with the `addVector()` method. Check Chapter 8 if you need a review on the use of this powerful method.

Improving the tank game

Although all the tank's basic functionality is in place, this game has a very simplistic behavior. Right now, the only enemy is a very stupid drone tank (which simply jitters around and doesn't even shoot back). The improvements you might make begin with these suggestions:

✔ **Improve the other tank.** Modify the other tank to have a real turret and the same general behavior as the first. (Note that you may want to invert the second tank so it generally fires to the left.)

✔ **Improve the AI.** The drone tank isn't very bright or fearsome. Give it the capability to shoot back periodically.

✔ **Add fixed defenses.** Maybe instead of an enemy tank, you have a target to destroy (the enemy command bunker or something) with defenses in the way. Add some obstacles that need to be blown up before you reach the bunker.

✔ **Make enemy artillery.** Build fixed-position artillery units that periodically fire. The user will have to destroy these or risk being blown up.

✔ **Make a two-player version.** The tank-style game is ideal for two players on a single keyboard. Add the second tank and a scoring mechanism.

✔ **Change the whole theme.** This general game can be rebuilt along many themes. You can be a gunner defending your bomber from enemy aircraft, or manning a turret defending from hordes of onrushing enemies. (This is the foundation of the famous tower defense style of games.)

Miles and Miles of Tiles and Tiles

A tile-based world isn't really a game type. Instead, it's a technique used in many other games to provide interesting flexible backgrounds without huge memory costs. The basic idea is to take a number of small images and use them in combination to build a complete background image. Figure 13-9 shows a simple map drawn with a tile-based world.

Typically, you'll build a tile object, which contains a number of small (32 x 32 pixel) images. Each tile object can display any of the images on command. This scheme has a number of interesting advantages:

✔ **Memory requirements can be very small.** Each image loads into memory only once, so you can create a very large world (much larger than the visible screen) with a small memory footprint.

✔ **You can use many different tiles.** My example uses only three small tiles (grass, dirt, and water), but you can build an extremely complex world with any of the beautiful tile sets you can download from sites like `OpenGameArt.org`.

✔ **The map is dynamic.** The image displayed in each tile can be modified at runtime. In my example, you can click on any tile to change the terrain type. This allows the map state to change during gameplay (for example, a block becomes molten slag after a nuclear attack). This also allows you to add a map editor.

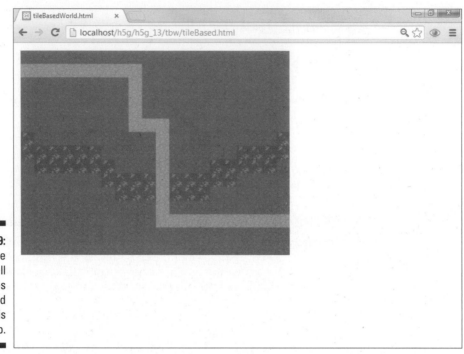

Figure 13-9:
Only three
small
images
were used
to draw this
map.

✔ **Tiles can have gameplay effects.** You can use tiles to create interesting tactical situations, like water that cannot be crossed or mountains that give an advantage to a defender.

✔ **Maps are simply arrays of integers.** To store a tile-based map, you don't need to store the tiles at all. Instead, you simply keep track of the tile states. See the code in this section for an example.

✔ **Maps can be much larger than the screen.** A tile map can be any two-dimension array of integers. If you want to display a huge game world, you can build it as large as you want and simply reflect a subset of that world as the tiles shown on the screen.

✔ **Scrolling a tileset is simple.** It's easy to make large scrolling worlds with a tile system, because the display is separated from the data. The tiles themselves rarely move. Instead, a different subset of the map data is displayed, giving the illusion that the player is moving in a larger world.

✔ **Tiles are suitable for multiple game types.** Tiles are frequently used for role-playing games, as well as board games, tactical games, and side-scrolling platform games.

Creating a Tile object

The Tile object is (naturally enough) the foundation of tile-based maps. Here's my code for a simple tile prototype:

```
var GRASS = 0;
var DIRT = 1;
var WATER = 2;
var NUMSTATES = 3;

function Tile(){
    tTile = new Sprite(scene, "grass.png", 32, 32);
    tTile.setSpeed(0);
    tTile.state = GRASS;
    tTile.images = new Array("grass.png", "dirt.png",
        "water.png");
    tTile.row = 0;
    tTile.col = 0;

    tTile.setState = function(state){
        this.state = state;
        this.setImage(this.images[this.state]);
    } // end setState

    tTile.getRow = function(){
        return this.row;
    } // end getRow

    tTile.getCol = function(){
        return this.col;
    } // end getCol;

    tTile.getState = function(){
        return this.state;
    } // end getState

    tTile.checkMouse = function(){
        if (this.isClicked()){

            newState = this.state;
            newState++;
            if (newState >= NUMSTATES){
                newState = 0;
            } // end if

            this.setState(newState);
        } // end if
    } // end if

    return tTile;
} // end Tile constructor
```

The most significant part of a tile is its multi-state nature. It has multiple states. Each state displays a different image. Here's how to write it:

1. **Prepare your images.**

   The most visible parts of the tile-based system are the various images. Build or obtain (with the necessary permissions, of course) some tiles you can use. Mine came from the excellent lpc tile atlas at `http://opengameart.org`. I broke each image into a separate 32-by-32 image. Each image should be the same size, and usually these sizes will be a power of two (16 x 16, 32 x 32, and 64 x 64 are the most common sizes).

2. **Build constants for the states.**

   The easiest way to work with states is to assign constants for them. Constants have the advantage of being easily readable by humans and straightforward integers to the computer. I created a constant for each state in my tileset, as well as a constant describing the number of states. (My example has only three states, but you can easily expand it to make as many as you want.) I also added constants for the number of ROWS and COLS in my map.

3. **Build a standard sprite.**

   The tile is still essentially a sprite. It doesn't typically move, so you can set its speed to 0. Use any of the sprite images you want as the default.

4. **Assign a default state.**

   The `state` property is the most important aspect of a tile. It indicates which state the tile is currently displaying. The `state` value should always be one of the state constants.

5. **Create an array of images.**

   Each tile will have access to all the possible images. Store them in an array. Make sure the array order lines up with the constant values. For example, "grass.png" is element zero in my array, and the GRASS constant is zero, so `images[GRASS]` will be "grass.png"

6. **Set a row and column.**

   Tiles are usually placed in a two-dimensional grid, so it can be very useful to track the current tile's row and column.

7. **Add a `setState()` method.**

   This method allows you to easily change a tile to any of the state values. Use a constant to assure the state is recognized by your tiles. The `state` property is modified to reflect the current state, and the image is also changed, so the correct image will display on the next update.

8. **Provide data retrieval techniques.**

   These functions return the row, column, and current state of the tile.

9. **Allow an editing behavior.**

   In my example, I'm actually making a map editor, so I'll allow the user to modify each tile by clicking on it. The checkMouse() method determines whether the tile has been clicked. If so, the state is incremented and the new state is displayed.

Building a map from tiles

Each tile is a powerful tool, but the real power of the tile-based structure is how tiles are combined to create a complete map. The tileset is a two-dimension array of tile objects. Like most two-dimension arrays, it's normally managed by a pair of nested loops. Here's the code for setting up the tileset:

```
function setupTiles(){
    tileset = new Array(ROWS);
    for (row = 0; row < ROWS; row++){
        tRow = new Array(COLS);
        for (col = 0; col < COLS; col++){
            tRow[col] = new Tile();
            xPos = 16 + (32 * col);
            yPos = 16 + (32 * row);
            tRow[col].setPosition(xPos, yPos);
            tRow[col].row = row;
            tRow[col].col = col;
        } // end col for loop
        tileset[row] = tRow;
    } // end row for loop;
} // end setupTiles
```

There are only a few points to keep in mind here:

✔ **The tileset is an array.** Each member of the tileset array is actually a row (which is another array). Build an array of length ROWS.

✔ **Step through each row.** Use a standard for loop to step through all the rows.

✔ **Each row is an array of length COLS.** A two-dimension array is actually an array of arrays (at least, that's how it's implemented in JavaScript and many other languages). Make an array of length COLS for each row.

✔ **Step through the columns.** Make a for loop that happens once per column. You now have two counting variables (row and col), which together describe the position of each tile in the two-dimension structure.

✔ **Create a new tile.** Simply use the tile constructor to build a new tile.

✔ **Set the tile's position.** I used a little math to calculate the appropriate position of each tile in the scene. You can multiply the row and column by the width and height of the cell to determine a rough placement, but because the X and Y positions of a sprite refer to the center of the sprite, I added half the tile's width and height to make the tiles fit nicely in the screen.

✔ **Assign the row and column data to the sprite.** For easier access later, simply copy the row and col data to properties of the sprite.

Updating the tiles

Tiles are just sprites, so they are updated in the normal way. However, there are a lot of tiles, so it makes sense to use an organized approach to updating. Remember, nested for loops are the natural companions of 2D arrays, so a pair of loops is the best way to ensure every tile gets updated.

```
function updateTiles(){
    for (row = 0; row < ROWS; row++){
        for (col = 0; col < COLS; col++){
            tileset[row][col].checkMouse();
            tileset[row][col].update();
        } // end col for loop
    } // end row for
} // end updateTiles
```

My example is also a map editor, so I included a call to check the mouse inside the nested loops so I don't have to build another nested loop structure.

Loading a tile map

One of the most exciting things about tiles is how easily they're stored, loaded, and modified. It isn't necessary to store and load all the tiles. All you really need to know is the states! Take a look at the loadMap() function, and you'll see what I mean:

```
function loadMap(){
    // loads a map from an array
    map = new Array(
        new Array(0,0,0,0,0,0,0,0,0,0,0,0,0,0,0,0,0,0,0,0),
        new Array(1,1,1,1,1,1,1,1,1,0,0,0,0,0,0,0,0,0,0,0),
        new Array(0,0,0,0,0,0,0,0,1,0,0,0,0,0,0,0,0,0,0,0),
        new Array(0,0,0,0,0,0,0,0,1,0,0,0,0,0,0,0,0,0,0,0),
        new Array(0,0,0,0,0,0,0,0,1,0,0,0,0,0,0,0,0,0,0,0),
        new Array(0,0,0,0,0,0,0,0,1,1,1,0,0,0,0,0,0,0,0,0),
        new Array(2,0,0,0,0,0,0,0,0,0,1,0,0,0,0,0,0,0,0,2),
```

```
        new Array(2,2,2,2,2,2,0,0,0,0,1,0,0,0,0,2,2,2,2,2),
        new Array(0,2,2,2,2,2,2,0,0,0,1,0,0,0,2,2,2,2,2,0),
        new Array(0,0,0,0,0,0,2,2,2,2,1,2,2,2,2,2,0,0,0,0),
        new Array(0,0,0,0,0,0,0,2,2,2,1,2,2,2,0,0,0,0,0,0),
        new Array(0,0,0,0,0,0,0,0,0,0,1,0,0,0,0,0,0,0,0,0),
        new Array(0,0,0,0,0,0,0,0,0,0,0,1,1,1,1,1,1,1,1,1),
        new Array(0,0,0,0,0,0,0,0,0,0,0,0,0,0,0,0,0,0,0,0),
        new Array(0,0,0,0,0,0,0,0,0,0,0,0,0,0,0,0,0,0,0,0)
    );

    for (row = 0; row < ROWS; row++){
        for (col = 0; col < COLS; col++){
            currentVal = map[row][col];
            tileset[row][col].setState(currentVal);
        } // end col for loop
    } // end row for
```

The interesting part of this function is the map variable. This is nothing more than a two-dimension array of integer values. If you squint a little bit while staring at the array, you'll see the map pattern in the integers. Each integer represents the state for the corresponding tile.

Of course, you can have more than one such array, which means it's easy to store multiple maps. You can also make the integer array much larger than the screen, and simply display a screen-size subset of the main map.

The second part of the function simply maps through the integer array and sets each tile to the state indicated by the integer.

Improving the tile world

The tile-based world is really a technique more than a game, but you can use a few techniques to improve the system:

✔ **Collision states:** You can test to see if a sprite collides with any tile. You might have certain states that register collisions and other states (for example an "empty" state) that ignores collisions. You'll frequently want to use predictive collision detection (described in the RPG section of this chapter) to keep your sprite from intersecting a wall or barrier.

✔ **Editing maps:** You can build a map editor that allows you to graphically build a map with a given tileset. Then just have your program print out the corresponding state values. You can then embed these values in your code. Although it would be nice to load and save worlds in external files, JavaScript doesn't have this capacity (for security reasons). It's possible to do so, but the best solutions involve server-side languages like PHP, which are outside the scope of this book (but see one of my other books on this topic if you're interested).

- **Large scrolling worlds:** One of the nicest features of tile systems is the capability to have worlds that are larger than the visual screen. Just build a very large world array. Then create variables called something like `offsetLeft` and `offsetTop`. When you want to scroll the map, just change the values of these variables. When you display a map, just display `row + offsetTop` and `col + offsetLeft` to display the appropriate subset of the larger map.

- **Page maps:** An alternative to the scrolling world is a *page-based* tile system. For this system, you simply create a series of maps. When the character leaves a map, simply load the new map. This is frequently used in RPGs to simulate entering a building, for example.

While role-playing adventure games are the obvious use of tile-based worlds, they also appear in a number of other genres.

- **Playing cards:** Build a tile set based on playing cards. (There are some good card images at `http://openclipart.org`.) Use these tiles to illustrate a simple card game.

- **Platform:** Platform games are great for tile-based worlds, because they can be expanded in multiple directions. Use a collision-state mechanism to determine if a tile registers a collision.

- **Puzzle:** Certain kinds of puzzle games (like matching games and pipe games) are ideal tile games. Essentially, you'll store all possible elements in each cell, but display only the ones you need.

- **Strategy games:** Strategy games can be implemented quite well in a tile-based setting. Typically, the map is implemented in a tile setting to allow for combat and movement modifiers based on terrain types.

- **Board games:** Take a look at the tic-tac-toe game implemented next for another example of a tile-based implementation.

Tic-Tac-Toe Is the Way to Go

Like many programming teachers, I see a lot of tic-tac-toe games. This game seems pretty simple, but it can be surprisingly difficult to implement well. There are three main aspects to tic-tac-toe:

- **The visual and data interface:** The most obvious (and easy) problem is how to manage the visual layout: How do the players interact with the board to make their selections?

✓ **Determining a winner:** It seems straightforward to determine if somebody wins. After all, it's just a series of `if` statements. But this is where beginners usually get into a lot of trouble. The number of comparisons necessary gets out of control in a hurry. I show a better technique.

✓ **Building an AI:** Artificial intelligence is a topic in advanced classes in computer science. However, the AI problem in tic-tac-toe is easy enough for beginners to manage if you think carefully through the data problem.

My tic-tac-toe game is shown in Figure 13-10.

Creating the board

The best way to manage the user interface is to build a simplistic tile-based mechanism. (Look at the "Miles and Miles of Tiles and Tiles" section of this chapter for more on tile systems. The key to the tic-tac-toe game is a special sprite called a *cell.* Each cell represents a space on the board. It has three states (X, O, and blank). Clicking on the cell changes the internal state and (of course) the visual representation of the state.

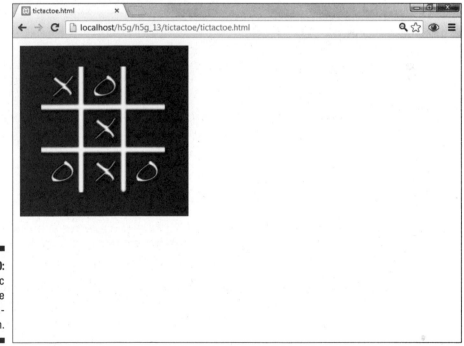

Figure 13-10:
A basic tic-tac-toe implementation.

The cell object is simply a subclass of the sprite:

```
function Cell(){
    tCell = new Sprite(game, "blank.png", 100, 100);
    tCell.setSpeed(0);
    tCell.state = BLANK;

    tCell.images = new Array("blank.png", "X.png",
        "O.png");

    tCell.checkClick = function(){
        if (this.isClicked()){
            if (this.state == BLANK){
                this.state = currentPlayer;
                this.setImage(this.images[currentPlayer]);

                //change the player
                if (currentPlayer == X){
                    currentPlayer = O;
                } else {
                    currentPlayer = X;
                } // end if
            } // end if
        } // end if
    } // end checkClick

    return tCell;
} // end cell
```

Here's how the `cell` code works:

1. **Create a** `currentPlayer` **variable.**

   This variable holds the value corresponding to the current player. The current player variable will rotate between X and O.

2. **Assign constants for the states.**

   The three states are integer constants.

3. **Create an array of images.**

   Assign images that correspond to the various states.

4. **Create a** `checkClick()` **method.**

    This method will change the cell's state appropriately. It will also change the `currentPlayer` variable so the next click will register for the other player.

5. **Build an array of cells.**

    Once a single cell does what you want, you can build an array of them.

Setting up the visual layout

The placement of the cells on the screen is interesting. It may seem natural to use a two-dimension array for the tic-tac-toe board, but the nested loop structure can be cumbersome on such a small data structure, and treating the board as a 2D array doesn't provide many benefits. Instead, I build this as a single-dimension array and use some tricks to get the visual appearance I want.

The cells are arranged like this:

```
0 1 2
3 4 5
6 7 8
```

To make them draw in the correct rectangular pattern, I use an old programmer's trick to turn the single dimension array into a two-dimension visual structure.

Try dividing all the values in the image above by 3. You'll see some interesting patterns. Every value in the first row (0, 1, and 2) yield zero (and some remainder) when divided by 3. Each element in the second row (3, 4, and 5) gives 1 remainder something, and each element of the third row produces a 2 remainder something. If you divide any of these numbers by 3 and convert the result into an integer, you'll get the row number. In JavaScript, you can use this line of code:

```
row = parseInt(i / 3);
```

There's another interesting pattern if you look at the remainders. All of the numbers in the first column (0, 3, and 6) are evenly divisible by 3, meaning they have remainders of 0. All the numbers in the next column (1, 4, and 7) have a remainder of 1, and the last column produces a remainder of 2. In other words, the remainder of division by 3 will give the column number. In

JavaScript, the *modulus* operator (%) will produce the remainder of an integer division, so you can get the column number with a similar formula:

```
col = i % 3
```

The code for creating the cells uses these formulas to extract the row and column number for each cell, and then places the cell on the screen by multiplying these values by the cell width and adding an offset (just as I did in the tile-based world, because this is another tile-based world).

```
function buildCells(){
    cells = new Array(9);
    xOffset = 100;
    yOffset = 100;
    for (i = 0; i < cells.length; i++){
        cells[i] = new Cell();
        row = parseInt(i / 3);
        col = i % 3;
        xPos = (col * 100) + xOffset;
        yPos = (row * 100) + yOffset;
        cells[i].setPosition(xPos, yPos);
    } // end for loop
} // end buildCells
```

Checking for a winning combination

It's very easy for a human to tell if one player or the other has won a game of tic-tac-toe: Just look for three in a row. The computer doesn't understand the concept of three in a row, and it needs to be taught. It's possible to use a complex series of `if` statements to check for all the possible winning combinations, but it takes a lot of code to do this. With a little thought, you can simplify the process tremendously. Take a look at the following code fragment:

```
winningCombos = new Array(
    new Array(0, 1, 2),
    new Array(3, 4, 5),
    new Array(6, 7, 8),
    new Array(0, 3, 6),
    new Array(1, 4, 7),
    new Array(2, 5, 8),
    new Array(0, 4, 8),
    new Array(2, 4, 6)
);
```

The code simply sets up a two-dimension array. This array is a list of all the winning combinations. If the same player controls cells 0, 1, and 2, that player has won the game. Each row represents a different winning combination.

It then becomes easy to check for a winner:

```
function checkWins(){
    winner = 0
    for (combo = 0; combo < winningCombos.length; combo++){
        a = winningCombos[combo][0];
        b = winningCombos[combo][1];
        c = winningCombos[combo][2];

        if (cells[a].state == cells[b].state){
            if (cells[b].state == cells[c].state){
                if (cells[a].state != BLANK){
                    winner = cells[a].state;
                } // end if
            } // end if
        } // end if
    } // end for
    return winner;
} // end checkWins
```

This code goes through the array of cells and checks each winning combination. If it discovers any combination with the same value (but not blank), the value in the cells indicates the winner of the game.

Adding an AI

The most common type of artificial intelligence for this sort of problem is called a *heuristic* algorithm. It's a trick that allows the computer to quickly come up with a good solution while not guaranteeing a perfect solution. In general, heuristic algorithms work by assigning a point value to each possible move and then selecting the best move available.

The general strategy is to build an array of cell rankings:

```
cellRank = new Array(3,2,3,3,4,3,3,2,3);
```

The rank of each cell indicates the number of winning combinations that go through it, so cell 4 (the center cell) is the most valuable cell at the beginning of the game.

As the game goes on, the computer reevaluates the grid according to the following simplistic calculations:

1. **If any cell is nonblank, demote it.**

    The only cells you should consider are those that are blank, so if a cell is already taken, subtract 99 from its cell ranking.

2. **Look for partially completed winning combinations.**

    Step through each winning combination. If any two cells have the same value but the third is blank, add a value to the third.

3. **Find the highest cell.**

    After going through all the combinations, loop through the cell rankings to see which is the highest cell ranking.

The `tttAI.html` program on the website (`www.aharrisbooks.net`) shows the `cellRank` heuristic and a hint for the next cell.

Improving the tic-tac-toe game

The tic-tac-toe game is reasonably complete, but it can be improved. Here are a few suggestions:

- ✔ **Implement a computer player.** My version calculates the best cell for the computer player, but it doesn't actually play. It's relatively easy to have the computer player pick the best cell.

- ✔ **Improve the heuristic.** While this heuristic will work, it could definitely be improved. It plays well, but it can be beaten. Learn its weakness, and see if you can improve on the performance.

- ✔ **Allow multiple plays.** Right now the game must be reset after every game. Add a mechanism to replay, keeping track of the score. Look into the `localStorage` mechanism for how to add this feature.

Index

• *X* •